A New Text
for a Modern China

Irene Liu with Li Xiaoqi

Cheng & Tsui Company

First edition 1998
Reprinted January 2000

Cheng & Tsui Company
25 West Street
Boston, MA 02111-1213 USA
(800)554-1963
FAX: (617)426-3669
http://www.cheng-tsui.com

Library of Congress Catalog Card Number: 92-071971

ISBN 0-88727-312-2

Printed in The United States of America

PUBLISHER'S NOTE

The Cheng & Tsui Company is pleased to announce *A New Text for a Modern China*, an updated version of the highly-praised *A Chinese Text for a Changing China*. New users, as well as those familiar with the preceding version, should find much of value here: the lesson topics have been kept current and dynamic.

This text will prove of even more value when used in conjunction with *Across the Straits: 22 Miniscripts for Developing Advanced Listening Skills*, another new title from Cheng & Tsui. *Across the Straits* is designed to hone the listening skills of third and fourth year students and presents audio materials which may be easily coordinated with the units and lessons in the present book.

A New Text for a Modern China directly addresses the difficulty experienced by third-year students of Chinese, who desire reading material which is both sufficiently engaging and within their lexical, grammatical and syntactic understanding. At the core of the five topical units in this text are short passages drawn from contemporary Chinese sources. The readings are followed by generous amplifying material, including vocabulary lists in *pinyin*, traditional and simplified Chinese characters, grammatical explanations, and exercises.

The *C&T Asian Language Series* is designed to publish and widely distribute quality language texts as they are completed by such leading institutions as the Beijing Language Institute, as well as other significant works in the field of Asian languages developed in the United States and elsewhere.

We welcome readers' comments and suggestions concerning the publications in this series. Please contact the following members of the Editorial Board:

Professor Shou-hsin Teng, Chief Editor
3 Coach Lane, Amherst, MA 01002

Professor Dana Scott Bourgerie
Asian and Near Eastern Languages, Brigham Young University, Provo, UT 84602

Professor Samuel Cheung
Dept. of Oriental Languages, University of California, Berkeley, CA 94720

Professor Ying-che Li
Dept. of East Asian Languages, University of Hawaii, Honolulu, HI 96822

Professor Timothy Light
Office of the Provost, Western Michigan University, Kalamazoo, MI 49008

Introduction

A New Text for a Modern China responds to the same needs, and observes the same guiding principles as its predecessor, *A Chinese Text for a Changing China*. It also reflects the changes in Chinese life and language (and the adaptations made to them in teaching Chinese at Columbia University) that have occurred in the intervening years. Those readers who have used the preceding version will find much that is new here. The present book is more expansive in scope, but guided by principles of clarity, conciseness, utility, and appropriateness for third-year students.

A challenge for third-year students of Chinese is that, after two years of studying the basic language, they are eager to read more sophisticated material but lack the necessary skills. We solve this problem in two ways: (1) by giving students readings that are intellectually stimulating, but not far beyond their lexical, grammatical, or syntactic understanding; and (2) by teaching reading strategies that make the job easier. The reading selections in this book comprise a body of sophisticated material which introduces the students to dynamic social phenomena; however, vocabulary and grammar have been carefully contained within students' probable range of comprehension. The exercises further help students acquire literacy in reading and writing.

This text consists of nineteen lessons, grouped into five units on specific topics. Each unit begins with a short introduction consisting of useful background information. This introductory material is designed to enhance understanding of the issues subsequently raised in the unit, and centers on the rapidly changing attitudes and values of modern China. The lessons, most of them in a humorous style to help sustain student interest, include language of varying degrees of difficulty. *A New Text for a Modern China* does not reproduce the structural arrangement common in first and second year texts. This approach is justifiable on the following grounds: (1) third-year students do not require strictly graded degrees of difficulty; (2) the intrinsic interest of coherent texts helps to hold students' attention; and (3) the texts are actually from Chinese sources, and thus present practical challenges to the students.

Each lesson is short, consisting of one page or at most one and one-half pages of text, and designed to be challenging but not overly difficult. Short passages of text more effectively sustain students' interest; furthermore, completing a short lesson gives students an immediate sense of achievement.

In order to build students' linguistic competence, this book stresses the learning of stock phrases. Each lesson includes a list of commonly used stock phrases, suitable for students at the advanced level. The purpose of learning stock phrases is to equip students with language that occurs repeatedly in actual Chinese texts, thus improving overall reading speed and competence.

The grammatical component of *A New Text for a Modern China* solidifies, expands and refines the fundamental knowledge of Chinese structure and syntax which students acquire at the elementary and intermediate levels. New words learned in the lessons are revisited in sentences which illustrate important grammar points. The constant re-presentation of words enables students to make rapid progress, since vocabulary retention is less difficult. The illustrative sentences are context-oriented so that students may achieve a more complete understanding of grammar specifics. Furthermore, grammar is explained in a simple, straightforward way, which promotes ready comprehension and enables students to prepare lessons at home, saving class time for discussions.

This book offers a variety of reading and writing exercises. Individual teachers may choose those best suited to the specific needs of their students. We have included an important set of exercises concerning stock phrases. It is not sufficient merely to memorize these stock phrases; students must learn them in their various contexts. This series of exercises serves that function.

People learn to read by reading: if the material is interesting and not oppressively difficult, students will enjoy reading and will be encouraged to read more. Therefore, we include one or two supplementary readings in each exercise, on topics that coincide with the concurrent lesson.

The Chinese parts of the book are in pinyin, and traditional and simplified Chinese characters. The vocabulary, lessons and illustrative sentences in the grammar sections are in both traditional and simplified Chinese characters. Each lesson includes: a) text; b) glossary; c) stock phrases constructed from lexical items in the same lesson; d) grammar notes with illustrative sentences; and e) exercises, which include one or two short essays for supplementary reading. These essays review most of the vocabulary words of the lesson and cover the same topic. Stock phrases and illustrative sentences are accompanied by their English equivalents.

It is our hope that *A New Text for a Modern China* will prove of use both to new students and teachers, and to those familiar with its predecessor.

Thanks are due John Meskill for editing the English, and for his encouragement.

I.C.L.

TABLE OF CONTENTS

目录

Unit One

1. 人口 住房

中国有许多社会问题。比如人口问题、房子问题、交通问题、失业问题、经济问题、腐败问题等等。

本单元选了两篇报道，第一篇谈的是人口问题。

中国人太多了，增长得太快了。1950 年，中国人口是 5 亿左右，三十年后，1982 年人口为 10.25 亿，增长了一倍，到 1990 年，已经超过 11 亿了。虽然中国政府早在七十年代末就提出了一家只能生一个孩子的政策，可是中国的人口增长还是太快了，世界上平均四个半人中就有一个是中国人。人口太多，给生活水平带来很大影响。生产在不断发展，可是人们的收入却提高得不快。

第二篇谈的是住房问题。

跟着人口问题，住房问题也产生了。1980 年，北京市居民平均每人住房面积才三点多平方米，后来，北京盖了许多新楼、高楼，到 1990 年，达到每个人平均六点七平方米。可是房子还是不够住，因为以前一家人住一套房子，现在孩子们长大了，结婚了，一人就要一套房子。

这两个问题非常严重，是中国当前急迫需要解决的问题。

1. 人口　住房

　　中國有許多社會問題。比如人口問題、房子問題、交通問題、失業問題、經濟問題、腐敗問題等等。

　　本單元選了兩篇報導，第一篇談的是人口問題。

　　中國人太多了，增長得太快了。1950 年，中國人口是 5 億左右，三十年後，1982 年人口為 10.25 億，增長了一倍，到 1990 年，已經超過 11 億了。雖然中國政府早在七十年代末就提出了一家只能生一個孩子的政策，可是中國的人口增長還是太快了，世界上平均四個半人中就有一個是中國人。人口太多，給生活水平帶來很大影響。生產在不斷發展，可是人們的收入却提高得不快。

　　第二篇談的是住房問題。

　　跟着人口問題，住房問題也產生了。1980 年，北京市居民平均每人住房面積才三點多平方米，後來，北京蓋了許多新樓、高樓，到 1990 年，達到每個人平均六點七平方米。可是房子還是不夠住，因為以前一家人住一套房子，現在孩子們長大了，結婚了，一人就要一套房子。

　　這兩個問題非常嚴重，是中國當前急迫需要解決的問題。

生词 NEW WORDS

1.人口	人口	rénkǒu	N. population
2.住房	住房	zhùfáng	N. housing; lodgings
3.比如	比如	bǐrú	for example
4.交通	交通	jiāotōng	N. traffic
5.失業	失业	shīyè	VO. to lose one's job
6.物價	物价	wùjià	N. (commodity) price
7.腐敗	腐败	fǔbài	SV. corrupt
8.本	本	běn	Det. this (literary)
9.單元	单元	dānyuán	N. unit
10.篇	篇	piān	M. for report, essay
11.報導	报道	bàodào	N. (news) report
12.增長	增长	zēngzhǎng	V. increase
13.億	亿	yì	Nu. a hundred million
14.為	为	wéi	V. is/was (literary)
15.超過	超过	chāoguò	V. exceed
16.七十年代末			
七十年代末		qīshí niándài mò	TW. the end of the 70's
17.提出	提出	tíchū	V. introduces (a policy); puts forward (a proposal)
18.政策	政策	zhèngcè	N. policy
19.平均	平均	píngjūn	V/MV. average; on the average
20.水平	水平	shuǐpíng	N. level; standard
21.生產	生产	shēngchǎn	N. production
22.不斷地	不断地	búduàn dì	Adv. uninterruptedly; continuously
23.收入	收入	shōurù	N. income
24.提高	提高	tígāo	V. as transitive V: to raise; as intransitive V: to rise; to improve
25.產生	产生	chǎnshēng	V. (problem) emerged; ...creates (problem)
26.居民	居民	jūmín	N. resident
27.面積	面积	miànjī	N. area

4

28. 平方米	平方米	píngfāng mǐ	N. square metre
29. 蓋	盖	gài	V. build
30. 套	套	tào	M. a suite of rooms
31. 嚴重	严重	yánzhòng	SV. serious
32. 當前	当前	dāngqián	TM. present; current
33. 急迫	急迫	jípò	SV. urgent; pressing
34. 需要	需要	xūyào	V. needs; requires
35. 解決	解决	jiějué	V. to solve

1.1. 人口大爆炸
人口面面观

在北京

　　1987 年 7 月 27 日，这一天的最高气温是三十五摄氏度。

　　从中午 12 点到 13 点，《北京日报》的一名记者和几名工作人员分别站在市内最大的一家百货商店的四个大门口，统计顾客流量。门外气温非常高而门内的热气也厉害得使人受不了。统计结果，在这一个小时内有 8240 人带着热浪进来，9680 人带着汗气出去。

　　7 月 30 日，北京电视台报道，北京火车站顾客流量非常高，日流量达 33 万人，可火车站设计的客流量不过是日五六万人。所有的检票厅都改成了临时候车室，但车站大厅前的广场上仍然是人山人海。

在广州

　　1988 年春季交易会期间，一批日商住在广州宾馆。一天黄昏的时候一位日商站在窗户前看街，像有新发现似的，指着窗外惊呼着说："hayaku, mite kudasai！"（日语:快来看！）立刻，四五名日商往窗前走去，眼睛都向海珠桥方面看过去。这时南来北往的自行车，如蝗虫般来来去去，在海珠桥的两边合起来，变成一条密密的人流、车流，像永远走不完的百万大军。

　　这些日商评价说:"简直是一大奇观！"

　　专家认为，中国人口，照这种速度增长下去，1995 年年底，就会达到 12 亿多了。

1.1. 人口大爆炸
人口面面觀

在北京

　　1987 年 7 月 27 日，這一天的最高氣溫是三十五攝氏度。

　　從中午 12 點到 13 點，《北京日報》的一名記者和幾名工作人員分別站在市內最大的一家百貨商店的四個大門口，統計顧客流量。門外氣溫非常高而門內的熱氣也厲害得使人受不了。統計結果，在這一個小時內有 8240 人帶着熱浪進來，9680 人帶着汗氣出去。

　　7 月 30 日，北京電視臺報導，北京火車站顧客流量非常高，日流量達 33 萬人，可火車站設計的客流量不過是日五六萬人。所有的檢票廳都改成了臨時候車室，但車站大廳前的廣場上仍然是人山人海。

在廣州

　　1988 年春季交易會期間，一批日商住在廣州賓館。一天黃昏的時候一位日商站在窗戶前看街，像有新發現似的，指着窗外驚呼着說："hayaku, mite kudasai！"（日語:快來看！)立刻，四五名日商往窗前走去，眼睛都向海珠橋方面看過去。這時南來北往的自行車，如蝗蟲般來來去去，在海珠橋的兩邊合起來，變成一條密密的人流、車流，像永遠走不完的百萬大軍。

　　這些日商評價説："簡直是一大奇觀！"

　　專家認為，中國人口，照這種速度增長下去，1995 年年底，就會達到 12 億多了。

9

生词 NEW WORDS

1.爆炸	爆炸	bàozhà	N. explosion
2.面面觀	面面观	miànmiàn guān	VP. (to view) from various aspects
3.氣溫	气温	qìwēn	N. (air) temperature
4.攝氏	摄氏	shèshì	N. Celsius
5.度	度	dù	N. degree (of temperature)
6.記者	记者	jìzhě	N. reporter
7.人員	人员	rényuán	N. personnel
8.百貨商店	百货商店	bǎihuò shāngdiàn	N. department store
9.統計	统计	tǒngjì	V. to add up (the number)
10.顧客	顾客	gùkè	N. customer
11.流量	流量	liúliàng	N. rate of flow
12.熱氣	热气	rèqì	N. steam; heat
13.厲害	厉害	lìhài	SV. devastating
14.使	使	shǐ	V. to cause, make
15.受不了	受不了	shòubùliǎo	VP. cannot bear
16.結果	结果	jiéguǒ	N. result
17.小時	小时	xiǎoshí	N. hour
18.熱浪	热浪	rèlàng	N. heat wave
19.汗氣	汗气	hànqì	N. sweaty atmosphere
20.電視臺	电视台	diànshìtái	N. television station
21.達	达	dá	V. to reach
22.設計	设计	shèjì	N/V. design; to design
23.檢票廳	检票厅	jiǎnpiàotīng	NP. a room where tickets are checked
24.臨時	临时	línshí	Adv. temporary
25.候車室	候车室	hòuchē shì	NP. waiting room (in a railway or bus station)
26.廣場	广场	guǎngchǎng	N. public square
27.仍然	仍然	réngrán	Adv. still
28.春季	春季	chūnjì	N. spring
29.交易	交易	jiāoyì	N. trade; business

30. 期間	期间	qījiān	N. a period of time (specific)
31. 黃昏	黄昏	huánghūn	N. dusk
32. 發現	发现	fāxiàn	N/V. discovery; to discover
33. 驚呼	惊呼	jīnghū	V. to cry out in amazement
34. 立刻	立刻	lìkè	Adv. immediately
35. 眼睛	眼睛	yǎnjīng	N. eye
36. 蝗蟲	蝗虫	huángchóng	N. locust
37. 密	密	mì	Adv. dense; thick
38. 百萬大軍 百万大军		bǎiwàn dàjūn	NP. an army a million strong (here: a metaphor)
39. 評價	评价	píngjià	V. to comment
40. 奇觀	奇观	qíguān	NP. a spectacular sight
41. 專家	专家	zhuānjiā	N. a specialist
42. 認為	认为	rènwéi	V. to deem; consider
43. 速度	速度	sùdù	N. speed

地名　Place Names

1. 廣州	广州	Guǎngzhōu	Canton
2. 海珠橋	海珠桥	Hǎizhū-qiáo	the largest bridge in Canton

常用词组　STOCK PHRASES

1. 工作人員	工作人员	worker; staff
2. 報道經過	报道经过	to report on what happened
3. 新聞報道	新闻报道	news report
4. 加快速度	加快速度	to increase speed
5. 增長知識	增长知识	to broaden (or enrich) knowledge

11

语法 GRAMMAR

1.分别

Syntactically, 分别 is an adverb which may precede a preposition (or co-verb) of a verb. Even though 分别 precedes a verb, semantically, it does not modify the verb. It qualifies the noun or nouns in the sense that "one person does the same thing to several individuals separately", or "several individuals each do the same thing to the same person." It can mean either that "one entity deals separately with different conditions or situations" or "several entities each cope with the same thing the same way."

Examples:

(1)你分别跟他们谈谈吧。

你分別跟他們談談吧。

Why don't you talk to each of them?

(2)你们分别跟他谈谈吧。

你們分別跟他談談吧。

Why don't you each talk to him separately

(3)市长跟副市长分别接见了他。

市長跟副市長分別接見了他。

The mayor and the deputy mayor each received him separately.

(4)市长分别见了他们三个人。

市長分別見了他們三個人。

The mayor received the three of them separately.

2. 而

而 is basically a syntactic marker that connects two verb phrases or two clauses. Having no intrinsic meaning 而 derives its meaning from the verb phrases or clauses it links together. 而 may be interpreted as "and" if the two elements supplement each other, and as "but" if they contrast each other. Moreover, if the two elements are clauses, 而 may also be rendered

12

as a comma or a colon placed between the two clauses. In this lesson we only take up the first of these uses.

A. 而 connects two qualitatively similar verb phrases.

Examples:

(1)这条河长而宽。

這條河長而寬。

This river is long and wide.

(2)他们正在紧张而高兴地工作着

他們正在緊張而高興地工作着。

They are working intensely and happily.

B. 而 connects two clauses whose meanings supplement each other.

Examples:

(1)各组的研究都得到很好的结果而第三组的特别好。

各組的研究都得到很好的結果而第三組的特別好。

Each group achieved good results in research, and the third group was especially good.

(2)门外的气温非常高而门内的热气也很利害。

門外的氣溫非常高而門內的熱氣也很利害

Outside, the temperature is unusually high; inside, the heat is severe.

3.使

S_1 + 使 + (S_2 + VP)

Syntactically, 使 is a causative verb that takes a clause as its object. Semantically, this pattern expresses the idea that a person or a condition, S_1, causes another person or situation, S_2, to be in a specific state that is presented in the verb phrase.

Examples:

(1)这样作才能使大家高兴。

這樣作才能使大家高興。

Only by handling it this way will it make everyone (feel) happy.

(2)他的话并不使我生气。

他的話並不使我生氣。

His words did not make me angry at all.

(3)他的态度使他变得朋友越来越少。

他的態度使他變得朋友越來越少。

His attitude has caused him to become a person with
fewer and fewer friends.

4.在...duration...内

This is a specific time phrase that may go before or after the subject of
a sentence. Within the phrase the duration of time can be minutes, days,
months or years. Although this interval of time is not made definite by the
use of a specifier such as 这 or 那, the time of its occurrence is known in the
speaker's mind. 在 is optional in this time phrase.

Examples:

(1)三年内我就毕业了。

三年內我就畢業了。

I'll graduate in three years (from now).

(2)昨天在几个小时内就下了几寸的雨。

昨天在幾個小時內就下了几寸的雨。

Yesterday within a few hours it rained several inches.

(3)几天内那个商店就卖了几万元的商品。

幾天內那個商店就賣了幾萬元的商品。

Within a few days that store sold commodities worth
tens of thousands of yuan.

5.在...X...期间

Like the pattern above, this is a definite time phrase which may occur
before or after the subject. The preposition 在 must be included when the
entire phrase follows the subject, but may be dropped when preceding it.

The "X" inserted in the phrase represents a specific event which took
place or will take place at a definite time. Syntactically, "X" may take the

form of a noun phrase or a verb+object construction.

Examples:

(1)我在念研究院期间认识了许多学者。

我在念研究院期間認識了許多學者。

During the time that I studied in graduate school, I became acquainted with quite a few scholars.

(2)春季交易会期间广州市卖了不少商品。

春季交易會期間廣州市賣了不少商品。

Canton city sold a great amount of merchandise during (the very time of) the spring trade fair.

(3)他在上海开会期间去看了几位老同学。

他在上海開會期間去看了幾位老同學。

During the time that he attended the conference in Shanghai he visited several of his old classmates.

6.(好)像.....(似的)　S + (好)像 + predicate (+似的)

Syntactically, (好)像 must follow the subject and precede the rest of the sentence, 似的 is optional but when included it must be placed at the end of the sentence. Semantically, a sentence including the (好)像.....似的 structure is not a statement of fact. The sentence merely states the speaker's impression that something is the case.

Examples:

(1)他像不怎么舒服(似的)。

他像不怎麼舒服(似的)。

He appears to be a little sick.

(not so comfortable)

(2)他好像只告诉了小王一个人。

他好像只告訴了小王一個人。

It looks as if he informed only one person, xiao Wang.

(3)这个人我像看见过他似的。

這個人我像看見過他似的。

I seem to have seen this person before.

7.如...X...般(地)

S + 如...X...般(地) + VP

Syntactically, "如...X...般" is an adverbial phrase that precedes the verb phrase of a sentence. The adverb marker 地 is optional. Semantically, "X", in the form of a noun, is a simile, used to describe a quality or action of the subject.

Examples:

(1)她的眼睛如秋水般地明亮。

她的眼睛如秋水般地明亮。

Her eyes are clear like the autumn waters.

(clear, bright looking, like the beauty of "autumn ripples")

(2)上百上千的自行车如蝗虫般地来来去去。

上百上千的自行車如蝗蟲般地來來去去。

Like locusts, hundreds and thousands of bicycles coming and going.

一、选词填空

A. 记者、顾客、气温、热浪、度、统计、百货、门口、汗气、在…之内

有一天，北京市非常热，最高（　　　　）是三十八（　　　）。几位（　　　　）
来到市内最大的一家（　　　　）商店，他们站在商店（　　　　），（　　　　）
着（　　　　）流量。统计结果，（　　　）半个小时（　　　　），有五千一百二十
人带着（　　　　）进来，六千二百三十人带着（　　　　）出去。

B.　商人，南来北往，惊呼，密密，来来去去，像…似的，宾馆，合

有一天，一位美国（　　　　）站在（　　　　）的窗前向外看，突然，
他（　　　）有新发现（　　　　），指着窗外（　　　　）："快来看！
快来看！"　原来，马路上（　　　　）的自行车，像蝗虫似的（　　　　），
在一座桥的两边（　　　）起来，成为一条（　　　　）的人流、车流。

二、用本课的生词写出
　　a.六个跟天气最有关系的词：
　　b.两个跟电视台最有关系的词：
　　c.六个跟研究或调查最有关系的词：

三、用下面的语法点造句。每个语法点一句。
　　a.分别　　　　b.而　　　　c.使
　　d.在……内　　e.在……期间　　f.好像……似的

四、用约二百五十字写出你对中国人口问题的看法(多用本课的生词和语法)

五、泛读下面短文：

十一点六亿人口意味着甚么？

根据中国第四次人口调查，到1990年7月1日零点，中国总人口是11.6亿。这个数字说明，中国的计划生育工作作得不错，人口大爆炸得到了一定的控制。八十年代前期，中国实行了计划生育政策:一个家庭只能生一个孩子。从那时起，中国大约少生了两亿多人，这是一个非常好的结果。但是中国已经有11.6亿人口，并且每年还要增加1500多万，差不多是一个澳大利亚的人口！这说明中国人口问题还是非常严重，中国真非实行计划生育不可。

中国的土地是世界第三位大，但是人均土地还不到世界人均土地的三分之一。1989年中国粮食生产达到历史最高水平，但是因为人口增加太多太快，人均粮食比1984年还低30公斤。河流、湖泊，中国有那么多，而人均水量是世界第88位。交通、运输等发展得很快，但是坐车难、看病难、住房难等问题总解决不了……因为人口数量太多。

专家们认为，90年代是中国经济发展的重要的时期，也是人口控制的重要时期。90年代前期，中国第三次人口出生高峰到了，如果控制不好，中国人口就会很快地增长到十二亿了。

1.根据	gēnjù	according to
2.人口调查	rénkǒu diàochá	census
3.计划生育	jìhuà shēngyù	family planning; birth control
4.控制	kòngzhì	to control
5.实行	shíxíng	to carry out; to implement
6.澳大利亚	Aòdàlìyà	Australia
7.人均土地	rénjūn tǔdì	land per person
8.公斤	gōngjīn	kilogram; kilo
9.运输	yùnshū	transport
10.高峰	gāofēng	peak
11.解决	jiějué	to solve
12.如果	rúguǒ	if

一、選詞填空

A. 記者、顧客、氣溫、熱浪、度、統計、百貨、門口、汗氣、在…之內

有一天，北京市非常熱，最高（　　　）是三十八（　　）。幾位（　　　　）
來到市內最大的一家（　　　）商店，他們站在商店（　　　），（　　　　）
着（　　　）流量。統計結果，（　　）半個小時（　　　），有五千一百二十
人帶着（　　　）進來，六千二百三十人帶着（　　　）出去。

B.　商人，南來北往，驚呼，密密，來來去去，像…似的，賓館，合

有一天，一位美國（　　　）站在（　　　）的窗前向外看，突然，
他（　　　）有新發現（　　　），指着窗外（　　　）：“快來看！
快來看！”原來，馬路上（　　　）的自行車，像蝗蟲似的（　　　），
在一座橋的兩邊（　　　）起來，成為一條（　　　）的人流、車流。

二、用本課的生詞寫出
　　a.六個跟天氣最有關係的詞：
　　b.兩個跟電視台最有關係的詞：
　　c.六個跟研究或調查最有關係的詞：

三、用下面的語法點造句。每個語法點一句。
　　a.分別　　　　b.而　　　　c.使
　　d.在……內　　e.在……期間　f.好像……似的

四、用約二百五十字寫出你對中國人口問題的看法(多用本課的生辭和語法)

五、泛讀下面短文：

十一點六億人口意味着甚麽？

　　根據中國第四次人口調查，到 1990 年 7 月 1 日零點，中國總人口是 11.6 億。這個數字説明，中國的計劃生育工作作得不錯，人口大爆炸得到了一定的控制。八十年代前期，中國實行了計劃生育政策:一個家庭只能生一個孩子。從那時起，中國大約少生了兩億多人，這是一個非常好的結果。但是中國已經有 11.6 億人口，並且每年還要增加 1500 多萬，差不多是一個澳大利亞的人口！這説明中國人口問題還是非常嚴重，中國真非實行計劃生育不可。

　　中國的土地是世界第三位大，但是人均土地還不到世界人均土地的三分之一。 1989 年中國糧食生産達到歷史最高水平，但是因爲人口增加太多太快，人均糧食比 1984 年還低 30 公斤。河流、湖泊，中國有那麼多，而人均水量是世界第 88 位。交通、運輸等發展得很快，但是坐車難、看病難、住房難等問題總解決不了……因爲人口數量太多。

　　專家們認爲，90 年代是中國經濟發展的重要的時期，也是人口控制的重要時期。 90 年代前期，中國第三次人口出生高峰到了，如果控制不好，中國人口就會很快地增長到十二億了。

1.	根據	gēnjù	according to
2.	人口調查	rénkǒu diàochá	census
3.	計劃生育	jìhuà shēngyù	family planning; birth control
4.	控制	kòngzhì	to control
5.	實行	shíxíng	to carry out; to implement
6.	澳大利亞	Aòdàlìyà	Australia
7.	人均土地	rén jūn tǔdì	land per person
8.	公斤	gōngjīn	kilogram;kilo
9.	運輸	yùnshū	transport
10.	高峰	gāofēng	peak
11.	解決	jiějué	to solve
12.	如果	rúguǒ	if

1.2　住宅

　　改革开放以来中国人在基本上解决了吃和穿的问题；但是，住宅到目前都还是一个很大的社会问题。在一般的大中城市，人均面积只有 7 平方米。在有的地区，人均面积还有在 3 平方米以下的。近年来，中国盖了大批的住房，但是，却出现了一个怪现象：一方面是有房没人买，另一方面是有人没房住，同时也有人分配到住宅不去住，私下出租给别人，这是为什么呢？

　　有房没人买是因为住宅价格太高，居民买不起。居民想要买得起，要存款 50 年。国际标准是：住宅价格是家庭年收入的 3 到 6 倍，在中国却是 20 倍。

　　有人没房住的原因是多方面的。一个原因是，中国人口多，增长快，但是因为经济发展得较慢，房子盖得少，所以总是不够住。

　　还有一个原因，就是以前的住房制度有严重的问题。1949 年以来，中国不允许有私人住宅。国家盖好的房子不卖给私人，而是由政府分配。由于政府收的房租非常低，大家就都想住大房，住好房。一些有权力的人，就利用他们手中的权力，为自己，自己的儿子，甚至为自己的孙子分配好房子，大房子。这就造成了机会不均等的情况，出现了有人没房住，有人分配了房子而不去住的怪现象。

　　有关专家指出，解决中国住房问题的根本办法是改革住房制度，使住房商品化。但老百姓怎么能住上商品房，政府还需要想很多办法。因此，住房在很长的时期内将还会是中国社会上的一个大问题。

1.2　住宅

　　改革開放以來中國人在基本上解決了吃和穿的問題；但是，住宅到目前都還是一個很大的社會問題。在一般的大中城市，人均面積只有 7 平方米。在有的地區，人均面積還有在 3 平方米以下的。近年來，中國蓋了大批的住房，但是，却出現了一個怪現象：一方面是有房沒人買，另一方面是有人沒房住，同時也有人分配到住宅不去住，私下出租給別人，這是為甚麼呢？

　　有房沒人買是因為住宅價格太高，居民買不起。居民想要買得起，要存款 50 年。國際標準是：住宅價格是家庭年收入的 3 到 6 倍，在中國却是 20 倍。

　　有人沒房住的原因是多方面的。一個原因是，中國人口多，增長快，但是因為經濟發展得較慢，房子蓋得少，所以總是不夠住。

　　還有一個原因，就是以前的住房制度有嚴重的問題。1949 年以來，中國不允許有私人住宅。國家蓋好的房子不賣給私人，而是由政府分配。由於政府收的房租非常低，大家就都想住大房，住好房。一些有權力的人，就利用他們手中的權力，為自己，自己的兒子，甚至為自己的孫子分配好房子，大房子。這就造成了機會不均等的情況，出現了有人沒房住，有人分配了房子而不去住的怪現象。

　　有關專家指出，解決中國住房問題的根本辦法是改革住房制度，使住房商品化。但老百姓怎麼能住上商品房，政府還需要想很多辦法。因此，住房在很長的時期內將還會是中國社會上的一個大問題。

生词　NEW WORDS

1.住宅	住宅	zhùzhái	N. residence; dwelling
2.改革開放	改革开放	gǎigé kāifàng	Ph. reform and open door (policy)
3.基本	基本	jīběn	N. basic; fundamental
4.社會	社会	shèhuì	N. society
5.大批	大批	dàpī	Det. a large number of
6.現象	现象	xiànxiàng	N. phenomenon
7.分配	分配	fēnpèi	V. allot; distribute
8.私下	私下	sīxià	Adv. privately; secretly
9.價格	价格	jiàgé	N. price
10.存款	存款	cúnkuǎn	V/N. deposit in the bank; savings in the bank
11.國際	国际	guójì	Attr. international
12.標準	标准	biāozhǔn	N. standard; criterion
13.却	却	què	Adv. but; yet (a literary term for 可是)
14.原因	原因	yuányīn	N. cause; reason
15.經濟	经济	jīngjì	N. economy
16.發展	发展	fāzhǎn	V. develop; expand
17.制度	制度	zhìdù	N. system
18.允許	允许	yǔnxǔ	V. permit; allow
19.私人	私人	sīrén	Attr. privately (owned); personal
20.由於	由于	yóuyú	Con. due to; as a result of
21.政府	政府	zhèngfǔ	N. government
22.利用	利用	lìyòng	V. exploit; make use of; utilize
23.權力	权力	quánlì	N. power; authority
24.甚至	甚至	shènzhì	Adv. even go so far as to; even to the point of
25.不均等	不均等	bù jūnděng	SV. unequal; unfair
26.指出	指出	zhǐchū	V. point out
27.根本	根本	gēnběn	Attr. basic; fundamental

28 商品	商品	shāngpǐn	N. commercial product; thing for sale
29....化	....化	....huà	Suffix. -ize; -ify
30.老百姓	老百姓	lǎobǎixìng	NP. the common people
31.因此	因此	yīncǐ	Con. for this reason; consequently
32.将	将	jiāng	Adv. will (in the future)

常用词组　STOCK PHRASES

1.解决.....问题	解决.....问题	to solve a/the problem (of)
2.出现.....现象	出现.....现象	there appears a phenomenon (of)
3.造成.....情况	造成.....情况	resulted in a situation of

语法　GRAMMAR

1. 在......上

$$S + (在......上) + VP$$

In this lesson, 在......上 is not used concretely, but figuratively. In this usage, 在......上 is a prepositional phrase, which may appear either before or after the subject of a sentence. Semantically, this phrase is used to put the matter stated by the sentence in a particular perspective. It may be translated as "pertaining to ...," "in terms of ...," or "....-ly."

Examples:

(1)在文化上中国和美国有许多不同的地方。

在文化上中國和美國有許多不同的地方。

In terms of culture, there exist many different aspects between China and America.

(2)中国在经济上发展得还是比较慢，所以老百姓的生活水平
不能提高得很快。

中國在經濟上發展得還是比較慢，所以老百姓的生活水平
不能提高得很快。

Pertaining to the economy, China is developing rather slowly. As a result, the living standard of the Chinese cannot be raised quickly.

(3)改革开放以来，中国人在基本上解决了吃和穿的问题。

改革開放以來，中國人在基本上解決了吃和穿的問題。

Since the reform and open door policy, the problem of (related to) food and clothing has been basically resolved.

2. V + 到 (+ 了)

This is a resultative verb phrase in its actual form, indicating that the expectation of an action is reached. The resultative ending 到 is used to show that the action has succeeded in obtaining a positive result. For example, a) 买到了: bought (succeeded in buying)

b) 看到了: saw (succeeded in seeing)

c) 租到了: rented (succeeded in renting)

d) 分配到了: allocated (succeeded in allocating)

Examples:

(1)他在一个环境很好的地方买到了一所房子。

他在一個環境很好的地方買到了一所房子。

He bought a house in a good location (good environment).

(2)他已经看到那几辆进口的法国汽车了。

他已經看到那幾輛進口的法國汽車了。

He has already seen those imported French cars.

(3)我租到了一间光线很好的屋子。

我租到了一間光線很好的屋子。

I was able to rent (was successful in renting) a bright room.

(4)等了半年，老张终于分配到了一个好的工作。

等了半年，老張終於分配到了一個好的工作。

After waiting for 6 months, Lao Zhang was finally assigned a good job.

3. V + 给

A.　　　A + Adv. + (把 + O) + V-给 + B　（了）

When we want to talk about a transaction of commodities between two parties, A and B, we use the "把" structure where A represents the originating party, B the terminating party. "O" represents the commodity. The "V" shows the manner of transaction, such as 卖,借 or 租, etc. "给" is included to show that the transaction is directed toward B. Thus, 卖给 B means "sell (it) to B," 租给 B "rent (it) out to B," and 借给 B "lent (it) to B."

Examples:

(1)政府不把盖好的房子卖给私人。

政府不把蓋好的房子賣給私人。

The government will not sell fully built houses to individual persons.

(2)上个月我不必用汽车，所以把车借了给一个朋友用。

27

上個月我不必用汽車，所以把車借了給一個朋友用。

I had no need to use my car last month; so I lent it to a friend.

(3)要是你能把你这所大房子租给别人，一定可以租到不少钱。

要是你能把你這所大房子租給別人，一定可以租到不少錢。

If you could rent out your big house, you could get a lot of money.

B. This structure "A + Adv + (把 + O) + V-给 + B" may be rewritten as "O, A + Adv. + V-给 + B."

Examples:

(1)a.政府不把盖好的房子卖给私人。

　　b.盖好的房子，政府不卖给私人。

(2)a.我把不用的那张桌子借了给一个朋友。

　　b.不用的那张桌子，我借了给一个朋友。

(3)a.要是你能把你的大房子租给别人，一定可以租到不少钱。

　　b.你的大房子，要是能租给别人，一定可以租到不少钱。

4. 由　　　O + 由 + S + V, the semantic interpretation is the following "matter + 由 + actor + action"

As you see, 由 is used to introduce the actor who assumes an official capacity to carry out the designated action of an event. 由 is translated as "by" in English. However, a 由 sentence is <u>not</u> a passive sentence in Chinese.* 由+actor, in fact, is to be interpreted as "It is for the actor to ...." (Yuen Ren Chao)

Further, this structure is used only in written language, not spoken. The verbs appearing in this structure belong to a closed list which represents formal actions, such as 参加 cānjiā "to attend (a meeting), to take part in, to join," 决定 juédìng "to decide," 陪同 péitóng "to accompany," 主持 zhǔchí "to take charge of, to preside over (a meeting),"

*The Chinese passive sentence differs from the English passive sentence. While the English passive sentence is a purely syntactical maneuvering of the positions of the subject and object, the Chiense passive sentence is semantically oriented. The object must be the recipient of the action and directly affected by the action.

办理 bànlǐ "to handle, to conduct," 分配 fēnpèi "to districute, to allocate, to assign," 领导 lǐngdǎo "to lead," etc.

Examples:

(1) 今年春季交易会的情况将由北京电视台报道。

今年春季交易會的情況將由北京電視台報道。

The situation (the general atmosphere) of the Spring Trade Fair of this year will be reported by the Beijing TV station.

(2) 公司新用的三名设计人员，工作由李广分配。

公司新用的三名設計人員，工作由李廣分配。

As to the three newly hired personnel for the designing jobs, their work will be assigned by Lǐ Guǎng.

(3) 我们找到了两个方法可以解决那个问题，用哪一个方法得由钱文决定。

我們找到了兩個方法可以解決那個問題，用哪一個方法得由錢文決定。

We have found two ways to solve that problem. It is for Qián Wén to decide which way we are going to use.

5. S + (一方面.........) + (另一方面.........)

This structure conveys the idea that the person, the subject of the sentence, has two matters of concern that occur simultaneously. It may be translated as "on the one hand.....on the other......" The predicate following 另一方面 often includes adverbs such as 又, 也, 却 or 还.

Examples:

(1) 他一方面很想帮助我，另一方面又怕负责。

他一方面很想幫助我，另一方面又怕負責。

On the one hand, he wanted to help me; on the other, he was afraid of the responsibility.

(2) 中国现在一方面是人民的生活水平提高了不少，另一方面是失业的人却越来越多。

中國現在一方面是人民的生活水平提高了不少，另一方面是失業的人却越來越多。

Presently in China, on the one hand, the people's standard of living has risen quite a lot; on the other hand, however, unemployment has increased.

(3)他一方面想搬到南方去住，另一方面又受不了南方的夏天。

他一方面想搬到南方去住，另一方面又受不了南方的夏天。

On the one hand, he was thinking of moving to the South to live; on the other hand, he couldn't stand the summer in the South.

6. .....化　　X + 化

This is an unusual structure, theorized by some to reflect foreign influence. Its word order represents "object+verb" rather than the regular Chinese word order which is "verb+object." Syntactically, 化 "to change" is a verb. "X" is the object of 化. Thus, in normal Chinese word order, the order should be "化+X." In this particular usage, however, the word order is reversed to become "X+化," "object+verb." In further development, the "化" has become a suffix. It may be added to a noun or a stative verb to convert the "N/SV+化" into a verb phrase. Thus, 工业化 gōngyè huà means "industrialize," 商品化 shāngpǐn huà "commercialize," 现代化 xiàndài huà "modernize," etc.

Examples:

(1)住房商业化

住房商業化

to commercialize housing

(2)农业科学化

農業科學化

to make agriculture scientific

(3)制度合理化

制度合理化

to rationalize the system

(4)中国现在需要工业现代。

中國現在需要工業現代化。

At present, China needs to modernize its industry.

Note that the usage of "AB化" is limited.

30

练习　EXERCISES

一、常用词组练习：用本课的常用词组填空
1.中国目前急迫地需要（　）住房问题。
2.世界上不少地区受到 El Niño 的影响，天气出现了很多奇怪的（　）。
3.这个小城的居民越来越多，开车的人也越来越多，（　）了一个城市交通混乱的情况。
4.如果政府不立刻想办法（　）失业问题，社会不久就会大乱。

二、猜测词的意思（不用字典）
（猜测 cāicè "to guess"）
1.人均面积的意思是（　　）。
2.商品房的价格太高，一般老百姓都买不起。
　买不起的意思是（　　）。
3.那家公寓的房租是每个月 $1,500，我每个月工作只能拿到 $1,000，
　住不起。
　住不起的意思是（　　）。
4.中国的住房问题很严重，有的地区一个居民平均住的面积是
　3 平方米以下。
　3 平方米以下大概是（　　）。

三、改写句子（用本课的语法改写）
1.九十年代以前的情况是，政府把工作分配给人民。（用"由"改写）
2.中国的经济发展得很快，但是也造成失业问题越来越严重的情况。
　（用"一方面……另一方面……"改写）
3.他在银行的存款只有两千块，你的房子千万不要卖给他。（用"把"）
4.有人认为，中国解决住房问题的方法是把政府拥有的房子变成商品房，
　老百姓可以随便买。（用"……化"）
5.李越的工作是决定我们公司商品的价格。（用"由"）

四、阅读理解（根据本课内容回答问题）

A.1.这课怎么说明在中国每个居民住的地方都非常小？
2.政府为了解决住房问题，做了什么？
3.在住房上，中国现在出现了什么情况？
4.在住宅价格上，国际标准和中国标准怎么不一样？
5.老百姓需要有什么条件才能买一所住宅？
6.在住房制度上，政府的政策是什么？
7.你认为这种政策最严重的问题是什么？（说一点）
8.专家们认为可以用什么方法解决住房问题？
9.你认为这个方法能很快地解决住房问题吗？为什么？

B.下面的问题，你的回答不能比五句话多。
1.第一段的主题是说虽然中国人吃和穿的问题现在基本上解决了，
但是住宅仍然是一个严重的问题。这一段用了几个例子说明住宅的各种
情况？（回答只说一共有几个情况，不必说情况的内容。）
2.第二段的主要目的是什么？
3.第三段的主要目的是什么？
4.第四段的主要目的是什么？
5.这一课的主题是什么？

五、用大约二百个字总结本课的意思。总结的格式（格式: form）如下：
a.住房问题的起因
b.政府原有的住房政策和新做法
c.你对解决住房问题的意见

六、阅读下面的两篇短文：

A. 市长的头疼

中国共有 381 个城市。每天，市长要遇到许许多多的麻烦事，其中最让他们头疼的就是房子问题。

北京虽然是政府的所在地，也是全国的政治文化中心，住房却十分紧张。到 1988 年，全北京有 50 多万住房严重困难户，他们平均每人住房面积不到三平方米。一些青年人结婚四，五年了还没有一间房..........在一所中学的对面，有一排很旧，很危险的房子，本来应该拆除的，可是，这所学校的校长和许多老师都住在这里。一家一间，男女老少四，五个人挤在一起。

上海，中国最大的、人口最多的城市，也是住房最挤的城市。一间小小的屋子要挤上男男女女两，三代人。晚上在地上睡觉的家庭很多。成千上万的学生和老师，家里放不下一张桌子，只好在床上看书，写字。在外滩，一到晚上就会出现一个奇观..........恋爱河岸，一对对情人排成一条人的长河，在那里谈情说爱。

天津，中国北方的名城。改革开放后这里发生了很大的变化，但住房问题还是市长的头疼。不少住房，院子比大街低，屋子比院子低，所以一下雨水就往屋里流..........市长们下决心盖了许多新房，可是现在仍有几万户平均每人住房面积不到三平方米。

1.市长	shìzhǎng	mayor
2.头疼	tóuténg	headache
3.户	hù	household
4.危险	wēixiǎn	danger
5.拆除	chāichú	to demolish
6.挤	jǐ	crowded; packed
7.两，三代	liǎng, sān dài	two or three generations
8.外滩	wài tān	The Bund
9.排（队）	pái(duì)	to queue up; to form a line
10.院子	yuànzi	courtyard
12.流	liú	to flow

B. 改变中的住房制度

多年来，中国政府都在想办法解决人民住房困难的问题，最近南京市试着实行一个新的政策，就是实行一种住房只售不租的新规定。下面简单地说明这种规定的做法：

　　根据《规定》，南京市的国家单位，社会团体，企业单位等，在新分配公有住房给职工时，有下面的规定：（公有住房包括新盖的住房，新购买的商品房，腾空成套住房等。）

　　一、由职工根据当时房改售房政策的规定购买。

　　二、职工可根据盖房子的实际成本价，或比盖房的实际成本价低而比房改成本价高的钱数，大家合起来盖房子。每套住宅的产权是各人自己的。

　　在实行住房新制度时，南京市还考虑到一些居民的实际购买能力，对各种家庭作了不同的具体规定：

　　一，中低收入家庭中，要购买住房的居住困难户，可向工作单位申请帮助一部分钱，数目是这一户房价的 40%。

　　二，对不能一次把钱给完的职工，可根据有关规定申请贷款。贷款数目是房价的 70%，在 15 年内还清贷款。

　　三，对差不多是完全沒有收入的家庭，更可以批准他们不购买住房。

　　这个制度能不能真正实行，并解决了住房困难问题，要经过一段时间才能知道，但我们可以看到政府在不断地设计新政策来解决这个困难的问题。

1.实行	shíxíng	to implement; to put into practice
2.规定	guīdìng	regulation
3.根据	gēnjù	according to
4.团体	tuántǐ	group; organization
5.企业	qǐyè	business
6.腾空	téngkōng	to empty out
7.成套住房	chéngtào zhùfáng	the entire flat
8.职工	zhígōng	staff and workers
9.实际	shíjì	actual
10.成本价	chéngběn jià	cost of production
11.合起来	hé qǐlái	to pool (their money)
12.产权	chǎnquán	property right
13.具体	jùtǐ	specific; particular
14.贷款	dàikuǎn	a loan
15.收入	shōurù	income
16.批准	pīzhǔn	to approve; to ratify

練習　EXERCISES

一、常用辭組練習：用本課的常用辭組填空

1.中國目前急迫地需要（　　）住房問題。

2.世界上不少地區受到 El Niño 的影響，天氣出現了很多奇怪的（　　）。

3.這個小城的居民越來越多，開車的人也越來越多，（　　）了一個城市交
通混亂的情況。

4.如果政府不立刻想辦法（　　）失業問題，社會不久就會大亂。

二、猜測詞的意思（不用字典）

（猜測 cāicè "to guess"）

1.人均面積的意思是（　　）。

2.商品房的價格太高，一般老百姓都買不起。

買不起的意思是（　　）。

3.那家公寓的房租是每個月 $1,500，我每個月工作只能拿到 $1,000，
住不起。

住不起的意思是（　　）。

4.中國的住房問題很嚴重，有的地區一個居民平均住的面積是
3 平方米以下。

3 平方米以下大概是（　　）。

三、改寫句子（用本課的語法改寫）

1.九十年代以前的情況是，政府把工作分配給人民。（用"由"改寫）

2.中國的經濟發展得很快，但是也造成失業問題越來越嚴重的情況。
（用"一方面……另一方面………"改寫）

3.他在銀行的存款只有兩千塊，你的房子千萬不要賣給他。（用"把"）

4.有人認為，中國解決住房問題的方法是把政府擁有的房子變成商品房，
老百姓可以隨便買。（用"……化"）

5.李越的工作是決定我們公司商品的價格。（用"由"）

四、閱讀理解（根據本課內容回答問題）

A.1.這課怎麼説明在中國每個居民住的地方都非常小？
　2.政府為了解決住房問題，做了甚麼？
　3.在住房上，中國現在出現了甚麼情況？
　4.在住宅價格上，國際標準和中國標準怎麼不一樣？
　5.老百姓需要有甚麼條件才能買一所住宅？
　6.在住房制度上，政府的政策是甚麼？
　7.你認為這種政策最嚴重的問題是甚麼？（説一點）
　8.專家們認為可以用甚麼方法解決住房問題？
　9.你認為這個方法能很快地解決住房問題嗎？為甚麼？

B.下面的問題，你的回答不能比五句話多。
　1.第一段的主題是説雖然中國人吃和穿的問題現在基本上解決了，
　　但是住宅仍然是一個嚴重的問題。這一段用了幾個例子説明住宅的各種
　　情況？（回答只説一共有幾個情況，不必説情況的內容。）
　2.第二段的主要目的是甚麼？
　3.第三段的主要目的是甚麼？
　4.第四段的主要目的是甚麼？
　5.這一課的主題是甚麼？

五、用大約二百個字總結本課的意思。總結的格式（格式: form）如下：
　a.住房問題的起因
　b.政府原有的住房政策和新做法
　c.你對解決住房問題的意見

六、閱讀下面的兩篇短文：

A. 市長的頭疼

中國共有 381 個城市。每天，市長要遇到許許多多的麻煩事，其中最讓他們頭疼的就是房子問題。

北京雖然是政府的所在地，也是全國的政治文化中心，住房卻十分緊張。到 1988 年，全北京有 50 多萬住房嚴重困難戶，他們平均每人住房面積不到三平方米。一些青年人結婚四，五年了還沒有一間房..........在一所中學的對面，有一排很舊，很危險的房子，本來應該拆除的，可是，這所學校的校長和許多老師都住在這裡。一家一間，男女老少四，五個人擠在一起。

上海，中國最大的、人口最多的城市，也是住房最擠的城市。一間小小的屋子要擠上男男女女兩，三代人。晚上在地上睡覺的家庭很多。成千上萬的學生和老師，家裡放不下一張桌子，只好在床上看書，寫字。在外灘，一到晚上就會出現一個奇觀..........戀愛河岸，一對對情人排成一條人的長河，在那里談情說愛。

天津，中國北方的名城。改革開放後這裡發生了很大的變化，但住房問題還是市長的頭疼。不少住房，院子比大街低，屋子比院子低，所以一下雨水就往屋里流..........市長們下決心蓋了許多新房，可是現在仍有幾萬戶平均每人住房面積不到三平方米。

1.市長	shìzhǎng	mayor
2.頭疼	tóuténg	headache
3.戶	hù	household
4.危險	wēixiǎn	danger
5.拆除	chāichú	to demolish
6.擠	jǐ	crowded; packed
7.兩，三代	liǎng, sān dài	two or three generations
8.外灘	wài tān	The Bund
9.排（隊）	pái(duì)	to queue up; to form a line
10.院子	yuànzǐ	courtyard
12.流	liú	to flow

B. 改變中的住房制度

多年來，中國政府都在想辦法解決人民住房困難的問題，最近南京市試著實行一個新的政策，就是實行一種住房只售不租的新規定。下面簡單地說明這種規定的做法：

根據《規定》，南京市的國家單位，社會團體，企業單位等，在新分配公有住房給職工時，有下面的規定：（公有住房包括新蓋的住房，新購買的商品房，騰空成套住房等。）

一、由職工根據當時房改售房政策的規定購買。

二、職工可根據蓋房子的實際成本價，或比蓋房的實際成本價低而比房改成本價高的錢數，大家合起來蓋房子。每套住宅的產權是各人自己的。

在實行住房新制度時，南京市還考慮到一些居民的實際購買能力，對各種家庭作了不同的具體規定：

一，中低收入家庭中，要購買住房的居住困難戶，可向工作單位申請幫助一部分錢，數目是這一戶房價的 40%。

二，對不能一次把錢給完的職工，可根據有關規定申請貸款。貸款數目是房價的 70%，在 15 年內還清貸款。

三，對差不多是完全沒有收入的家庭，更可以批準他們不購買住房。

這個制度能不能真正實行，並解決了住房困難問題，要經過一段時間才能知道，但我們可以看到政府在不斷地設計新政策來解決這個困難的問題。

1.	實行	shíxíng	to implement; to put into practice
2.	規定	guīdìng	regulation
3.	根據	gēnjù	according to
4.	團體	tuántǐ	group; organization
5.	企業	qǐyè	business
6.	騰空	téngkōng	to empty out
7.	成套住房	chéngtào zhùfáng	the entire flat
8.	職工	zhígōng	staff and workers
9.	實際	shíjì	actual
10.	成本價	chéngběn jià	cost of production
11.	合起來	hé qǐlái	to pool (their money)
12.	產權	chǎnquán	property right
13.	具體	jùtǐ	specific; particular
14.	貸款	dàikuǎn	a loan
15.	收入	shōurù	income
16.	批準	pīzhǔn	to approve; to ratify

Unit Two

2. 教育 就业

中国的教育在文化大革命期间，曾经受到很大的损害。文革以后，政府才又能开始在教育上作出各种努力。二十年后的今天，各类学校都有了很大的发展。就拿大学来说，在过去的 10 年里增长了一倍：从 1979 年的 500 所发展到 1989 年的 1075 所。各类学校的学生人数也大大增长。特别是 1986 年以后，中国政府实行九年义务教育制度，所有六岁半的儿童都必须进入学校学习，学龄儿童入学率达到 97.1%。全国人口中文盲率下降到 20% 左右。同时，各类业余大学，职业中学也发展得很快。现在更有了私立学校，也正在发展中。

但是，由于教育经费不多(1989 年政府花在每个学生身上的钱平均数是 422 元)，办学条件比较差，特别是中小学，房子不够。在农村，学校房子的情况更坏。

中国的教育还是比较落后，能上大学的人还是不多。最近几年，中国的教育又出现了新问题，因为社会上做买卖的人越来越多，这些人的收入比知识分子的高得多，所以许多人认为读书没有用。于是一些农村的孩子不去上学，帮助父母工作、挣钱；大学生、研究生中有的退学去找好工作、有的出国…………，教师中也有的不教书了，去做买卖……

本单元的课文从不同方面写出了中国当前的教育，就业情况。

2. 教育 就業

　　中國的教育在文化大革命期間，曾經受到很大的損害。文革以後，政府才又能開始在教育上作出各種努力。二十年以後的今天各類學校都有了很大的發展。就拿大學來說，在過去的 10 年裡增長了一倍：從 1979 年的 500 所發展到 1989 年的 1075 所。各類學校的學生人數也大大增長。特別是 1986 年以後，中國政府實行九年義務教育制度，所有六歲半的兒童都必須進入學校學習，學齡兒童入學率達到 97.1%。全國人口中文盲率下降到 20% 左右。同時，各類業餘大學，職業中學也發展得很快。現在更有了私立學校，也正在發展中。

　　但是，由於教育經費不多(1989 年政府花在每個學生身上的錢平均數是 422 元)，辦學條件比較差，特別是中小學，房子不夠。在農村，學校房子的情況更壞。

　　中國的教育還是比較落後，能上大學的人還是不多。最近幾年，中國的教育又出現了新問題，因為社會上做買賣的人越來越多，這些人的收入比知識分子的高得多，所以許多人認為讀書沒有用。於是一些農村的孩子不去上學，幫助父母工作、掙錢；大學生、研究生中有的退學去找好工作、有的出國…………，教師中也有的不教書了，去做買賣……

　　本單元的課文從不同方面寫出了中國當前的教育，就業情況。

1.教育	教育	jiàoyù	N. education
2.就業	就业	jiùyè	VO. obtain employment; take up an occupation
3.文化大革命 　文化大革命		wénhuà dàgémìng	NP. the Great Cultural Revolution
4.受損害	受损害	shòu sǔnhài	VP. being damaged
5.類	类	lèi	M. kind; type
6.拿…來说 　拿…來说		ná…láishuō	Prep.Ph. take…for example
7.增長	增长	zēngzhǎng	V. increase; rise
8.人数	人数	rénshù	N. number of people
9.實行	实行	shíxíng	V. put into effect; implement
10.義務教育 　义务教育		yìwù jiàoyù	N. compulsory education
11.制度	制度	zhìdù	N. system
12.必須	必须	bìxū	Adv. must
13.學齡	学龄	xuélíng	N. school age
14.兒童	儿童	értóng	N. children
15.…率	…率	…lǜ	N. the percentage of…
16.達到	达到	dádào	V. reach
17.文盲	文盲	wénmáng	N. illiterate
18.下降	下降	xiàjiàng	V. fall; decline; drop
19.業餘大學 　业余大学		yèyú dàxué	N. college for people who attend after work
20.職業中學 　职业中学		zhíyè zhōngxué	N. vocational high school
21.私立學校 　私立學校		sīlì xuéxiào	N. private school
22.經費	经费	jīngfèi	N. funds; outlay

23.辦學	办学	bànxué	VO. operate schools
24.差	差	chà	SV. not up to standard; inferior
25.情況	情况	qíngkuàng	N. situation; circumstances
26.農村	农村	nóngcūn	N. farming village
27.落後	落后	luòhòu	SV/V. be backward; lag behind
28.知識分子 知识分子		zhīshǐ fènzǐ	NP. intellectuals
29.掙錢	掙钱	zhèngqián	VO. earn money
30.退學	退学	tuìxué	VO. quit school
31.教師	教师	jiàoshī	N. teacher
32.當前	当前	dāngqián	Attr. current; present

2.1 我是职业高中生

我是一个学财会的职业高中生，跟待业青年比，我是个幸运儿。

你了解待业青年吗？他们初中毕业后想继续上学却考不上，想找工作却找不到，只好在家里等待，心里苦恼极了。而我不但有学上，而且毕了业立刻就会有一个好工作……当会计。现在社会上缺会计，我们这些学会计的可是热门货。无论甚么人，听说我学会计都说："好！"

好是好，这我不否认，可是我也有烦恼。因为我们的学校是职业学校，所以要学的课程特别多。会计课程像会计原理、经济学、企业管理等当然都要学，普通高中的课程也都要学。我每天除了上课，就是做功课，很少有时间参加别的活动。另外，学校还有规定：两门主科考试不及格的取消职业高中生的资格。这可真压得我们喘不过气来，有时候我简直受不了啦，可是一想起那些待业的同龄人，我又觉得自己太幸运了。于是，我又忘了自己的烦恼，反而替他们着急，惋惜。

我们职业高中生学了东西可以立刻就用。比如我们班有几个同学，利用暑假，给个体户结帐、检查仓库。工作又轻松又新鲜，既实际又得钱。还有几个学美术的同学，给一些单位的商品画广告。画一次就拿一百来块，真是一举两得的美差事。

现在离毕业只有一年时间了，我想参加明年的全国高等学校统一招生考试。读了十多年书，不去考一考大学太遗憾了。也许我能考上大学呢！即使考不上，心里也不会太难过，因为我努力了。如果考不上，就去当会计，这也不错。

2.1 我是職業高中生

我是一個學財會的職業高中生，跟待業青年比，我是個幸運兒。

你瞭解待業青年嗎？他們初中畢業後想繼續上學却考不上，想找工作却找不到，只好在家裡等待，心裡苦惱極了。而我不但有學上，而且畢了業立刻就會有一個好工作……當會計。現在社會上缺會計，我們這些學會計的可是熱門貨。無論甚麼人，聽說我學會計都說："好！"

好是好，這我不否認，可是我也有煩惱。因為我們的學校是職業學校，所以要學的課程特別多。會計課程像會計原理、經濟學、企業管理等當然都要學，普通高中的課程也都要學。我每天除了上課，就是做功課，很少有時間參加別的活動。另外，學校還有規定：兩門主科考試不及格的取消職業高中生的資格。這可真壓得我們喘不過氣來，有時候我簡直受不了啦，可是一想起那些待業的同齡人，我又覺得自己太幸運了。於是，我又忘了自己的煩惱，反而替他們着急，惋惜。

我們職業高中生學了東西可以立刻就用。比如我們班有幾個同學，利用暑假，給個體戶結帳、檢查倉庫。工作又輕鬆又新鮮，既實際又得錢。還有幾個學美術的同學，給一些單位的商品畫廣告。畫一次就拿一百來塊，真是一舉兩得的美差事。

現在離畢業只有一年時間了，我想參加明年的全國高等學校統一招生考試。讀了十多年書，不去考一考大學太遺憾了。也許我能考上大學呢！即使考不上，心裡也不會太難過，因為我努力了。如果考不上，就去當會計，這也不錯。

生词　NEW WORDS

1.職業	职业	zhíyè	N. profession
2.高中生	高中生	gāozhōng shēng	NP. senior high school student
3.財會	财会	cáikuài	N. finance and accounting
4.待業	待业	dàiyè	VO. await job assignment (a term used only in China)
5.幸運兒	幸运儿	xìngyùnér	N. a lucky guy; a person who always gets good breaks
6.初中	初中	chūzhōng	N. junior high school
7.等待	等待	děngdài	V. wait
8.苦惱	苦恼	kǔnǎo	SV. distressed; be in misery
9.會計	会计	kuàijì	N. accountant
10.缺	缺	quē	V. be short of
11.熱門貨	热门货	rèmén huò	N. goods in great demand
12.否認	否认	fǒurèn	V. deny
13.煩惱	烦恼	fánnǎo	N. vexation; worries
14.課程	课程	kèchéng	N. course of study
15.原理	原理	yuánlǐ	N. principle
16.經濟學	经济学	jīngjì xué	N. economics (as a study)
17.企業管理　企业管理		qǐyè guǎnlǐ	NP. business management (as a study)
18.普通	普通	pǔtōng	SV. general; common
19.活動	活动	huódòng	N. activity
20.另外	另外	lìngwài	Con. in addition; besides
21.規定	规定	guīdìng	N. regulation
22.主科	主科	zhǔkē	N. required courses in the major subject
23.及格	及格	jígé	V. pass (a test)
24.取消	取消	qǔxiāo	V. cancel; nullify
25.資格	资格	zīgé	N. qualification; seniority in a working place/in a position

取消学生资格　to revoke a person's standing as a student

26. 壓	压	yā	V. press; pressure; oppress
27. 喘不過氣來			
喘不过气来		chuǎn bú guò qì lái	VP. cannot breath
28. 簡直(地)			
简直(地)		jiǎnzhí dě	Adv. simply
29. 同齡	同龄	tónglíng	VO. of the same age
30. 反而	反而	fǎnér	Con. on the contrary
31. 惋惜	惋惜	wǎnxī	V. feel sorry for a person over something that should have happened but did not; feel sorry for a person that he or she suffered something undesirable.
32. 暑假	暑假	shǔjià	N. summer vacation
33. 個體戶	个体户	gètǐhù	NP. a small private business (a term used only in China)
34. 結帳	结帐	jiézhàng	VO. to settle accounts
35. 檢查	检查	jiǎnchá	V. check up on; inspect
36. 倉庫	仓库	cāngkù	N. warehouse
检查仓库		to check warehouse stocks	
37. 輕鬆	轻松	qīngsōng	SV. relaxed; light (work)
38. 新鮮	新鲜	xīnxiān	SV. fresh (experience, food, etc.)
39. 實際	实际	shíjì	SV. practical
40. 美術	美术	měishù	N. arts
41. 商品	商品	shāngpǐn	N. merchandise
42. 廣告	广告	guǎnggào	N. advertisement
43. 一舉兩得			
一举两得		yījǔ liǎngdé	Idiom. kill two birds with one stone
44. 美差事			
美差事		měi chāishì	NP. a terrific job
45. 高等學校			
高等学校		gāoděng xuéxiào	NP. colleges and universities
46. 統一招生			

统一招生		tǒngyī zhāoshēng	NP/VP. an announcement of/to announce the national unified entrance examination for college students
47.遗憾	遗憾	yíhàn	SV. regrettable (that something happened or did not happen)
48.即使	即使	jíshǐ	Con. even if

常用词组

1.普通人	普通人		common people
2.普通话	普通话		common language (standard Chinese)
3.有资格	有资格		to be qualified
4.没资格	没资格		to lack qualification
5.老资格	老资格		old hand; veteran
6.取消资格	取消资格		to disqualify
7.取消决定	取消决定		to cancel a decision
8.工作单位	工作单位		work unit
9.生产单位	生产单位		production unit
10.统一招生	统一招生		(see 46.)

1. A ＋ 跟 ＋ B ＋ (相)比, A.....

When comparing A and B, A.....   This construction indicates that when a comparison is made between A and B, A has the following quality. In usage, it is not necessary to state both A's. One has an option to use the first A which is at the beginning of the sentence, or the second A which follows the phrase 跟....相比. The word 相, meaning "each other" or "mutually," may be omitted.

Examples:

(1)跟普通高中(相)比，职业高中的课程要多一些。

跟普通高中(相)比，職業高中的課程要多一些。

Compared to a regular high school, a vocational high school may have more courses.

(2)跟租私房(相)比，住政府分配的房子要便宜多了。

跟租私房(相)比，住政府分配的房子要便宜多了。

Compared to renting a room privately, living in a government assigned room is likely to be much cheaper.

(3)跟同龄人(相)比，他是个幸运儿。

跟同齡人(相)比，他是個幸運兒。

Compared to his peers, he is a lucky guy.

(4)中国现在有十一亿人口，跟一九四九年比，增加了六亿五千万。

中國現在有十一億人口，跟一九四九年比，增加了六億五千萬。

China now has a population of 1.1 billion. Compared to l949 it has increased by 650 million.

2.   SV＋是＋SV, ＋可是 (但是，就是)....   It's true that ..., but...

The first clause "S ＋ SV ＋ 是 ＋ SV" concedes a fact. The second clause asserts another fact which is true regardless of the first fact.

Examples:

(1)这件衣服好是好，就是太贵了，我买不起。

這件衣服好是好，就是太貴了，我買不起。

51

It's true that this piece of clothing is good, but so
expensive that I can't afford to buy it.

(2)学习汉语难是难，但是很有意思。

學習漢語難是難，但是很有意思。

It's true that studying Chinese is difficult, but it
is interesting.

(3)这台洗衣机便宜是便宜，就是质量不太好。

這台洗衣機便宜是便宜，就是質量不太好。

It's true that this washing machine is inexpensive, but its
quality is not too good.

(4)他瘦是瘦，但是身体很健康。

他瘦是瘦，但是身體很健康。

It's true that he is skinny, but he is healthy.

3. 除了+A+就是+B

The basic meaning of 除了 is "excluding or apart from." 除了
together with 就是 limits the matters of discussion to 2, A and B.
除了+A+就是+B, thus, may be interpreted as "other than A, only B"; or
even "aside from A, only B," depending on the context.

Examples:

(1)他每天除了上课就是作功课，没有时间作别的有意思的事情。

他每天除了上課就是作功課，沒有時間作別的有意思的事情。

Everyday, other than going to class, he only does
homework. He has no time for amusement.

(2)这几天除了刮风就是下雨，气温也非常低。

這幾天除了颱風就是下雨，氣溫也非常低。

These last few days, aside from being windy, it has also
been rainy. And the temperature has been extraordinarily
low.

(3)在食堂吃饭，除了米饭就是面条，没有别的。

在食堂吃飯，除了米飯就是麵條，沒有別的。

In the dining hall, aside from rice, there is only noodles to eat, nothing else.

4. 反而 instead;to the contrary(opposed to what has been expected)

反而 connects two clauses, the second expressing a situation opposite to what might have been expected, given the first clause.

Note that 反而 must be placed in the second clause directly preceding the opposing situation.

Examples:

(1)他不但沒有哭，反而笑了。

他不但沒有哭，反而笑了。

He did not cry. Instead, he laughed.

(2)风不但没有停，反而大了。

風不但沒有停，反而大了。

The wind has not stopped; to the contrary, it is even

stronger.

(3)他学汉语比我晚，可是汉语说得反而比我好。

他學漢語比我晚，可是漢語說得反而比我好。

He began studying Chinese later than I, but he speaks

better than I.

(4)已经四月了，天气怎么反而冷起来了。

已經四月了，天氣怎麼反而冷起來了。

It is already April, how can it have turned so cold?

5.即使....也....   even if....still....

即使 is used in the first clause to express an extreme supposition, and 也 in the second clause emphasizes what will happen regardless of the supposition.

Examples:

(1)即使大家都不去，我也要去。

即使大家都不去，我也要去。

Even if no one goes, I still want to go.

(2)即使下雨也不会下得太大。

即使下雨也不會下得太大。

Even if it rains, it cannot be too heavy.

(3)我的考试即使得不了100分，也会有90多分。

我的考試即使得不了100分，也會有90多分。

Even if I cannot get 100 in the exam, I will still get over 90.

一、填空：

　　初中毕业后小王考上了美术（　　）高中，在（　　）学校里，小王要学的（　　）很多，数学、语文、外语这些（　　）高中的课程要学，画画、广告、配色等这些美术课程也得学，所以忙的（　　　　），很少有时间（　　）别的活动。另外，学校还有（　　）：两门课程考试不及格的就（　　）职业高中生的（　　　）。虽然课程很多，可是，跟（　　）青年比，小王觉得（　　）得多，因为待业青年在家里等待，心里很（　　），而小王，不但（　　　　），而且毕业后会有一个好工作。

二、用前一课和本课的生词写出：

　　1. 22 个与"教育"最有关糸的词
　　2. 15 个与"就业"最有关糸的词

三、造句：

　　1.否认　　　2.规定　　　3.取消　　　4.反而　　　5.惋惜
　　6.遗憾　　　7.即使……也　8.… SV 是 SV，但是
　　9. A 跟 B 相比

四、阅读下面的短文：

沒有围墙的大学

　　在北京城北边有一座和普通居民住房一样的小四合院，小四合院的门口却挂着一块大牌子：中华社会大学。这是首都第一家民办(自费)大学。这所大学有 11 个糸、95 个班。这 95 个班分散在北京城的东南西北方的 22 个教室里，人们把它叫做"沒有围墙的大学"。这所小四合院就是这个大学的办公室。

　　中华社会大学是 1982 年成立的。老师是从各个大学请来的，都很有经验。学生是没有考上大学的高中生。这些学生想上大学，可是没考上，他们很苦恼。当他们知道北京有一所民办大学时，他们真高兴。和普通(公办)大学比，

这所大学的条件差多了。他们要自己交学费，他们没有校园，图书馆，更重要的是他们毕业以后国家不分配工作。可是这所大学的学生都学习得非常努力，因为他们知道有机会上大学是非常不容易的。

现在这所大学已经有了近5000名毕业生，这些学生大多数都受到社会的欢迎。一名学经济管理的女学生，毕业后去一家工厂工作，由于她工作努力，知识丰富，外语水平高，能够直接和外国商人谈判，很快地就当了丝绸出口部门的副经理。还有一个学生，毕业后到一所大学当系主任的秘书，他帮助系主任成立了德语系，中德语言中心....工作做得很好，现在已经被送到德国去学习。

中华社会大学越办越大，越办越好。他们已经得到了成功。

社会办学，自费大学，这是中国当前教育改革的一个方向。

1.	围墙	wéiqiáng	enclosing wall
2.	四合院	sìhéyuàn	a compound with houses around a courtyard
3.	牌子	páizi	signboard
4.	首都	shǒudū	capital (of a country)
5.	民办	mínbàn	privately run; privately administered
6.	系	xì	department (of a college or university)
7.	自费	zìfèi	paid by private tuition
8.	分散	fēnsàn	spread out (in all directions)
9.	公办	gōngbàn	run by the government
10.	校园	xiàoyuán	campus
11.	丰富	fēngfù	rich (here:in knowledge)
12.	直接地	zhíjiē dì	directly
13.	谈判	tánpàn	to negotiate
14.	丝绸	sīchóu	silk
15.	副经理	fù-jīnglǐ	assistant manager
16.	系主任	xì-zhǔrèn	department chair (in a college or university)
17.	秘书	mìshū	a secretary
18.	成功	chénggōng	succeed
19.	改革	gǎigé	reform

練習　EXERCISES

一、填空：

　　初中畢業後小王考上了美術（　　）高中，在（　　）學校裡，小王要學的（
　）很多，數學、語文、外語這些（　　）高中的課程要學，畫畫、廣告、配色等
這些美術課程也得學，所以忙的（　　　　），很少有時間（　　）別的活動。
另外，學校還有（　　）：兩門課程考試不及格的就（　　）職業高中生的（
　　）。雖然課程很多，可是，跟（　　）青年比，小王覺得（　　）得多，因為待
業青年在家裡等待，心裡很（　　），而小王，不但（　　　　），而且畢業後會有
一個好工作。

二、用前一課和本課的生辭寫出：
　　1. 22 個與 "教育" 最有關係的詞
　　2. 15 個與 "就業" 最有關係的詞

三、造句：
　　1.否認　　　2.規定　　　3.取消　　　4.反而　　　5.惋惜
　　6.遺憾　　　7.即使....也　　　　　8. .... SV 是 SV，但是
　　9. A 跟 B 相比

四、閱讀下面的短文：

沒有圍牆的大學

　　在北京城北邊有一座和普通居民住房一樣的小四合院，小四合院的門口
卻掛着一塊大牌子：中華社會大學。這是首都第一家民辦(自費)大學。這所大
學有 11 個系、95 個班。這 95 個班分散在北京城的東南西北方的 22 個教室裡，
人們把它叫做 "沒有圍牆的大學"。這所小四合院就是這個大學的辦公室。
　　中華社會大學是 1982 年成立的。老師是從各個大學請來的，都很有經驗。
學生是沒有考上大學的高中生。這些學生想上大學，可是沒考上，他們很苦
惱。當他們知道北京有一所民辦大學時，他們真高興。和普通(公辦)大學比，

這所大學的條件差多了。他們要自己交學費，他們沒有校園，圖書館，更重要的是他們畢業以後國家不分配工作。可是這所大學的學生都學習得非常努力，因為他們知道有機會上大學是非常不容易的。

　　現在這所大學已經有了近5000名畢業生，這些學生大多數都受到社會的歡迎。一名學經濟管理的女學生，畢業後去一家工廠工作，由於她工作努力，知識豐富，外語水平高，能夠直接和外國商人談判，很快地就當了絲綢出口部門的副經理。還有一個學生，畢業後到一所大學當系主任的祕書，他幫助系主任成立了德語系，中德語言中心....工作做得很好，現在已經被送到德國去學習。

　　中華社會大學越辦越大，越辦越好。他們已經得到了成功。

　　社會辦學，自費大學，這是中國當前教育改革的一個方向。

1.	圍牆	wéiqiáng	enclosing wall
2.	四合院	sìhéyuàn	a compound with houses around a courtyard
3.	牌子	páizi	signboard
4.	首都	shǒudū	capital (of a country)
5.	民辦	mínbàn	privately run; privately administered
6.	系	xì	department (of a college or university)
7.	自費	zìfèi	paid by private tuition
8.	分散	fēnsàn	spread out (in all directions)
9.	公辦	gōngbàn	run by the government
10.	校園	xiàoyuán	campus
11.	豐富	fēngfù	rich (here:in knowledge)
12.	直接地	zhíjiē de	directly
13.	談判	tánpàn	to negotiate
14.	絲綢	sīchóu	silk
15.	副經理	fù jīnglǐ	assistant manager
16.	系主任	xì zhǔrèn	department chair (in a college or university)
17.	祕書	mìshū	a secretary
18.	成功	chénggōng	succeed
19.	改革	gǎigé	reform

2.2 从"退学风"到"考研热"

在中国，以前是一人考上研究生，全家都感到光荣。到了八十年代末，中国的大学里却出现了一个前所未有的现象：不少研究生要求退学。仅1988一年中，全国就有700多名研究生自动退学。当时研究生退学的原因主要有两个。

一、为了出国。当时的政府教育部门规定，正在攻读硕士学位的研究生不能申请留学，已经毕业的研究生也要工作两年后，才有资格自费留学。对急着出国留学的研究生来说，这当然是个障碍。

二、为了找一个理想的工作。当时，研究生毕业后，如果由政府分配到一个单位去工作，工资不会太高。可是如果去一个大的企业单位，特别是中外合资的企业单位工作，工资是一般研究生的两倍、三倍。因此，有些研究生在上学期间，一找到理想的工作就退学求职。

十年以后，在1997年人民大学研究生报名处，第一天报名交费的就有2000多人。近年来北京各所大学的"考研热"一天比一天高。在北京经济贸易大学班的一个英语考研班上，可以坐下1000人的大教室居然坐满了人，还有许多人自己带着椅子来听课。

短短的十年，怎么会有这么大的变化呢？其中一个重要的原因是社会对人才的需求。

十年前，研究生毕业以后主要分配到科研单位和学校工作。这些单位的工资比一些大公司或大企业要差得多，而当时这些大公司和大企业对人才的需求以本科生为主。因此，不少大学生一找到合适的企业单位就不再考研究生，甚至考上了也退学。

十年后，情况却有了很大的变化。社会对本科以上学历的人才需求一年比一年增加。据北京市人才市场介绍，北京市对本科以上学历的人才需求，1995 年是 74%，1996 年上升到 80%。一些重点大学，如北京大学，清华大学等也有新规定，新教师必须有博士学位。某些大公司对公司中硕士、博士占职工总数的比例也有了更高的要求。因此，已经工作了的人和本科毕业生都希望再回学校攻读硕士或博士学位，以后可以找到更好的工作。

2.2 從"退學風"到"考研熱"

在中國，以前是一人考上研究生，全家都感到光榮。到了八十年代末，中國的大學裡却出現了一個前所未有的現象：不少研究生要求退學。僅 1988 一年中，全國就有 700 多名研究生自動退學。當時研究生退學的原因主要有兩個。

一、為了出國。當時的政府教育部門規定，正在攻讀碩士學位的研究生不能申請留學，已經畢業的研究生也要工作兩年後，才有資格自費留學。對急着出國留學的研究生來説，這當然是個障礙。

二、為了找一個理想的工作。當時，研究生畢業後，如果由政府分配到一個單位去工作，工資不會太高。可是如果去一個大的企業單位，特別是中外合資的企業單位工作，工資是一般研究生的兩倍、三倍。因此，有些研究生在上學期間，一找到理想的工作就退學求職。

十年以後，在 1997 年人民大學研究生報名處，第一天報名交費的就有 2000 多人。近年來北京各所大學的"考研熱"一天比一天高。在北京經濟貿易大學班的一個英語考研班上，可以坐下1000 人的大教室居然坐滿了人，還有許多人自己帶着椅子來聽課。

短短的十年，怎麼會有這麼大的變化呢？其中一個重要的原因是社會對人才的需求。

十年前，研究生畢業以後主要分配到科研單位和學校工作。這些單位的工資比一些大公司或大企業要差得多，而當時這些大公司和大企業對人才的需求以本科生為主。因此，不少大學生一找到合適的企業單位就不再考研究生，甚至考上了也退學。

十年後，情況卻有了很大的變化。社會對本科以上學歷的人才需求一年比一年增加。據北京市人才市場介紹,北京市對本科以上學歷的人才需求,1995年是74%,1996年上升到80%。一些重點大學,如北京大學,清華大學等也有新規定,新教師必須有博士學位。某些大公司對公司中碩士、博士佔職工總數的比例也有了更高的要求。因此,已經工作了的人和本科畢業生都希望再回學校攻讀碩士或博士學位,以後可以找到更好的工作。

生词 NEW WORDS

1. 退學	退学	tuì xué	VO. leave school; withdraw from school
2. 風（氣）	风（气）	fēng(qì)	N. fashion; custom; common practice
3. 研究生	研究生	yánjiūshēng	N. graduate student
4. 感到	感到	gǎndào	VP. feel; have a sense of
5. 光榮	光荣	guāngróng	N. glory; honor
6. 八十年代末	八十年代末	bāshí niándài mò	TW. end of the eighties
7. 出現	出现	chūxiàn	V. appear; emerge; arise
8. 前所未有	前所未有	qián-suǒ-wèi-yǒu	Ph. unprecedented
9. 要求	要求	yāoqiú	V. demand; request
10. 僅	仅	jǐn	Adv. only; solely; merely
11. 自動	自动	zìdòng	Adv. voluntarily; of one's own accord
12. 部門	部门	bùmén	N. department
13. 攻讀	攻读	gōngdú	VP. work for ("actively study")
14. 碩士	硕士	shuòshì	N. Master of Arts (M.A.)
15. 博士	博士	bóshì	N. Doctor (of Philosophy, etc.)
16. 學位	学位	xuéwèi	N. (academic) degree
17. 申請	申请	shēnqǐng	V. apply for
18. 自費	自费	zìfèi	Attr. at one's own expense
19. 障礙	障碍	zhàng'ài	N. obstacle; barrier
20. 理想	理想	lǐxiǎng	SV. ideal
21. 工資	工资	gōngzī	N. wages; pay
22. 單位	单位	dānwèi	N. unit (of organization)
23. 企業	企业	qǐyè	N. enterprise; business
24. 中外合資	中外合资	zhōngwài hézī	N. Chinese-foreign joint venture
25. 求職	求职	qiúzhí	VO. look for a job
26. 報名處	报名处	bàomíngchù	N. registration office
27. 交費	交费	jiāofèi	VO. pay a fee

28.教室	教室	jiàoshì		N. classroom
29.居然	居然	jūrán		Adv. surprisingly; (it) actually (happened that); unexpectedly
30.坐满	坐满	zuòmǎn		RVC. full to the last seat
31.人才	人才	réncái		N. talented person; qualified person
32.需求	需求	xūqiú		N. demand; requirement
33.以.....為主	以.....为主	yǐ..... wéi zhǔ		VP. regard....as the main (requirement)
34.本科生	本科生	běnkēshēng		N. undergraduate (degree)
35.....以上	.....以上	.....yǐshàng		Det. ...and above
36.學歷	学历	xuélì		N. record of schooling
37.增加	增加	zēngjiā		V. increase; add
38.上升	上升	shàngshēng		V. rise; go up
39.重點大學	重点大学	zhòngdiǎn dàxué		N. top-ranked university
40.必須	必须	bìxū		V. must; have to
41.某	某	mǒu		Det. such and such (N); a certain (N)

常用词组   STOCK PHRASES

1.前所未有	前所未有	unprecedented
2.申請學校	申请学校	to apply to a school
申請工作	申请工作	to apply for jobs
申請留學	申请留学	to apply for studying abroad
3.公費留學	公费留学	to study abroad at state expense
自費留學	自费留学	to study abroad at one's own expense
4.科研單位	科研单位	scientific research organization
企業單位	企业单位	business organization
中外合資企業	中外合资企业	Chinese-foreign joint venture

语法　GRAMMAR

1. 为

　　A. 为+NP　　　　　S + (为+NP) + VP

为 here functions as a preposition, which takes a noun phrase as its object. This 为+NP must be followed by a verb phrase. Semantically, 为 introduces 1) the beneficiary who profits from the action of the sentence, 2) the object of one's service or concern.

　　Examples:

　　(1)交易会为广州带来了很多各地游客。

　　　　交易會為廣州帶來了很多各地遊客。

　　　　The trade fair has brought many tourists from various places to the city of Canton. (Canton profits from the trade fair.)

　　(2)老李为孩子找到了一个很好的英语老师。

　　　　老李為孩子找到了一個很好的英語老師。

　　　　Lǎo Lǐ has found a very good English teacher for his child.

　　(3)我已经拿到了去中国的签证了，你不必为我着急了。

　　　　我已經拿到了去中國的簽證了，你不必為我着急了。

　　　　You don't have to worry about me, I have got the visa to go to China.

　　B. 为了+VP　　　　S + (为了+VP1) + VP2

In contrast to the previous usage in which 为 stands alone, 为 in this pattern includes 了 in its domain. This 为了 must be followed by a verb phrase rather than a noun phrase as in the pattern above. Semantically, 为了 is used to introduce a purpose or a reason (expressed by VP1) for an action (expressed by VP2) to take place.

　　Examples:

　　(1)那家商店为了能得到更多的顾客，从日本进口了很多新型的电视机。

　　　　那家商店為了能得到更多的顧客，從日本進口了很多新型的電視機。

　　　　For the purpose of getting more customers, that store has imported many new models of television sets from Japan.

66

(2)交易会为了作好工作，用了不少学过企业管理的大学生。

交易會為了作好工作，用了不少學過企業管理的大學生。

In order to do the job well, the trade fair hired many college students who had studied business management.

(3)老李为了给孩子找一个好的英语老师，化了很多钱。

老李為了給孩子找一個好的英語老師，化了很多錢。

Lǎo Lǐ has spent a lot of money for the purpose of finding a good English teacher for his child.

(Compare this sentence with sentence (3) in the previous section of the 为+NP pattern.)

Note that the phrase "为了出国" in this lesson is part of the sentence "研究生为了出国退学。"

2. 对.....来说   S + (对.....来说) + VP

"对......来说" is a prepositional phrase, which may appear either before or after the subject. Semantically, a sentence with this phrase expresses a personal opinion rather than a fact. "对.....来说" may be translated as "as far as ..... is concerned; to X ....."

Examples:

(1)汉字简化的政策，对我来说，可以提高工人和农民的教育水平。

漢字簡化的政策，對我來說，可以提高工人和農民的教育水平。

To me, the policy of simplification of characters can raise the educational level of workers and farmers.

(2)对王新民的父母来说，他念职业高中比普通高中好得多，因为职业高中一毕业就可以有工作。

對王新民的父母來說，他念職業高中比普通高中好得多，因為職業高中一畢業就可以有工作。

As far as Wáng Xīn Mín's parents are concerned, his attending a vocational high school is much better than a regular high school, because he will be able to get a job as soon as he graduates from that vocational high school.

(3)对很多研究生来说，拿到学位后不能迅速就业是很苦恼的事。

對很多研究生來說，拿到學位後不能迅速就業是很苦惱的事。

To many graduate students, it would be distressing if one could not quickly obtain employment right after getting a degree.

3. 一天比一天；一年比一年　　　一天比一天/一年比一年 + SV

Both phrases serve the function of an adverb. They express the fact that the quality or the state of the condition or the action is getting more and more so day by day or year by year.

Examples:

(1)那个城市的办学条件很差，所以教育水平一年比一年落后。

那個城市的辦學條件很差，所以教育水平一年比一年落後。

The conditions under which the schools are run in that city have been poor. As a resul, the educational level (in that city) is falling behind year by year.

(2)中国人民的生活水平现在一天比一天高了。

中國人民的生活水平現在一天比一天高了。

The living standard of the Chinese people at present is rising day by day.

(3)经过改革以后，那家中外合资企业生产的水平提高得一年比一年快。

經過改革以後，那家中外合資企業生產的水平提高得一年比一年快。

After the reform, that Chinese-foreign joint venture has raised the level of their production faster year by year.

4. 居然

Being an adverb, 居然 can only be placed before a verb phrase. It is used to express a strong feeling that some situation or happening exceeds the speaker's expectations or is contrary to them. For example, something which should not happen happens, something which is inconceivable happens or something which is thought to be difficult to accomplish is accomplished. Note that the speaker is not the subject of the sentence.

Examples:

(1)为了去看电影，小王居然没上课。

为了去看電影，小王居然沒上課。

Surprisingly, Xiǎo Wáng, simply for the purpose of going to a movie, didn't go to class.

(2)他已经是大学生了，居然不认识那个字。

他已經是大學生了，居然不認識那個字。

He is already a college student. It's amazing that he doen't know that character (word).

(3)他们结了婚才两个月，现在居然要离婚了。

他們結了婚才兩個月，現在居然要離婚了。

They have been married only for two months, yet they are actually now considering a divorce.

(4)他，一个小学生，居然写出了这么好的小说，真了不起。

他，一個小學生，居然寫出了這麼好的小說，真了不起。

He is only a grade school student. It is terrific that he actually wrote such a good novel.

5. 以 + X + 为 + Y   S + 以 + X + 为 + Y

This construction has two patterns, 1) both X and Y are noun phrases, 2) while X is an adjective/sv or a verb-object construction, Y is a noun phrase. Although both constructions literally mean "take X to be Y," the interpretation varies according to the context of the sentence. See the following:

A. Examples:

(1)纽约日报是以广告为主的报纸。

紐約日報是以廣告為主的報紙。

The New York Daily News is a newspaper which considers advertisements as central.

(2)他不但聪明而且非常努力，所以我们都以他为榜样。

他不但聰明而且非常努力，所以我們都以他為榜樣。

69

Since he is not only intelligent but also works extremely hard, we all take him to be our role model.

B. Examples:

(1)那个大公司对人才的需求以精明能干为主。

那個大公司對人才的需求以精明能幹為主。

That big company regards intelligence and capability as the major requirement for their recruitment of talents. (both 精明 and 能幹 are SV)

(2)老张答应帮助我，但以给他 100 元为条件。

老張答應幫助我，但以給他 100 元為條件。

Lǎo Zhāng promised to help me (but) on the condition that I give him one hundred yuan.

6. 甚至　　　A, B 甚至 C

甚至 links 2 or more situations or conditions. It appears only before the last one. Semantically, it is used 1) to invite a comparison between what happened and what might have happened, 2) to give an extreme example.

Examples:

(1)十几年前，美国失业的人很多，甚至很有能力的人也失业。

十幾年前，美國失業的人很多，甚至很有能力的人也失業。

Some ten years ago many Americans, even the most capable persons, lost their jobs.

(2) 八十年代末，不少大学生一找到合适的企业单位就不再考研究生，甚至考上了也退学。

八十年代末，不少大學生一找到合適的企業單位就不再考研究生，甚至考上了也退學。

In the late eighties, many college students, once they found a good job in a business organization, stopped trying to get into graduate school - even if they had been accepted, they would withdraw.

(3) 我们认识已经五六年了，他总是对我很不客气，甚至现在都还是对我不客气。

我們認識已經五六年了，他總是對我很不客氣，甚至現在都還是對我不客氣。

We have known each other for five or six years. He has always been rude to me, even to the present.

一、常用词组练习：用本课的常用词组填空

1.他是一个念科学的研究生，还有半年就可以拿到博士学位了，他希望拿到学位以后能申请到一个（　　）去工作。

2.小王知道，中国现在和将来都需要很多电脑方面的人才，所以决定到美国去学电脑，现在正在写信（　　），希望明年可以开始在美国的大学学习。

3.这个汽车工厂是一个（　　），工厂的地点和工人由中国方面供给（provide），其他方面由德国方面供给。

4.我妹妹申请到（　　），八月就要到日本念书去了。在日本四年的学费和生活费都是由中国政府给。

5.李成龙是这个小农村里第一个考上大学的人，他下个月就要到北京上学去了。这是村里（　　）的情况。整个村子的人都感到光荣和兴奋。

二、猜测词的意思（不用字典）

1.经贸大学是什么意思？

2.人才市场是什么地方？

3.他到美国去留学的主要原因是学习电脑，次要原因是有机会到美国各地去看看。

次要是什么意思？

三、造句：用下面的语法点和常用词组造句，每项造一句。(Simple sentences will not be acceptable. Your sentences must provide context such as time, location, condition, personal opinion, etc.)

1.为了+VP　　　　4.以……为……　　　7.申请工作

2.对……来说　　　5.甚至　　　　　　　8.公费留学

3.居然　　　　　　6.前所未有　　　　　9.中外合资企业

四、阅读理解（根据本课内容回答问题）

1.一般中国人对攻读硕士、博士学位的人是什么态度？

2.八十年代中国政府的留学生政策是什么？

3.这个政策产生了什么问题？

4.当时研究生毕业后都有工作，不会失业，但是为什么他们不满意？

5.那时候研究生认为理想的工作是什么？

6.九十年代很多学生对念研究院的态度有了很大的改变，本课给了三个例子是什么？（简单说明）

7.九十年代，中国对有硕士、博士学位的人才，需求越来越增加。

请简单写出书上给的三个例子：

a.用数字说明

b.用重点大学的情况说明

c.用一些大公司的情况说明

五、作文：《经济改革对高等教育(higher education)的影响》

可用下面的格式。

a.研究生对上学态度的改变

b.八十年代研究生的情况（原因和结果：只谈经济方面的原因）

c.九十年代研究生情况的改变（用一两个例子说明情况的改变：改变的原因，改变的结果）

d.你自己的观点（viewpoint）

六、阅读下面的短文：

大学的改变

近年来社会发生了很大的改变；同时，大学也发生了改变。这些改变可以从四个方面看出来：

一，收费方面。以前，上大学不必交学费，所有的学杂费都是国家给，但现在国家不再给了。国家认为：第一，高等教育不是义务教育，不应该由国家给。第二，培养一名学生每年要化四，五千元。目前国家在教育方面的经费不够，给了学生的学杂费以后就没有钱再用在先进的设备和良好的教学环境上。这对大学的发展一定会是一个障碍。因此，从 1989 年起，大学开始向学生收学杂费。目前在收费方面国家还没有统一的标准。一般的收费情况大概是公费生学杂费每学年几百元，自费生每学年几千元。今后情况改变了，收费标准也还会有新的改变。

　　二、分配工作方面。以前公费生毕业后工作由国家统一分配，但自费生毕业后可以自己找工作。现在各地都有人才市场、大学生就业市场。用人单位可以挑选大学生，大学生也可以挑选用人单位。双方同意后，跟有关部门办一下手续就行了。今后要实行在国家政策指导下，毕业生自己选择工作的办法。

　　三、课余时间方面。现在不少大学生利用课余时间工作。有的去做买卖，有的转让自己的研究成果，干什么的都有。这是前所未有的现象。

　　四、大学内部的改变。为了适应社会的需要，许多大学加了很多新的专业。有的大学为了适应国际上交往的需要，改了校名。学校内部的管理也在发生变化。

　　就像社会上许多方面在改革一样，大学也在不断地改变中。

1.	收费	shōufèi	to charge (to collect fees)
2.	学杂费	xué-zá-fèi	tuition and miscellaneous fees
3.	培养	péiyǎng	to nurture
4.	先进设备	xiānjìn shèbèi	advanced facilities
5.	标准	biāozhǔn	standard
6.	挑选	tiāoxuǎn	to choose; select
7.	同意	tóngyì	to agree
8.	办手续	bàn shǒuxù	to make arrangements (go through procedures)
9.	在....指导下	zài.....zhǐdǎo xià	under the guidance of.....
10.	课余时间	kèyú shíjiān	free time (after class hours)
11.	转让	zhuǎnràng	to transfer
12.	成果	chéng guǒ	achievement; (positive) results
13.	适应需要	shìyìng xūyào	to meet the needs
14.	专业	zhuānyè	special field of study

一、常用辭組練習：用本課的常用辭組填空
 1.他是一個念科學的研究生，還有半年就可以拿到博士學位了，他希望拿
 到學位以後能申請到一個〔 〕去工作。
 2.小王知道，中國現在和將來都需要很多電腦方面的人才，所以決定到美
 國去學電腦，現在正在寫信〔 〕，希望明年可以開始在美國的大
 學學習。
 3.這個汽車工廠是一個〔 〕，工廠的地點和工人由中國方面供給
 (provide)，其他方面由德國方面供給。
 4.我妹妹申請到〔 〕，八月就要到日本念書去了。在日本四年的學
 費和生活費都是由中國政府給。
 5.李成龍是這個小農村裡第一個考上大學的人，他下個月就要到北京上學
 去了。這是村裡〔 〕的情況。整個村子的人都感到光榮和興奮。

二、猜測詞的意思（不用字典）
 1.<u>經貿大學</u>是什麼意思？
 2.<u>人才市場</u>是什麼地方？
 3.他到美國去留學的主要原因是學習電腦，<u>次要</u>原因是有機會到美國各地
 去看看。
 <u>次要</u>是什麼意思？

三、造句：用下面的語法點和常用辭組造句，每項造一句。(Simple sentences
 will not be acceptable. Your sentences must provide context such as
 time, location, condition, personal opinion, etc.)
 1.為了+VP   4.以⋯⋯為⋯⋯   7.申請工作
 2.對⋯⋯來說   5.甚至   8.公費留學
 3.居然   6.前所未有   9.中外合資企業

四、閱讀理解（根據本課內容回答問題）
 1.一般中國人對攻讀碩士、博士學位的人是甚麼態度？
 2.八十年代中國政府的留學生政策是甚麼？

3.這個政策產生了甚麼問題?

4.當時研究生畢業後都有工作,不會失業,但是為甚麼他們不滿意?

5.那時候研究生認為理想的工作是甚麼?

6.九十年代很多學生對念研究院的態度有了很大的改變,本課給了三個
例子是甚麼? (簡單說明)

7.九十年代,中國對有碩士、博士學位的人才,需求越來越增加。
請簡單寫出書上給的三個例子:
a.用數字說明
b.用重點大學的情況說明
c.用一些大公司的情況說明

五、作文:《經濟改革對高等教育(higher education)的影響》
可用下面的格式。
a.研究生對上學態度的改變
b.八十年代研究生的情況 (原因和結果:只談經濟方面的原因)
c.九十年代研究生情況的改變 (用一兩個例子說明情況的改變:
改變的原因,改變的結果)
d.你自己的觀點 (viewpoint)

六、閱讀下面的短文:

大學的改變

近年來社會發生了很大的改變;同時,大學也發生了改變。這些改變可
以從四個方面看出來:

一,收費方面。以前,上大學不必交學費,所有的學雜費都是國家給,
但現在國家不再給了。國家認為:第一,高等教育不是義務教育,不應該由
國家給。第二,培養一名學生每年要化四,五千元。目前國家在教育方面的
經費不夠,給了學生的學雜費以後就沒有錢再用在先進的設備和良好的教學
環境上。這對大學的發展一定會是一個障礙。因此,從 1989 年起,大學開始
向學生收學雜費。目前在收費方面國家還沒有統一的標準。一般的收費情況
大概是公費生學雜費每學年幾百元,自費生每學年幾千元。今後情況改變了,

收費標準也還會有新的改變。

　　二、分配工作方面。以前公費生畢業後工作由國家統一分配，但自費生畢業後可以自己找工作。現在各地都有人才市場、大學生就業市場。用人單位可以挑選大學生，大學生也可以挑選用人單位。雙方同意後，跟有關部門辦一下手續就行了。今後要實行在國家政策指導下，畢業生自己選擇工作的辦法。

　　三、課餘時間方面。現在不少大學生利用課餘時間工作。有的去做買賣，有的轉讓自己的研究成果，幹甚麼的都有。這是前所未有的現象。

　　四、大學內部的改變。為了適應社會的需要，許多大學加了很多新的專業。有的大學為了適應國際上交往的需要，改了校名。學校內部的管理也在發生變化。

　　就像社會上許多方面在改革一樣，大學也在不斷地改變中。

1. 收費　　　　shōufèi　　　　to charge (to collect fees)

2. 學雜費　　　xué-zá-fèi　　　tuition and miscellaneous fees

3. 培養　　　　péiyǎng　　　　to nurture

4. 先進設備　　xiānjìn shèbèi　advanced facilities

5. 標準　　　　biāozhǔn　　　　standard

6. 挑選　　　　tiāoxuǎn　　　　to choose; select

7. 同意　　　　tóngyì　　　　　to agree

8. 辦手續　　　bàn shǒuxù　　　to make arrangements (go through procedures)

9. 在....指導下　zài.....zhīdǎo xià　　under the guidance of.....

10. 課餘時間　kèyú shíjiān　　free time (after class hours)

11. 轉讓　　　　zhuǎnràng　　　to transfer

12. 成果　　　　chéng guǒ　　　achievement; (positive) results

13. 適應需要　　shìyìng xūyào　　to meet the needs

14. 專業　　　　zhuānyè　　　　special field of study

2.3 "读书无用"论的新冲击

浙江大学有一对夫妇都是副教授，有三个孩子。他们工作几十年，家里除了书，没有多少其他的东西。后来，老大老二大学毕业了，但他们的生活仍然是那么清苦。前几年，他们的小女儿高考失利，就去杭州一家高级宾馆作经理助手，几年时间，这个家庭发生了很大的变化，彩电，冰箱等现代化用品进了这个穷教授家门。老教授骄傲地说："家里值钱的东西都是小女儿买的"但骄傲之后，却又非常难过。一辈子献身教育，培养了许多人才，著作也很多，可以说为教育事业作出了很大的贡献，为甚么待遇还不如没有读过大学的小女儿！

像这一类的事情还有很多。某大学有一位工程师，生活一直很困难，自从没文化的妻子摆了个点心摊以后，一年时间就还清了一切债务，这位工程师多病的脸上也有了红光。另外，还有位二十六岁的青年教师，他家兄弟三人，小学毕业的大哥化十万造了一栋四层楼，高中毕业的二哥造了一栋三层楼。他大学毕业，却只能住父母留下的小平房，别说造房子，就是结婚也结不起，他考虑了很久，决定不教书了。

现在，许多教师不愿意教书，学生不愿意读书，主要是因为知识分子的生活水平太低。于是，许多学校办起了商店，小卖部等赚钱企业，许多教师到校外兼职，增加收入。

2.3 "讀書無用"論的新衝擊

浙江大學有一對夫婦都是副教授，有三個孩子。他們工作幾十年，家裡除了書，沒有多少其他的東西。後來，老大老二大學畢業了，但他們的生活仍然是那麼清苦。前幾年，他們的小女兒高考失利，就去杭州一家高級賓館作經理助手，幾年時間，這個家庭發生了很大的變化，彩電，冰箱等現代化用品進了這個窮教授家門。老教授驕傲地說："家裡值錢的東西都是小女兒買的"但驕傲之後，卻又非常難過。一輩子獻身教育，培養了許多人才，著作也很多，可以說為教育事業作出了很大的貢獻，為甚麼待遇還不如沒有讀過大學的小女兒！

像這一類的事情還有很多。某大學有一位工程師，生活一直很困難，自從沒文化的妻子擺了個點心攤以後，一年時間就還清了一切債務，這位工程師多病的臉上也有了紅光。另外，還有位二十六歲的青年教師，他家兄弟三人，小學畢業的大哥化十萬造了一棟四層樓，高中畢業的二哥造了一棟三層樓。他大學畢業，卻只能住父母留下的小平房，別說造房子，就是結婚也結不起，他考慮了很久，決定不教書了。

現在，許多教師不願意教書，學生不願意讀書，主要是因為知識分子的生活水平太低。於是，許多學校辦起了商店，小賣部等賺錢企業，許多教師到校外兼職，增加收入。

生词 NEW WORDS

1.副教授	副教授	fù jiàoshòu	N. associate professor
2.辛苦	辛苦	xīnkǔ	SV. harsh; hardships
3.清苦	清苦	qīngkǔ	SV. penurious; in straitened circumstances
4.高考	高考	gāokào	NP. college entrance examination
5.失利	失利	shīlì	VP. suffer a setback
6.賓館	宾馆	bīnguǎn	NP. hotel (a term used in mainland China)
7.經理	经理	jīnglǐ	N. manager
8.助手	助手	zhùshǒu	N. assistant
9.發生	发生	fāshēng	V. take place; occur
10.變化	变化	biànhuà	N/V. change
11.彩電	彩电	cǎidiàn	N. color television
12.冰箱	冰箱	bīngxiāng	N. refrigerator
13.現代化	现代化	xiàndàihuà	SV. modernized
14.驕傲	骄傲	jiāo'ào	SV. proud
15.值錢	值钱	zhíqián	SV. valuable
16.獻身	献身	xiànshēn	VO. give one's life for; dedicate oneself to
17.培養	培养	péiyǎng	V. cultivate (the mind, manner, etc.)
18.人才	人才	réncái	N. a person of ability; a talented person
19.著作	著作	zhùzuò	N. publications
20.待遇	待遇	dàiyù	N. compensation (pay and benefits)
21.工程師	工程师	gōngchéngshī	N. engineer
22.文化	文化	wénhuà	N. culture; education; schooling
23.攤	摊	tān	N. vendor's stand; stall
24.債務	债务	zhàiwù	N. debt; liabilities
25.兄弟	兄弟	xiōngdì	N. brothers
26.棟	栋	dòng	M. for building
27.論	论	lùn	N. theory; discussion
28.興起	兴起	xīngqǐ	V. rise
29.生活水平 生活水平		shēnghuó shuǐpíng	N. standard of living

30.小賣部	小卖部	xiǎomàibù	NP. a small shop (attached to a school or work place)
31.賺錢	赚钱	zhuànqián	VO. make money
32.兼職	兼职	jiānzhí	VO. hold two or more jobs concurrently
33.平房	平房	píngfáng	N. single-story house

常用词组 STOCK PHRASES

1.發生變化	发生变化	a change takes/has taken place
2.發生問題	发生问题	problems arise/rose
3.專門人才	专门人才	a person with special professional skills
4.培養人才	培养人才	to cultivate people's talents; to train professionals
5.提高待遇	提高待遇	to raise salary and benefits
6.提高水平	提高水平	to raise the level/standard
7.提高生活水平	提高生活水平	to raise the standard of living
8.提高文化水平	提高文化水平	to raise the standard of education

1.....之后(以后)

之后 is generally interchangeable with 以后 but is more literary. 之后 follows a NP or VP, and the entire phrase may go either before the subject or after.

A. NP + 之后

Examples:

(1)1949 年之后，中国增加了 6 亿多人口。

1949 年之後，中國增加了 6 億多人口。

Since 1949, the Chinese population has increased more than 6 hundred million.

(2)那次会议之后，我们没再见过面。

那次會議之後，我們沒再見過面。

We have not seen each other since that meeting.

(3)三天之后，他又回来了。

三天之後，他又回來了。

He came back again after three days.

B. VP + 之后

(4)起床之后，应该到室外活动活动。

起床之後，應該到室外活動活動。

After getting up, one should go outside to move one's muscles.

(5)听了他的话之后，我才明白是怎么回事。

聽了他的話之後，我才明白是怎麼回事。

Not until I heard what he said did I understand what was going on.

(6)他毕业之后就去国外了。

他畢業之後就去國外了。

He went abroad after graduation.

2. ....不如....

不如 has two usages.

A. A + 不如 + B   A is not as good as B.

Both A and B are nouns. 不如,in this case, conveys the idea that the quality/condition of A cannot match that of B.

Examples:

(1)他的汉语很好，我们几个人都不如他。

他的漢語很好，我們幾個人都不如他。

His Chinese is very good. None of us is as good as he.

(2)他的健康，现在不如从前。

他的健康，現在不如從前。

His health is declining. (His health at present is not as good as that of former days.)

(3)为甚么老教授的待遇还不如一个没上过大学的女孩子的？

為甚麼老教授的待遇還不如一個沒上過大學的女孩子的？

Why is the old professor's salary not as good as that of the girl who has never attended a college?

B. ....不如 + clause + 吧。   had better (suggestion)

The clause in this construction expresses a suggestion. 不如 introduces the suggestion that what follows is preferable.

Examples:

(4)今天天气不好，咱们不如明天再去吧。

今天天氣不好，咱們不如明天再去吧。

The weather is not good today. We had better go tomorrow instead.

(5)我看不如让小王去办这件事吧。

我看不如讓小王去辦這件事吧。

I feel that we had better let Xiao Wang take care of this matter.

3. 某

某 goes before either a noun or a combination of a measure word and a noun to indicate a meaning equivalent to "such and such " or "a certain ...".

Examples:

(1)他出生在美国东部的某城市。

他出生在美國東部的某城市。

He was born in a certain city in the eastern U.S.

(2)他把护照丢在旅行路上的某个地方了。

他把護照丟在旅行路上的某個地方了。

He lost his passport at a certain place on the road while travelling.

(3)由于某种原因，我不能跟你一起去看电影。

由於某種原因，我不能跟你一起去看電影。

For a certain reason I can't go to see a movie with you.

练习　EXERCISES

一、根据课文内容判断下面的句子，对的在括号里写 "T"，错的写 "F".。
 1.浙江大学的一对副教授家里生活很清苦。(　　)
 2.他们的三个孩子都大学毕业了。(　　)
 3.老三在一家大宾馆当经理。(　　)
 4.这对教授小女儿的工资比她父亲的工资高得多。(　　)
 5.老二为老教授买了许多现代化的家具。(　　)
 6.老教授感到骄傲，不是因为他的女儿能挣很高的工资而是他
  自己为教育事业作出了很大的贡献。(　　)
 7.有一位二十六岁的青年教师，他大学毕业后造了一栋二层楼
  的房子。(　　)
 8.这位青年教师的二哥有一栋三层楼的房子，大哥有一栋四层
  楼的房子。(　　)
 9.目前"读书无用"的思想对中国的教育影响很大。(　　)
 10.为了挣钱，现在有不少教师找兼职的工作。(　　)

二、用约三百字写本课的大纲。

三、阅读下面的短文：
谁也沒想到
 谁也沒想到一切发生得那么快，发生得那么突然。
 十几年前，大家差不多都一样，你一个月几十块工资，我也几十块；你
穿一件蓝衣服，我穿一件灰的；你每月吃两次用鱼票买的鱼，我也没有第三
次可以吃。
 然而，改革了、开放了、政策改变了，变得使有些人富了起来。这些人
富得那么快，又富得那么让一些人心里不是滋味。下面是作者和一位老师的
一段对话。
 老师："有一天我去市场买菜，我买了些白菜，萝卜，听见有人叫我老
师，一看是个几年前我教过的学生。这个学生学习很差，考试常不及格，初
中一毕业就离开学校了。现在他在市场上卖菜，长得白白胖胖的。你猜他一
个月挣多少钱？"

作者："有七八百块吧？"

老师："一千多！他亲口告诉我的。我估计这还是个保守的数字。一个月挣我一年的工资。聊了几句，这个学生就把一只鸡和一块火腿放进我的包里，还说上学时没听老师的话，现在帐都算不好……"

作者："你要了吗？"

老师："当然没要！老师怎么能要学生的东西？我把鸡和火腿放回去了，他很不高兴。"

作者："看来他是真心的。"

老师："真心的也不能要。回到家里，我心里很不平静，晚饭也没吃。"

作者："你是不是觉得不公平？"

老师："是，无论如何我的价值也不会只等于他的十分之一。"

作者："那当然，你文化比他高，能力比他强，要是你也去卖菜，一定比他挣得还要多！"

1.突然	tūrán	sudden
2.鱼票	yúpiào	a ration coupon for fish
3.然而	rán'ér	however; nevertheless
4.富	fù	rich
5.不是滋味	búshì zīwèi	be upset; feel bad
6.白菜	báicài	Chinese cabbage
7.萝卜	luóbǒ	radish
8.白白胖胖	báibái-pàngpàng	fat and sassy/saucy
9.估计	gūjì	to estimate; reckon
10.保守	bǎoshǒu	conservative
11.火腿	huǒtuǐ	ham
12.算帐	suànzhàng	keep accounts
13.平静	píngjìng	calm
14.公平	gōngpíng	fair
15.无论如何	wúlùn rúhé	at any rate; in any case

練習　EXERCISES

一、根據課文內容判斷下面的句子，對的在括號裡寫 "T"，錯的寫 "F"。

1.浙江大學的一對副教授家裡生活很清苦。（　　）

2.他們的三個孩子都大學畢業了。（　　）

3.老三在一家大賓館當經理。（　　）

4.這對教授小女兒的工資比她父親的工資高得多。（　　）

5.老二為老教授買了許多現代化的家具。（　　）

6.老教授感到驕傲，不是因為他的女兒能掙很高的工資而是他自己為教育事業作出了很大的貢獻。（　　）

7.有一位二十六歲的青年教師，他大學畢業後造了一棟二層樓的房子。（　　）

8.這位青年教師的二哥有一棟三層樓的房子，大哥有一棟四層樓的房子。（　　）

9.目前"讀書無用"的思想對中國的教育影響很大。（　　）

10.為了掙錢，現在有不少教師找兼職的工作。（　　）

二、用約三百字寫本課的大綱。

三、閱讀下面的短文：

誰也沒想到

誰也沒想到一切發生得那麼快，發生得那麼突然。

十幾年前，大家差不多都一樣，你一個月幾十塊工資，我也幾十塊；你穿一件藍衣服，我穿一件灰的；你每月吃兩次用魚票買的魚，我也沒有第三次可以吃。

然而，改革了、開放了、政策改變了，變得使有些人富了起來。這些人富得那麼快，又富得那麼讓一些人心裡不是滋味。下面是作者和一位老師的一段對話。

老師："有一天我去市場買菜，我買了些白菜，蘿蔔，聽見有人叫我老師，一看是個幾年前我教過的學生。這個學生學習很差，考試常不及格，初中一畢業就離開學校了。現在他在市場上賣菜，長得白白胖胖的。你猜他一個月掙多少錢？"

作者:"有七八百塊吧?"

老師:"一千多!他親口告訴我的。我估計這還是個保守的數字。一個月掙我一年的工資。聊了幾句,這個學生就把一隻雞和一塊火腿放進我的包裡,還說上學時沒聽老師的話,現在帳都算不好........"

作者:"你要了嗎?"

老師:"當然沒要!老師怎麼能要學生的東西?我把雞和火腿放回去了,他很不高興。"

作者:"看來他是真心的。"

老師:"真心的也不能要。回到家裡,我心裡很不平靜,晚飯也沒吃。"

作者:"你是不是覺得不公平?"

老師:"是,無論如何我的價值也不會只等於他的十分之一。"

作者:"那當然,你文化比他高,能力比他強,要是你也去賣菜,一定比他掙得還要多!"

1.突然	tūrán	sudden
2.魚票	yúpiào	a ration coupon for fish
3.然而	rán'ér	however; nevertheless
4.富	fù	rich
5.不是滋味	búshì zīwèi	be upset; feel bad
6.白菜	báicài	Chinese cabbage
7.蘿蔔	luóbǒ	radish
8.白白胖胖	báibái-pàngpàng	fat and sassy/saucy
9.估計	gūjì	to estimate; reckon
10.保守	bǎoshǒu	conservative
11.火腿	huǒtuǐ	ham
12.算帳	suànzhàng	keep accounts
13.平靜	píngjìng	calm
14.公平	gōngpíng	fair
15.無論如何	wúlùn rúhé	at any rate; in any case

3. 恋爱 婚姻

在几千年的封建社会里，中国人的恋爱、婚姻一直受到许多限制。青年男女不能自由恋爱，他们的婚姻要由父母决定。社会地位高的，有钱人家的儿子要找有钱人家的女儿。社会地位低的，穷人的女儿只能嫁给穷人的儿子。结婚以前男女双方不能见面，更不能谈话，结婚以后，不管有没有感情都不能离婚。如果妻子死了，丈夫可以再一次结婚。但是如果丈夫死了，即使妻子很年轻也不能再结婚。因此，在中国，"家庭"一直非常稳定，但是，这种稳定需要牺牲个人的感情。

从本世纪中期开始，父母决定婚姻的情况有了根本的改变，青年人可以自由恋爱，自由结婚了。但是传统的婚姻观念还存在，找对象时还必须看对方的社会地位，结婚后不幸福也不愿意离婚，怕别人笑话、看不起，老年人的恋爱会受到子女和周围人的反对。不同的人仍然在用不同的方式压抑自己的感情。

进入九十年代以后，随着经济的不断发展，人们的思想得到了很大的解放，再也不用压抑自己的感情了，可以勇敢地追求爱情和幸福。于是，大学生找农民企业家、离婚、老年人第二次结婚等事越来越多，甚至有了公证婚前财产协议的作法。可以说，中国人保守的婚姻观念终於发生了变化。

3. 戀愛 婚姻

在幾千年的封建社會裡，中國人的戀愛、婚姻一直受到許多限制。青年男女不能自由戀愛，他們的婚姻要由父母決定。社會地位高的，有錢人家的兒子要找有錢人家的女兒。社會地位低的，窮人的女兒只能嫁給窮人的兒子。結婚以前男女雙方不能見面，更不能談話，結婚以後，不管有沒有感情都不能離婚。如果妻子死了，丈夫可以再一次結婚。但是如果丈夫死了，即使妻子很年輕也不能再結婚。因此，在中國，"家庭"一直非常穩定，但是，這種穩定需要犧牲個人的感情。

從本世紀中期開始，父母決定婚姻的情況有了根本的改變，青年人可以自由戀愛，自由結婚了。但是傳統的婚姻觀念還存在，找對象時還必須看對方的社會地位，結婚後不幸福也不願意離婚，怕別人笑話、看不起，老年人的戀愛會受到子女和週圍人的反對。不同的人仍然在用不同的方式壓抑自己的感情。

進入九十年代以後，隨着經濟的不斷發展，人們的思想得到了很大的解放，再也不用壓抑自己的感情了，可以勇敢地追求愛情和幸福。於是，大學生找農民企業家、离婚、老年人第二次結婚等事越來越多，甚至有了公証婚前財产协议的作法。可以说，中國人保守的婚姻觀念終於發生了變化。

生词　NEW WORDS

1.婚姻	婚姻	hūnyīn	N. marriage
2.封建	封建	fēngjiàn	N. feudalism
3.限制	限制	xiànzhì	N. restriction
4.自由戀愛 自由恋爱		zìyóu liàn'ài	VP. to love based on one's own feelings (without parents' constraint)
5.社會地位 社会地位		shèhuì dìwèi	N. social status; social position
6.雙方	双方	shuāngfāng	N. both sides; the two parties
7.不管	不管	bùguǎn	Adv. no matter(what,who,how.. etc.)
8.感情	感情	gǎnqíng	N. feelings; emotion
9.離婚	离婚	líhūn	V. divorce
10.妻子	妻子	qīzǐ	N. wife
11.犧牲	牺牲	xīshēng	V. sacrifice; do sth. at the expense of
12.世紀	世纪	shìjì	N. century
13.中期	中期	zhōngqī	N. middle period
14.傳統	传统	chuántǒng	N. tradition
15.觀念	观念	guānniàn	N. concept; idea
16.存在	存在	cúnzài	V. exist
17.幸福	幸福	xìngfú	SV. happy; blissful
18.受到	受到	shòudào	VP. be subjected (subject) to
19.周圍	周围	zhōuwéi	N. around; surroundings
20.反對	反对	fǎnduì	N/V. opposition; oppose
21.方式	方式	fāngshì	N. way; fashion
22.壓抑	压抑	yāyì	V. hold back; constrain
23.隨着	随着	suízhě	V. along with
24.經濟	经济	jīngjì	N. economy
25.勇敢	勇敢	yǒnggǎn	SV. brave
26.追求	追求	zhuīqiú	V. seek
27.企業家	企业家	qǐyè jiā	N. entrepreneur

28.	公證	公证	gōngzhèng	V. notarize
29.	財產	财产	cáichǎn	N. property
30.	協議	协议	xiéyì	N. agreement
31.	保守	保守	bǎoshǒu	SV. conservative
32.	終於	终于	zhōngyú	Adv. at long last; finally

3.1 一则征婚启事和应征者

一九八八年五月的一天，上海《新民晚报》上出现了一则征婚启事："某男，三十四岁，农民企业家，年薪万余元，在农村有四百平方米楼房，在本市有带厨房和卫生间的私房六十平方米。希望找一位家住本市，会社交，能作秘书工作，长得较好，具有高中以上文化水平，二十四至三十岁的未婚姑娘为伴侣。"

没想到，才过了三天，就收到了约四百封信，而且有不少是大学生写来的。下面介绍其中三位姑娘的情况：

A姑娘先来与征婚者见面。她说："我去年从电视大学毕业，是优越的经济条件吸引我来应征的，但更重要的是，我喜欢在事业上有所作为的男子汉，并愿意用我所学到的知识去帮助他。"接着，她又向征婚者提了许多企业管理方面的问题，征婚者回答着，头上出现了细细的汗珠。

B姑娘今年二十六岁，眼睛又大又圆，说话非常痛快。她说："我正在上夜大学，我的想法是，不愿平平淡淡地度过一生，喜欢冒险。我想，一个农民企业家敢到大上海来找伴侣，就是一种冒险，这就是我要追求的。"征婚者说："我虽然有房子，但那是借钱盖的。"B姑娘说："我们可以努力工作，共同还这笔钱。"

C姑娘的到来最有意思。一天中午，征婚者忽然收到一封电报，上面写着："十四日晚七时上海咖啡馆等。"下面没有名字，也没有地址。征婚者正在感到奇怪的时候，又收到一封信，上面写着："非常非常想见到你，到时请拿一份当天的日报，寻找一位手拿着花的姑娘。"还是没地址没姓名。到了那天，征婚者终于见到了这位神秘的姑娘。她说："我是某大学的学生，今年毕业，对公共关系十分感兴趣。您不是想找一位会社交，能做秘书工作的伴侣吗？我想我一定可以。"征婚者问："你还会些什么？"姑娘回答："会说英语、日语，会打字、跳舞，字写得也不错。对了，还会喝酒，可以了吗？""你怎么会想到打电报这个主意呢？""我想，你的条件优越，一定会有许多姑娘来应征，所以，我就想出了这个主意，来显示一下我的社交才能。其实，我也想试试自己的能力，谢谢你给了我一次实践的机会。"

现在，征婚者已经找到了自己满意的女朋友，正在热恋中。

3.1　一則徵婚啓事和應徵者

　　一九八八年五月的一天，上海《新民晚報》上出現了一則徵婚啓事："某男，三十四歲，農民企業家，年薪萬餘元，在農村有四百平方米樓房，在本市有帶廚房和衛生間的私房六十平方米。希望找一位家住本市，會社交，能作祕書工作，長得較好，具有高中以上文化水平，二十四至三十歲的未婚姑娘爲伴侶。"

　　沒想到，才過了三天，就收到了約四百封信，而且有不少是大學生寫來的。下面介紹其中三位姑娘的情況：

　　A 姑娘先來與徵婚者見面。她說："我去年從電視大學畢業，是優越的經濟條件吸引我來應徵的，但更重要的是，我喜歡在事業上有所作爲的男子漢，並願意用我所學到的知識去幫助他。"接着，她又向徵婚者提了許多企業管理方面的問題，徵婚者回答着，頭上出現了細細的汗珠。

　　B 姑娘今年二十六歲，眼睛又大又圓，說話非常痛快。她說："我正在上夜大學，我的想法是，不願平平淡淡地度過一生，喜歡冒險。我想，一個農民企業家敢到大上海來找伴侶，就是一種冒險，這就是我要追求的。"徵婚者說："我雖然有房子，但那是借錢蓋的。"B姑娘說："我們可以努力工作，共同還這筆錢。"

　　C 姑娘的到來最有意思。一天中午，徵婚者忽然收到一封電報，上面寫着："十四日晚七時上海咖啡館等。"下面沒有名字，也沒有地址。徵婚者正在感到奇怪的時候，又收到一封信，上面寫着："非常非常想見到你，到時請拿一份當天的日報，尋找一位手拿着花的姑娘。"還是沒地址沒姓名。到了那天，徵婚者終於見到了這位神秘的姑娘。她說："我是某大學的學生，今年畢業，對公共關係十分感興趣。您不是想找一位會社交，能做祕書工作的伴侶嗎？我想我一定可以。”徵婚者問：“你還會些什麼？”姑娘回答：“會說英語、日語，會打字、跳舞，字寫得也不錯。對了，還會喝酒，可以了嗎？”“你怎麼會想到打電報這個主意呢？”“我想，你的條件優越，一定會有許多姑娘來應徵，所以，我就想出了這個主意，來顯示一下我的社交才能。其實，我也想試試自己的能力，謝謝你給了我一次實踐的機會。”

　　現在，徵婚者已經找到了自己滿意的女朋友，正在熱戀中。

生词 NEW WORDS

1. 則　　　则　　　zé　　　　　　　M. for news report, advertisement, etc.
2. 徵婚　　征婚　　zhēnghūn　　　VO. to advertise for a marriage partner
3. 啓事　　启事　　qǐshì　　　　　N. announcement
4. 應徵者　应征者　yìngzhēng zhě　N. the person who responds to the advertisement
5. 年薪　　年薪　　niánxīn　　　　N. annual pay
6. 餘　　　余　　　yú　　　　　　　N. more than; in excess of (here: 万余: ten thousand and over)
7. 廚房　　厨房　　chúfáng　　　　N. kitchen
8. 衛生間　卫生间　wèishēngjiān　N. bathroom
9. 私房　　私房　　sīfáng　　　　　N. private house
10. 社交　　社交　　shèjiāo　　　　N. social activities
11. 祕書　　秘书　　mìshū　　　　　N. secretary
12. 具有　　具有　　jùyǒu　　　　　V. have
13. 未婚　　未婚　　wèihūn　　　　V. unmarried
14. 伴侶　　伴侣　　bànlǚ　　　　　N. companion
15. 電視大學
　　电视大学　　diànshì dàxué　N. television university
16. 優越　　优越　　yōuyuè　　　　SV. superior
17. 吸引　　吸引　　xīyǐn　　　　　V. attract
18. 事業　　事业　　shìyè　　　　　N. career
19. 有所作為
　　有所作为　　yǒu suǒ zuòwéi　VO. be accomplished
20. 細細　　细细　　xìxì　　　　　　SV. very fine
21. 汗珠　　汗珠　　hànzhū　　　　N. beads of sweat
22. 痛快　　痛快　　tòngkuài　　　SV. straightforward
24. 夜大學　夜大学　yè dàxué　　　N. night university
25. 平平淡淡地
　　平平淡淡地　　píngpíngdàndànde Adv. plainly; unexcitedly
26. 度過　　度过　　dùguò　　　　　V. spend(time)

27.冒險	冒险	màoxiǎn	V/N. take a risk; adventure
28.電報	电报	diànbào	N. telegram; cable
29.咖啡館	咖啡馆	kāfēi guǎn	N. cafe
30.神秘	神秘	shénmì	SV. mysterious
31.公共關係 公共关系		gōnggòng guānxì	N. public relations
32.(對...)感興趣 (对...)感兴趣		(duì...)gǎn xīngqù	VO. be interested in; have interest in...
33.其實	其实	qíshí	Adv. in fact
34.實踐	实践	shíjiàn	V. to practice, carry out

常用词组 STOCK PHRASES

1.社交活動	社交活动	social activities
2.文化水平	文化水平	educational level
3.很有水平	很有水平	have high standards; be capable
4.水平很高	水平很高	the standard is high
5.終身伴侶	终身伴侣	lifelong companion (referring to one's husband or wife)
6.條件優越	条件优越	the terms/factors/conditions are excellent
7.優越感	优越感	sense of superiority; superiority complex
8.事業心	事业心	devotion to one's work; business ambition
9.痛快人	痛快人	a forthright person
10.說話痛快	说话痛快	talks simply and directly
11.做事痛快	做事痛快	get things done promptly, quickly
12.追求自由	追求自由	to seek freedom
13.追求幸福	追求幸福	to seek happiness

语法　GRAMMAR

1. 本　　本+N

Used only in written Chinese. 本 can be translated as "this," but it expresses the idea of "our" (belonging to this place).

Examples:

(1) 本市　　本市　this city; our city

(2) 本校　　本校　our (or this) school

(3) 本地　　本地　this place

(4) 本国　　本國　this country; one's own country

本周发　　本人（myself）

2. 具有　　S+具有+(modifier)+N

Functioning as a verb, 具有 is used only in written Chinese. The object of 具有 must be an abstract noun with two syllables, and that abstract noun often has a modifier. Examples of abstract nouns which may be used as objects of 具有 are: 意义(yìyì; meaning, significance); 精神 (jīngshén; drive spirit); 信心(xìnxīn; confidence); 力量(lìliang; strength); 特色(tèsè; distinguishing feature); 传统(chuántǒng; tradition); 思想(sīxiǎng; ideology, thinking, idea); 作用(zuòyòng; function, effect); 水平(shuǐpíng; level, standard).

对忠义

Examples:

(1) 应婚者必须具有高中以上文化水平。

应婚者必須具有高中以上文化水平。

The person who responds to the marriage proposal must have an educational level above high school.

(2) 1972 年中美上海公报具有伟大的历史意义。

1972 年中美上海公報具有偉大的歷史意義。

The 1972 Sino-American Shanghai Joint Communique has great historical significance.

3. ...以上

Syntactically, either a simple noun phrase of two syllables or a number may appear before 以上.

A. N+以上 expresses a position above a certain (focal) point.

Examples:

(1)云层以下下大雨，云层以上是晴空。

云層以下下大雨，雲層以上是晴空。

Below the clouds it rained heavily, above the clouds was

a clear boundless sky.

(2)她们都具有高中以上文化水平。

她們都具有高中以上文化水平。

They all have an educational level above high school.

B. NU+以上 expresses a number (or quantity) above a certain point.

Interest is focused on the level above the focal point.

Examples:

(3)六十分以上为及格。

六十分以上為及格。

The passing mark is above sixty.

(4)这件事四十岁以上的人可能还记得。

這件事四十歲以上的人可能還記得。

People above forty may still remember this matter.

(5)今年的产量比去年的增加了百分之三十以上。

今年的產量比去年的增加了百分之三十以上。

This year's output increased thirty percent over last year's.

4. 接着

Appearing in the second clause 接着 is a connector. It expresses the meaning of continuing on with another (different) action after the first action is concluded. The translation varies with the context (she went on..., she then..., and then...).

Examples:

(1)你说完了，我接着说几句。

你説完了，我接着説幾句。

I'll add a few words when you finish.

(2)我给他写了一封信，接着又发了一个电报。

我給他寫了一封信，接着又發了一個電報。

I wrote him a letter. After that I also sent him a telegram.

(3)接着我们又讨论了明年的计划。

接着我們又討論了明年的計劃。

Next (or then, after that) we discussed plans for

the following year.

5. ...来/去...　　　　S+(V1+O1)+来/去+(V2+O2)

In this construction, 来/去 appears between two verb phrases to show the relationship between the means to an end or some purpose. While the first verb phrase expresses the means or the action, the second verb phrase expresses an end or some purpose. The order of these two phrases may not be reversed. 来 is used to express a more intimate relationship to the speaker, 去 a more remote relationship to the speaker.

Examples:

(1)学校开了个晚会来欢迎新同学。

學校開了個晚會來歡迎新同學。

The school gave an (evening)party to welcome new students.

(2)我们应该想个办法来解决这个问题。

我們應該想個辦法來解決這個問題。

We should think of a way to solve this problem.

(3)他用偷来的钱去买新衣服。

他用偷來的錢去買新衣服。

He used the money that he stole to buy a new outfit.

(4)我要用学到的知识去帮助他。

我要用學到的知識去幫助他。

I want to use the knowledge I've acquired to help him.

6. 正在...之中

Used only in written Chinese this construction expresses the idea that the subject of the sentence is involved in an action or a condition which clearly has a beginning and an end. The verb used in this construction is normally a process verb of two syllables, such as 设计(shèjì, to design), 恢复 (huīfù, to resume), 修建(xiūjiàn, to construct), 建设(jiànshè, to build), 拍摄 (pāishè, to film), 热恋(rèliàn, be head over heels in love), etc.

Examples:

(1)他们正在热恋之中。

他們正在熱戀之中。

They are passionately in love.

(2)这部电影正在拍摄之中。

這部電影正在拍攝之中。

This movie is in the process of being filmed.

(3)这个飞机场正在修建之中。

這個飛機場正在修建之中。

The airport is in the process of being built.

一、填空：

条件、身高、希望、打字、秘书、热恋、企业家、住房
普通、考虑、应征、年龄、公共、收入、结婚、征婚

有一位农民（ 1 ），38 岁了，还沒有（ 2 ）。他各方面的（ 3 ）都非常好，（ 4 ）很大，有一栋二层楼房。（ 5 ）很高，每年赚一万多块钱，是（ 6 ）人的五倍。他在报上登了一则（ 7 ）启事。启事说，他（ 8 ）认识一位女朋友，这位女朋友（ 9 ）在 1.65 以上，（ 10 ）在 30 岁以下，长得漂亮，大学毕业，懂英语，会（ 11 ），能做（ 12 ）工作。征婚启事登出后，（ 13 ）者很多，这位农民企业家经过（ 14 ），找了一位在大学里学（ 15 ）关系的姑娘作朋友。现在，他们正在（ 16 ）之中。

二、造句：用下面的词造句

1. 具有　2. ……以上　3. 接着　4. 出现　5. 感兴趣

三、回答问题：

1. 在上海《新民晚报》上征婚的是一个什么人？
2. 他征婚的条件都是什么？
3. 应征的姑娘的文化水平如何？
4. A 姑娘是什么样的人？
5. B 姑娘长得如何？他喜欢什么样的人？
6. C 姑娘有什么特别的地方？她是否是一个很有才能的人？
7. 你最喜欢哪一个姑娘？为什么？要是你都不喜欢也请说明理由。

四、阅读下列短文：

A. 北京出现"电话红娘"

北京有一个"电话红娘"，"8317722"，每天接到一百多个电话。

这家服务台的一位小姐介绍说：打电话的人告诉我们地址，我们就寄去"电话红娘"登记卡，填本人的情况和对伴侣的要求。这张表经过计算机，把条件合适的人找到。"电话红娘"把两张表分别寄给男、女双方，为他们安排见面。

打电话的人有三分之一是未结过婚的女子，也有不少是离了婚的中年男女。

B. 上海电视征婚

上海出现了一件新鲜事。星期六晚上电视台增加了一个电视征婚节目。一九九零年的一个周末，晚上七点，五名勇敢的人第一次在电视上出现了。他们一起谈话、跳舞……介绍自己。几天之后，电视台就收到1650多封应征信。

对电视征婚，社会上看法很不一样。一些女青年认为，恋爱是个人的事，怎么能上电视呢？上了电视一定会被朋友笑话，说她们找不到对象，这多不好意思！一些男青年认为，一辈子不结婚也不能在电视里征婚，这样做不像男子汉。中国旧的传统思想对他们影响太大了！

电视征婚到底怎么样？

一位长得很漂亮的女工人，在报纸上登过几次征婚启事，可是因为她是工人，工作比较累，一些小伙子连面也不愿意见。现在这位姑娘高兴地说："有电视征婚，太好了，我在电视里一出现，一定行！"果然，电视征婚后，向这位漂亮姑娘求爱的信像雪片一样飞来。

一位四十二岁的商场经理，性格不太活泼，一直没找到对象。在朋友们的帮助下，他勇敢地走进电视台。他的条件、他的才能，吸引了许多女青年，现在他已经找到了满意的伴侣，他们不久就要结婚了。

1.红娘	hóngniáng	matchmaker
2.服务台	fúwùtái	service desk
3.登记卡	dēngjìkǎ	a registration card
4.计算机	jìsuànjī	computer
5.电视节目	diànshì jiémù	a television progrm
6.周末	zhōumò	weekend
7.跳舞	tiàowǔ	dance
8.上电视	shàng diànshì	appear on television
9.被…笑话	bèi…xiàohuà	to be laughed at
10.小伙子	xiǎohuǒzǐ	a young fellow
11.雪片	xuěpiàn	snowflake
12.性格	xìnggé	personality
13.活泼	huópǒ	lively

練習　EXERCISES

一、填空：
　　條件、身高、希望、打字、祕書、熱戀、企業家、住房
　　普通、考慮、應徵、年齡、公共、收入、結婚、徵婚

　　有一位農民(　　)，38 歲了，還沒有(　　)。他各方面的(　　)都非常好，
(　　)很大，有一棟二層樓房。(　　)很高，每年賺一萬多塊錢，是(　　)人
的五倍。他在報上登了一則(　　)啓事。啓事說，他(　　)認識一位女朋友，
這位女朋友(　　)在 1.65 以上，(　　)在 30 歲以下，長得漂亮，大學畢業，
懂英語，會(　　)，能做(　　)工作。徵婚啓事登出後，(　　)者很多，這位
農民企業家經過(　　)，找了一位在大學裡學(　　)關係的姑娘作朋友。現在，
他們正在(　　)之中。

二、造句：用下面的詞造句

1. 具有　2.….以上　3. 接着　4. 出現　5. 感興趣

三、回答問題：
　1.在上海《新民晚報》上徵婚的是一個什麼人？
　2.他徵婚的條件都是什麼？
　3.應徵的姑娘的文化水平如何？
　4.A 姑娘是什麼樣的人？
　5.B 姑娘長得如何？他喜歡什麼樣的人？
　6.C 姑娘有什麼特別的地方？她是否是一個很有才能的人？
　7.你最喜歡哪一個姑娘？為什麼？要是你都不喜歡也請說明理由。

四、閱讀下列短文：
A. 北京出現"電話紅娘"
　　北京有一個"電話紅娘"，"8317722"，每天接到一百多個電話。
　　這家服務台的一位小姐介紹說：打電話的人告訴我們地址，我們就寄去
"電話紅娘"登記卡，填本人的情況和對伴侶的要求。這張表經過計算機，
把條件合適的人找到。"電話紅娘"把兩張表分別寄給男、女雙方，為他們
安排見面。

打電話的人有三分之一是未結過婚的女子，也有不少是離了婚的中年男女。

B. 上海電視徵婚

上海出現了一件新鮮事。星期六晚上電視台增加了一個電視徵婚節目。一九九零年的一個週末，晚上七點，五名勇敢的人第一次在電視上出現了。他們一起談話、跳舞……介紹自己。幾天之後，電視台就收到1650多封應徵信。

對電視徵婚，社會上看法很不一樣。一些女青年認為，戀愛是個人的事，怎麼能上電視呢？上了電視一定會被朋友笑話，説她們找不到對象，這多不好意思！一些男青年認為，一輩子不結婚也不能在電視裡徵婚，這樣做不像男子漢。中國舊的傳統思想對他們影響太大了！

電視徵婚到底怎麼樣？

一位長得很漂亮的女工人，在報紙上登過幾次徵婚啓事，可是因為她是工人，工作比較累，一些小伙子連面也不願意見。現在這位姑娘高興地説："有電視徵婚，太好了，我在電視裡一出現，一定行！"果然，電視徵婚後，向這位漂亮姑娘求愛的信像雪片一樣飛來。

一位四十二歲的商場經理，性格不太活潑，一直沒找到對象。在朋友們的幫助下，他勇敢地走進電視台。他的條件、他的才能，吸引了許多女青年，現在他已經找到了滿意的伴侶，他們不久就要結婚了。

1. 紅娘	hóngniáng	matchmaker
2. 服务台	fúwùtái	service desk
3. 登記卡	dēngjì kǎ	a registration card
4. 計算機	jìsuànjī	computer
5. 电视节目	diànshì jiémù	a television program
6. 周末	zhōumò	weekend
7. 跳舞	tiàowǔ	dance
8. 上电视	shàng diànshì	appear on television
9. 被...笑话	bèi...xiàohuà	to be laughed at
10. 小伙子	xiǎohuǒzǐ	a young fellow
11. 雪片	xuěpiàn	snowflake
12. 性格	xìnggé	personality
13. 活泼	huópò	lively

3.2 黄昏之恋

"聪聪，走吧，爷爷送你上幼儿园。"

"不去，爷爷，我不去，幼儿园老师要我表演，我不要表演，我不去。"

爷爷一听可着了急，上星期六就约好了，星期一把聪聪送进幼儿园，他就到"她"那里去。谁知道今天聪聪特别不听话，说什么也不肯去。他不禁叹息起来；想当年，自己能指挥一个团，现在却连一个五岁的孙子都指挥不了。

于是他只好带着聪聪一起到"她"那里去。"她"住在北海公园附近，虽然只有一间小小的屋子，但是屋内收拾得很干净，而且屋前还种着各种好看的花草。

他推门进去，让聪聪叫"奶奶"。

"奶奶"——聪聪甜甜地叫了一声。

她一愣，没想到他把聪聪带来了。"唉"，她忙把聪聪拉过来，让他坐下，然后端出一碗鸡蛋羹来。这碗鸡蛋羹原来是为"他"做的，既然聪聪来了，就一分为二，让他和聪聪各吃半碗。

他吃了一口蛋羹，叹息一声，"唉，星期天最不好过，儿子儿媳在家，不好意思出来，可心里老是想着你。"

"等哪天你把事情向他们说明了，咱们去登记一下，就好了。"她说。

小聪聪疑惑地看看爷爷，又看看"奶奶"，不知道他们说的"登记"是什么意思，他只知道爷爷奶奶一"登记"，他就有蛋羹吃，所以，他希望他们天天都去"登记"，这样他一定能天天吃到蛋羹。

因为遇到一个好奶奶，聪聪一定要玩到吃完晚饭才走。晚饭后，爷孙两个终于回家了。聪聪边走边唱，高兴极了。

但是他们不知道家里已经闹翻天了。

原来，幼儿园的老师看见聪聪一天没来，着了急，下班后赶到聪聪家，想看看聪聪是不是病了。这样一来，可就急坏了聪聪的妈妈。

"都怪你！都怪你！自己不送孩子，一定要那么早去上班，现在可好，老爷子送孙子连自己都送丢了！呜……"

"妈妈，爸爸，"聪聪猛然推开门，飞跑进来。妈妈一看见宝贝儿子就立刻上去搂住孩子，又高兴又着急地问："宝贝儿，上哪儿去了，快告诉妈。"

"到奶奶家去了"聪聪高兴地说，"奶奶可好了，给我鸡蛋羹吃，带我到公园玩儿，还说给爷爷做衣服呢"

小俩口子先是对看了一下。然后一起看着老爷子，心想：哪来的这位"奶奶"？怎么从来没听说过？可嘴里又不好明明白白地问。

"是这样的"，老爷子不自然地看了看他们说："我给聪聪找了个奶奶，我们俩很合得来。你们小俩口商量商量吧，要是没意见，就把她那间房子换过来；要是有意见，我就搬到她那里去住。"

儿子一听就觉得别扭，可又很难反对，于是看了看妻子。

倒是儿媳来得快，她心想老爷子可不能走，走了谁看聪聪？来个奶奶也不错，一定比爷爷能干活，而且还带来一间房子呢，就很快地表了态："爸爸，当初我们结婚，您没反对过，现在您要办事，我们怎么能反对呢？我一百个同意！"

"是啊！我们完全赞成！"儿子立刻接着说。不用说，小聪聪也主动举了手。

3.2 黃昏之戀

"聰聰，走吧，爺爺送你上幼兒園。"

"不去，爺爺，我不去，幼兒園老師要我表演，我不要表演，我不去。"

爺爺一聽可着了急，上星期六就約好了，星期一把聰聰送進幼兒園，他就到"她"那裡去。誰知道今天聰聰特別不聽話，說甚麼也不肯去。他不禁嘆息起來；想當年，自己能指揮一個團，現在却連一個五歲的孫子都指揮不了。

於是他只好帶着聰聰一起到"她"那裡去。"她"住在北海公園附近，雖然只有一間小小的屋子，但是屋內收拾得很乾淨，而且屋前還種着各種好看的花草。

他推門進去，讓聰聰叫"奶奶"。

"奶奶"—聰聰甜甜地叫了一聲。

她一愣；沒想到他把聰聰帶來了。"唉"，她忙把聰聰拉過來，讓他坐下，然後端出一碗雞蛋羹來。這碗雞蛋羹原來是為"他"做的，既然聰聰來了，就一分為二，讓他和聰聰各吃半碗。

他吃了一口蛋羹，嘆息一聲，"唉，星期天最不好過，兒子兒媳在家，不好意思出來，可心裡老是想着你。"

"等哪天你把事情向他們說明了，咱們去登記一下，就好了。"她說。

小聰聰疑惑地看看爺爺，又看看"奶奶"，不知道他們說的"登記"是什麼意思，他只知道爺爺奶奶一"登記"，他就有蛋羹吃，所以，他希望他們天天都去"登記"，這樣他一定能天天吃到蛋羹。

因為遇到一個好奶奶，聰聰一定要玩到吃完晚飯才走。晚飯後，爺孫兩個終於回家了。聰聰邊走邊唱，高興極了。

但是他們不知道家裡已經鬧翻天了。

原來，幼兒園的老師看見聰聰一天沒來，着了急，下班後趕到聰聰家，想看看聰聰是不是病了。這樣一來，可就急壞了聰聰的媽媽。

"都怪你！都怪你！自己不送孩子，一定要那麼早去上班，現在可好，老爺子送孫子連自己都送丟了！嗚……"

"媽媽，爸爸，"聰聰猛然推開門，飛跑進來。媽媽一看見寶貝兒子就立刻上去摟住孩子，又高興又着急地問："寶貝兒，上哪兒去了，快告訴媽。"

"到奶奶家去了"聰聰高興地說，"奶奶可好了，給我雞蛋羹吃，帶我到公園玩兒，還說給爺爺做衣服呢"

小倆口子先是對看了一下。然後一起看着老爺子，心想：哪來的這位"奶奶"？怎麼從來沒聽說過？可嘴裡又不好明明白白地問。

"是這樣的"，老爺子不自然地看了看他們說："我給聰聰找了個奶奶，我們倆很合得來。你們小倆口商量商量吧，要是沒意見，就把她那間房子換過來；要是有意見，我就搬到她那裡去住。"

兒子一聽就覺得彆扭，可又很難反對，於是看了看妻子。

倒是兒媳來得快，她心想老爺子可不能走，走了誰看聰聰？來個奶奶也不錯，一定比爺爺能幹活，而且還帶來一間房子呢，就很快地表了態："爸爸，當初我們結婚，您沒反對過，現在您要辦事，我們怎麼能反對呢？我一百個同意！"

"是啊！我們完全贊成！"兒子立刻接着說。不用說，小聰聰也主動舉了手。

生词　NEW WORDS

1. 爺爺	爷爷	yéyẻ	N. grandpa
2. 幼兒園	幼儿园	yòu'éryuán	N. nursery school
3. 表演	表演	biǎoyǎn	V. perform
4. 約好	约好	yuēhǎo	RVC. (two people) have agreed on (sth.)
5. 聽話	听话	tīnghuà	VO. heed what an elder or superior says; SV. be obedient
6. 不禁	不禁	bújìn	Adv. can't help (doing sth.)
7. 嘆息	叹息	tànxī	V. sigh
8. 指揮	指挥	zhǐhuī	N/V. command; direct
9. 團	团	tuán	N. regiment
10. 附近	附近	fùjìn	N. in the vicinity of
11. 花草	花草	huācǎo	N. flowers and plants
12. 推	推	tuī	V. push
13. 甜	甜	tián	SV. sweet
14. 奶奶	奶奶	nǎinǎi	N. grandma
15. 愣	愣	lèng	V. be dumbfounded
16. 拉	拉	lā	V. pull
17. 雞蛋羹	鸡蛋羹	jīdàn gēng	N. egg custard(usually salty)
18. 既然（.....就） 既然（.....就）		jìrán(⋯jiù)	Adv. such being the case...(then)...
19. 一分為二 一分为二		yī fēn wéi èr	Ph. one divides into two
20. 不好過	不好过	bù hǎoguò	V. difficult to get through
21. 兒媳	儿媳	érxí	N. daughter-in-law
22. 登記	登记	dēngjì	V. register
23. 遇到	遇到	yùdào	V. meet
24. 鬧得翻天 鬧得翻天		nàodẻfāntiān	VP. raise a rumpus; create havoc
25. 都怪你	都怪你	dōu guài nǐ	Ph. It's all your fault.
26. 猛然	猛然	měngrán	Adv. suddenly

27.摟	摟	lǒu	V. hug; embrace
28.寶貝	宝贝	bǎobèi	N. darling; treasure
29.不自然	不自然	bú zìrán	SV. awkward
30.合得來	合得来	hédělái	RVC. get along well; compatible
31.意見	意见	yìjiàn	N. opinion
32.彆扭	别扭	bièniǔ	SV. awkward; uncomfortable
33.幹活	干活	gànhuó	VO. work
34.表態	表态	biǎotài	VO. make known one's position
35.同意	同意	tóngyì	N/V. agreement, approval; to agree
36.贊成	赞成	zànchéng	V. endorse
37.舉手	举手	jǔshǒu	VO. put up one's hand or hands

常用词组 STOCK PHRASES

1.談戀愛	谈恋爱	to be in love
2.失戀	失恋	to be jilted; to lose one's love
3.指揮交通	指挥交通	to direct traffic
4.各國	各国	every nation; various countries; all nations (emphasizing the individuality of each nation)
5.各種各樣	各种各样	all kinds (stressing a large variety of patterns to choose from)
6.提意見	提意见	to put forward one's opinions (make a criticism; make comments or suggestions)
7.交換意見	交换意见	to exchange ideas/opinions

语法　GRAMMAR

1. 可……了

    A. S+可+SV+了.

In this pattern 可 is an adverb which must be placed before the SV; 了, a sentence particle, must occur at the end of the sentence. Semantically, 可 together with 了 expresses an excessive degree of a quality described by the SV in the sentence. (with reference to the subject, a person, thing or condition)

    Examples:

(1) 小王告诉父亲，他要退学不念大学了。父亲听了可生气了。

    小王告訴父親，他要退學不唸大學了。父親聽了可生氣了。

    Xiǎo Wáng told his father that he wanted to quit school, not to study at the college any more. After listening to him, his father became extremely angry.

(2) 虽然他是外国人，汉语说得可好了。

    雖然他是外國人，漢語説得可好了。

    Although he is a foreigner, he speaks Chinese really well.

(3) 几年没见，那个小姑娘现在长得可漂亮了。

    幾年沒見，那個小姑娘現在長得可漂亮了。

    I have not seen that little girl for a few years. She has grown up quite beautiful.

    B. S+可+VP+了.

Again, 可 must occur before the VP and 了 must occur at the end of the sentence. The VP in this pattern may take the forms of V+O or V+V+O. Semantically, 可…了 shows that the condition or attitude of the subject of the sentence, which is described by the verb phrase, is being emphasized.

Examples:

(1)昨天我睡了一天觉，今天可有精神了。

昨天我睡了一天覺，今天可有精神了。

I slept the whole day yesterday; today I am really energetic.

(I really have energy.)

(2)老张可喜欢看电影了，常常看得连书都不念。

老張可喜歡看電影了，常常看得連書都不念。

Lǎo Zhāng really likes to see movies, to the point that he doesn't even study.

C. Sometimes 可 by itself can function as an emphatic marker.

Examples:

(1)他可不是个好人，别跟他作朋友。

他可不是個好人，别跟他作朋友。

(Beware) He is not a nice person. Don't make friends with him.

(2)我可知道他的脾气，他一生气就打人骂人。

我可知道他的脾氣，他一生氣就打人罵人。

Indeed, I know his temper. He will scream and hit people whenever he gets angry.

2. 于是   clause 1, 于是 clause 2

Functioning as a connective, 于是 shows the relationship between two clauses. Semantically, 于是 indicates that the 2nd clause is the consequence, result or outcome of an earlier event which is represented by the 1st clause. Both clauses refer to actual events, not abstractions. Thus, 于是 would be more accurately translated as "consequently, as a result, in consequence of that or thereupon." Notice that 于是 differs from 所以 "therefore", in that 所以 implies a logical cause and effect relation, which may be an abstract one.

Examples:

(1)看完电影以后，小妹说什么也不肯自己回家，于是我只好带着她一起到我男朋友那儿去。

看完電影以後，小妹說甚麼也不肯自己回家，於是我只好帶着她一起到我男朋友那兒去。

After the movie, little sister simply refused (didn't want) to go home alone. As a result, I had no choice but to take her with me to my boy friend's place.

(2)下课以后回家，饿极了，开开冰箱，看到同屋做好的饭，于是就把她的饭吃了。

下課以後回家，餓極了，開開冰箱，看到同屋作好的飯，於是就把她的飯吃了。

When I got home after class, I was extremely hungry. I opened the refrigerator and saw the food my roommate made, so I ate it.

(3)我哥哥昨天来跟我借钱。我昨天刚拿到工资，于是就借了给他五十块钱。

我哥哥昨天來跟我借錢。我昨天剛拿到工資，於是就借了給他五十塊錢。

My older brother came to borrow money from me yesterday. I just got paid yesterday. Accordingly, I lent him $50.

3. 既然....就....

A. S+既然+VP1, 就+VP2   or   既然+S+VP1, 就+VP2

Syntactically, 既然 can appear either before or after the subject, 就 before the second verb phrase only. Semantically, 既然 introduces an already existing condition or situation (expressed by VP1). 就 introduces a second clause which describes a conclusion reached by the speaker or writer (expressed by VP2).

Both 既然...就... and 因为...所以... express a cause and effect relationship. The basic difference is that 既然....就.... is a subjective opinion of the speaker or writer. 因为....所以.... states a logical relationship.

Examples:

(1)既然你已经来了，就别走了，在这儿吃晚饭吧。

既然你已經來了，就別走了，在這兒吃晚飯吧。

Since (it is the case that) you are already here, don't leave. Have dinner with us.

(2)他既然病了，就好好休息吧，别去公园了。

他既然病了，就好好休息吧，別去公園了。

Since (it being the case that) he is sick, he should take a good rest and not go to the park.

B. S1 既然..., S2 就...   or   既然 S1..., S2 就...

Notice that the clause introduced by 既然 can never come as a second clause. 就 can only be placed after the second subject of the second clause. When S2 is understood it may be dropped from the sentence.

Examples:

(1)去法国那么贵，你既然今年没有钱，就别去了，明年再去吧。

去法國那麼貴，你既然今年沒有錢，就別去了，明年再去吧。

It is so expensive to go to France. Since you don't have money this year, why don't you go next year, not this year?

(2)你既然对企业管理那么有兴趣，在大学就应该主修企业管理，不应该该主修英国文学。

你既然對企業管理那麼有興趣，在大學就應該主修企業管理，不應該主修英國文學。

Since you are so interested in business management, you should major in Business Management at college, not English Literature.

4. 先....然后....   S + 先 + VP1, 然后 + VP2

Syntactically, both 先 and 然后 are adverbs. These two adverbs are used to indicate a sequence of events and the order in which they occur.

Examples:

(1)别那么着急，那件事得先讨论一下，然后再作决定。

别那麼着急，那件事得先討論一下，然後再作決定。

Don't be so anxious. We ought to first have a discussion about that matter, and then make our decision.

(2)上个月的天气真坏，先是刮了十几天的大风，然后又下了十几天的大雨。

上個月的天氣真壞，先是刮了十幾天的大風，然後又下了十幾天的大雨。

The weather was really bad last month. It blew hard for more than ten days and then rained heavily for (another) ten more days.

5. 从来

从来 is an adverb of time. It always goes with a negative adverb, 不 or 沒. In cases where the negative 沒 is used, 过 must be included. Semantically, 从来 stresses the fact that at no time or on no occasion has a specific condition arisen. The time frame starts at a point in the past and extends to the present or even to the future.

A. 从来 + 沒 (有) + V/SV + 过

This pattern stresses that the time starts in the past and continues to the moment of speaking.

Examples:

(1)我从来沒抽过烟。

我從來沒抽過煙。

(So far) I have never smoked.

122

(2)那是一种新药吗？怎么我从来没听说过？

那是一種新藥嗎？怎麼我從來沒聽説過？

Is that a new medicine? How is it that I have never heard about it?

(3)他的考试从来没好过。

他的考試從來沒好過。

(So far) His examination results have never been good.

B.　从来 + 不 + V/SV

A sentence using this pattern refers to a habitual condition that starts in the past and may continue to exist in the future.

(1)他上课从来不迟到。

他上課從來不遲到。

He is never late for class.

(2)小王喜欢帮助别人。请他帮忙，他从来不推辞。

小王喜歡幫助別人。請他幫忙，他從來不推辭。

Xiǎo Wáng likes to help people. When people ask him for

help, he never refuses.

(3)他每次考试成绩都很好，但从来不骄傲。

他每次考試成績都很好，但從來不驕傲。

Every time she takes an examination, the marks are

good, but she is never conceited.

6. 倒是

Syntactically, 倒是 may function as a conjunction which appears either before or after the subject of the clause. Semantically, 倒是 is highly versatile. Its interpretation depends on the linguistic envionment, and it is difficult to have a good English equivalent without taking the entire sentence into consideration. In this lesson, we limit 倒是 to only one meaning among many. It is used to soften the tone of the sentence, and often functions as a comment on a preexisting clause. It may be translated as "actually" or "really" (in the sense of an expression of interest, surprise, mild protest, etc., according to context). Almost always the 倒是 clause is placed after the first clause.

Examples:

(1)有机会去南方旅游一次，倒是不错。

有機會去南方旅遊一次，倒是不錯。

It would be nice if there was a chance to tour the south.

(2)退休以后，养点儿金鱼，种点儿花，倒是很有意思。

退休以後，養點兒金魚，種點兒花，倒是很有意思。

It would be interesting if one could keep goldfish

(as pets) and grow flowers after retirement.

那倒不一点
那倒不是

124

练习　EXERCISES

一、根据课文内容判断句子，对的在括号里写"T"错的在括号里写"F"：

1.聪聪家有五口人：爷爷、奶奶、爸爸、妈妈和他。(F)
2.聪聪喜欢幼儿园的生活，每天高高兴兴地去。(F)
3.聪聪的爷爷每天都去看奶奶。(F)
4.奶奶给爷爷作了一件新衣服。(T)
5.爷爷和奶奶打算申请结婚。(T)
6.聪聪希望爷爷和奶奶天天都"登记"，这样他可以天天不去幼儿园。(F)
7.聪聪的妈妈认为爷爷找到了一位合适的伴侣，她很高兴。(F)
8.聪聪的妈妈希望爷爷和奶奶都帮助她看聪聪，帮助她干活，所以很同意
　爷爷再结婚。(T)
9.聪聪的爸爸对爷爷结婚不满意，可是又没有表示反对。(T)
10.爷爷和奶奶正在热恋中，他们很快就要结婚了。(T)

二、造句：每个词造一句(Simple sentences are not acceptable. Your sentences must provide context such as time, place, condition, personal opinions, etc.)

1.不禁　　2.倒是　　3.原来　　4.先…然后…
5.于是　　6.既然　　7.约好　　8.从来 (2 usages)

三、用约两百个字写你对老年人恋爱的意见。

四、阅读下面短文：

女儿为妈妈找伴侣

　　他，六十六岁。她，五十七岁。他们虽然离得很远，却成为一对好伴侣。
　　男的叫王路中，以前是一个企业单位的经理，现在已经退休了。三十年前他和妻子离了婚，一个人带着四个孩子生活。现在孩子们都长大了，结婚了，只剩下他一个人过日子。他白天看青天，晚上数星星，日子真不好过。他需要一个老伴。一天，他给《老人天地》杂志寄出了一则证婚启事，很快，

125

启事登了出来。几天以后，他收到了十几封应征者的来信。应征者有教师、医生、工程师等，她们的经济条件和住房条件都不错，其中一封广州姑娘的来信吸引了他。信上写着：

"母亲只有我一个女儿，虽然我想了各种办法让母亲生活好，可是母女感情和夫妻感情不同，母亲总觉得孤独，她缺少一个生活中的伴侣……我认为老人晚年应该生活得更幸福，他们也要追求爱情。请您不要笑我，女儿为妈妈找伴侣，在九十年代这已经不是新闻……"信里还有一张她妈妈的照片。看着照片，王路中的心跳了，他拿起了笔，把自己要说的话全都写了下来。

为什么女儿会为妈妈找伴侣？

原来，妈妈也是一个很有文化的人，年轻时长得很美。结婚后，生了一儿一女，生活很幸福。没想到，儿子忽然得病死了，丈夫又有了别的女人，和她离了婚。她的生活一下子全变了。虽然女儿关心她、爱她，但是在她的生活里缺少了一种感情————夫妻情。不过，她从来不好意思跟女儿说。

女儿最了解妈妈。为了妈妈的晚年生活，她注意报上登的各种征婚启事。当她从《老人天地》杂志上看到王路中的证婚启事后，认为他的条件很合适。她没有告诉妈妈，就给王路中写了那封信。现在，回信收到了，她把信交给了妈妈。妈妈看着信封，觉得很奇怪，但当她知道了一切后，被女儿的爱深深地感动了。

半年后，两颗孤独的心紧紧地连在一起，两位老人开始了新的生活。

1.退休	tuìxiū	to retire
2.剩	shèng	be left
3.青天	qīngtiān	blue sky
4.数	shǔ	to count
5.星星	xīngxīng	stars
6.杂志	zázhì	magazine
7.医生	yīshēng	(medical) doctor
8.孤独	gūdú	lonely
9.缺少	quēshǎo	lack
10.深深地	shēnshēn dì	deeply
11.感动	gǎndòng	be moved/touched

練習　EXERCISES

一、根據課文內容判斷句子，對的在括號裡寫"T"錯的在括號裡寫"F"：

1.聰聰家有五口人：爺爺、奶奶、爸爸、媽媽和他。(　　)
2.聰聰喜歡幼兒園的生活，每天高高興興地去。(　　)
3.聰聰的爺爺每天都去看奶奶。(　　)
4.奶奶給爺爺作了一件新衣服。(　　)
5.爺爺和奶奶打算申請結婚。(　　)
6.聰聰希望爺爺和奶奶天天都"登記"，這樣他可以天天不去幼兒園。(　　)
7.聰聰的媽媽認為爺爺找到了一位合適的伴侶，她很高興。(　　)
8.聰聰的媽媽希望爺爺和奶奶都幫助她看聰聰，幫助她幹活，所以很同意
　爺爺再結婚。(　　)
9.聰聰的爸爸對爺爺結婚不滿意，可是又沒有表示反對。(　　)
10.爺爺和奶奶正在熱戀中，他們很快就要結婚了。(　　)

二、造句：每個詞造一句(Simple sentences are not acceptable.　Your
sentences must provide context such as time, place, condition, personal
opinions, etc.)

1.不禁　　.2.倒是　　3.原來　　4.先...然後...
5.於是　　6.既然　　7.約好　　8.從來 (2 usages)

三、用約兩百個字寫你對老年人戀愛的意見。

四、閱讀下面短文：

女兒為媽媽找伴侶

　　他，六十六歲。她，五十七歲。他們雖然離得很遠，却成為一對好伴侶。
　　男的叫王路中，以前是一個企業單位的經理，現在已經退休了。三十年
前他和妻子離了婚，一個人帶着四個孩子生活。現在孩子們都長大了，結婚
了，只剩下他一個人過日子。他白天看青天，晚上數星星，日子真不好過。
他需要一個老伴。一天，他給《老人天地》雜誌寄出了一則徵婚啓事，很快，
啓事登了出來。幾天以後，他收到了十幾封應徵者的來信。應徵者有教師、

127

醫生、工程師等，她們的經濟條件和住房條件都不錯，其中一封廣州姑娘的來信吸引了他。信上寫着：

"母親只有我一個女兒，雖然我想了各種辦法讓母親生活好，可是母女感情和夫妻感情不同，母親總覺得孤獨，她缺少一個生活中的伴侶......我認為老人晚年應該生活得更幸福，他們也要追求愛情。請您不要笑我，女兒為媽媽找伴侶，在九十年代這已經不是新聞......"信裡還有一張她媽媽的照片。看着照片，王路中的心跳了，他拿起了筆，把自己要說的話全都寫了下來。

為什麼女兒會為媽媽找伴侶？

原來，媽媽也是一個很有文化的人，年輕時長得很美。結婚後，生了一兒一女，生活很幸福。沒想到，兒子忽然得病死了，丈夫又有了別的女人，和她離了婚。她的生活一下子全變了。雖然女兒關心她、愛她，但是在她的生活裡缺少了一種感情————夫妻情。不過，她從來不好意思跟女兒說。

女兒最瞭解媽媽。為了媽媽的晚年生活，她注意報上登的各種徵婚啟事。當她從《老人天地》雜誌上看到王路中的徵婚啟事後，認為他的條件很合適。她沒有告訴媽媽，就給王路中寫了那封信。現在，回信收到了，她把信交給了媽媽。媽媽看着信封，覺得很奇怪，但當她知道了一切後，被女兒的愛深深地感動了。

半年後，兩顆孤獨的心緊緊地連在一起，兩位老人開始了新的生活。

1.	退休	tuìxiū	to retire
2.	剩	shèng	be left
3.	青天	qīngtiān	blue sky
4.	數	shǔ	to count
5.	星星	xīngxing	stars
6.	雜誌	zázhì	magazine
7.	醫生	yīshēng	(medical) doctor
8.	孤獨	gūdú	lonely
9.	缺少	quēshǎo	lack
10.	深深地	shēnshēn di	deeply
11.	感動	gǎndòng	be moved/touched

3.3　中国婚姻观念变化的新现象：
公证婚前财产协议

　　中国的婚姻观念在不断地变。已经从传统的作法变为现代的自由恋爱结婚，而且离婚的人也随着时代的变化而逐渐增加。现在更有了"公证婚前财产协议"的新情况。造成这种情况的原因是，中国的市场经济发展了十几年后，今天，部分人开始拥有了相当数目的私有财产。

　　据调查，在中国，现代婚姻中的经济情况是：一、一方有相当数目的动产和不动产而另一方几乎"一穷二白"的占一定比例。二、在再婚者中，中、老年人大多双方都有动产和不动产。于是，财产就开始成为婚姻关系间的障碍———有产的一方或财产较多的一方，在婚前甚至婚后的一段时间内，心里常会怀疑对方的婚姻意图。这种心理状态自然会影响到婚姻的美满。而在再婚者中，老年人的情况更复杂，因为他们的财产问题直接牵扯到各自子女的利益。因此，有人主张，要想婚后生活安宁，得先在婚前处理好各自的财产。

　　九十年代初，广州开始有人选用"公证婚前财产协议"的办法来解决这一问题。上海在 1994 年也出现了第一个婚前财产公证的例子。由于媒体的宣传，"公证"很快地就成了热门话题。但去公证处咨询的人多，真正去公证的人还是少。据一般资料证明，进行婚前财产公证的人以白领、私营业主、台胞为多。早期要求公证的以再婚者为多，现在却以新婚的白领为主。

　　这种现象反映出当中国人开始有了"值得看管"的私有财产后，婚姻的内容就变得越来越复杂了。中国长期以来形成的婚前财产婚后共有的婚姻观，对很多婚前已有财产而婚后感情破裂的夫妇，现在已经不是一种爱情的表现，而是一种苦恼，使他们经常生活在痛苦中。这也是产生出公证婚前财产协议做法的原因之一。

对于公证"婚前财产协议"的做法，各方面的意见不同。赞成此种做法的专家们认为，"公证"能避免离婚时的财产纠纷，而且离婚后双方都不可能因借口"穷"而不承担子女的赡养义务。这些专家认为，"公证"是中国婚姻制度上的一个有历史性的进步。

3.3　中國婚姻觀念變化的新現象：
公證婚前財產協議

　　中國的婚姻觀念在不斷地變。已經從傳統的作法變為現代的自由戀愛結婚，而且離婚的人也隨着時代的變化而逐漸增加。現在更有了"公證婚前財產協議"的新情況。造成這種情況的原因是，中國的市場經濟發展了十幾年後，今天，部分人開始擁有了相當數目的私有財產。

　　據調查，在中國，現代婚姻中的經濟情況是：一、一方有相當數目的動產和不動產而另一方幾乎"一窮二白"的佔一定比例。二、在再婚者中，中、老年人大多雙方都有動產和不動產。於是，財產就開始成為婚姻關係間的障礙———有產的一方或財產較多的一方，在婚前甚至婚後的一段時間內，心裡常會懷疑對方的婚姻意圖。這種心理狀態自然會影響到婚姻的美滿。而在再婚者中，老年人的情況更複雜，因為他們的財產問題直接牽扯到各自子女的利益。因此，有人主張，要想婚後生活安寧，得先在婚前處理好各自的財產。

　　九十年代初，廣州開始有人選用"公證婚前財產協議"的辦法來解決這一問題。上海在 1994 年也出現了第一個婚前財產公證的例子。由於媒體的宣傳，"公證"很快地就成了熱門話題。但去公證處諮詢的人多，真正去公證的人還是少。據一般資料證明，進行婚前財產公證的人以白領、私營業主、臺胞為多。早期要求公證的以再婚者為多，現在却以新婚的白領為主。

　　這種現象反映出當中國人開始有了"值得看管"的私有財產後，婚姻的內容就變得越來越複雜了。中國長期以來形成的婚前財產婚後共有的婚姻觀，對很多婚前已有財產而婚後感情破裂的夫婦，現在已經不是一種愛情的表現，而是一種苦惱，使他們經常生活在痛苦中。這也是產生出公證婚前財產協議做法的原因之一。

對於公證"婚前財產協議"的做法，各方面的意見不同。贊成此種做法的專家們認為，"公證"能避免離婚時的財產糾紛，而且離婚後雙方都不可能因借口"窮"而不承擔子女的贍養義務。這些專家認為，"公證"是中國婚姻制度上的一個有歷史性的進步。

生词 NEW WORDS

1. 公証	公证	gōngzhèng	N/V. notarize; notarization
2. 財產	财产	cáichǎn	N. property
3. 逐漸	逐渐	zhújiàn	Adv. gradually
4. 造成	造成	zàochéng	V. create; bring about
5. 市場	市场	shìcháng	N. market
6. 相當數目	相当数目	xiāngdāng shùmù	NP. considerable number of; considerable amount of
7. 據調查	据调查	jù diàochá	Prep.phrase. according to surveys
8. 動產	动产	dòngchǎn	N. movables (personal property)
9. 幾乎	几乎	jīhū	Adv. nearly; almost
10. 一窮二白	一穷二白	yī-qióng-èr-bái	Idiom. completely without money
11. 佔	占	zhàn	V. constitute; make up; account for
12. 比例	比例	bǐlì	N. proportion; scale
13. 於是	于是	yúshǐ	Con. from this; consequently; thereupon; hence
14. 意圖	意图	yìtú	N. intention
15. 心理狀態	心理状态	xīnlǐ zhuàngtài	N. psychological state
16. 複雜	复杂	fùzá	SV. complicated; complex
17. 利益	利益	lìyì	N. interests; benefits; gains
18. 主張	主张	zhǔzhāng	V. advocate; maintain
19. 安寧	安宁	ānníng	N/SV. tranquillity; peaceful
20. 選用	选用	xuǎnyòng	V. select; make a choice for
21. 媒體	媒体	méitǐ	N. media
22. 諮詢	咨询	zīxún	V. consult; seek advice from
23. 資料	资料	zīliào	N. data; reference material
24. 證明	证明	zhèngmíng	V. prove; testify
25. 進行	进行	jìnxíng	V. proceed with; go ahead with
26. 白領	白领	báilǐng	N. white collar (worker)
27. 值得	值得	zhídé	SV. be worth
28. 看管	看管	kānguǎn	VP. look after; attend to

29.内容	内容	nèiróng	N. contents
30.形成	形成	xíngchéng	V. take shape; form
31.破裂	破裂	pòliè	VP. split; broken
32.痛苦	痛苦	tòngkǔ	N. pain; suffering
33.避免	避免	bìmiǎn	V. avoid; refrain from
34.糾紛	纠纷	jiūfēn	N. dispute; issue
35.借口	借口	jièkǒu	VO. (use as an) excuse; pretext
36.承擔	承担	chéngdān	V. bear; assume
37.義務	义务	yìwù	N. duty; obligation

常用词组　STOCK PHRASES

1.據調查	据调查	according to surveys
2.經濟情況	经济情况	financial situation; economic situation
3.成爲障礙	成为障碍	becomes an obstacle; becomes a barrier
4.感情破裂	感情破裂	friendly feelings has broken up; marriage has broken up
5.避免糾紛	避免纠纷	to avoid an issue; to avoid a dispute
6.承擔義務	承担义务	to assume an obligation

语法　GRAMMAR

1. 随着+X

随着+X has two patterns:

A. (S1 + V1 + 了 + O1)，随着 + (S2 + 就/又 + V2 + O2)

This pattern is used to indicate that right after the first event, the second follows. In usage, S2 will be dropped if it corresponds with S1.

Examples:

(1) 昨天下午三点，我到机场接了他，随着就把他带到旅馆去了。

昨天下午三點，我到機場接了他，隨着就把他帶到旅館去了。

Yesterday at three, right after I picked him up at the airport, I took him to the hotel.

(2) 他早上报了名，随着就去交学费。十二点以前就把上学的事都办好了。

他早上報了名，隨着就去交學費。十二點以前就把上學的事都辦好了。

Right after registration he went to pay the tuition. He finished the whole business of enrolling in school before 12.

(3) 昨天第一天上课，李老师跟大家说了几句话，随着就把书分了给大家。

昨天第一天上課，李老師跟大家説了幾句話，隨着就把書分了給大家。

Yesterday was the first day of classes. Teacher Lǐ first said a few words; she then distributed the books to everyone.

B. S + (随着+X) + V + O　　or　　(随着+X) + S + V + O

This pattern indicates that one event (S + V + O) develops/developed along with or keeping pace with another event (X). Syntactically, event "X" must be in the form of a noun phrase; the phrase "随着+X" may occur either before or after the subject.

Examples:

(1) 中国人的思想，随着经济的发展，得到了很大的解放。

中國人的思想，隨着經濟的發展，得到了很大的解放。

The Chinese people, keeping pace with the economic development, have greatly freed themselves from old ideas.

(2)随着时代的变化，离婚的人逐渐增加。

随着時代的變化，離婚的人逐漸增加。

With the passage of time, divorce has gradually increased.

(3)随着人口的增长，住房问题越来越严重。

隨着人口的增長，住房問題越來越嚴重。

Along with the growth of population, the problem of housing has become more and more serious.

2. 据+N　　　　　(据+NP) + S + V + O

A sentence with 据+NP, a prepositional phrase, provides information or opinion rather than a fact. The NP following "据" is the source of the information expressed by the sentence.

Examples:

(1)据报道北京市今年夏天的气温是五十年来最高的一年。

據報道北京市今年夏天的氣溫是五十年來最高的一年。

It is reported (according to a press report) that temperatures this summer in Beijing are the highest in 50 years.

(2)据调查现在一般人的经济状况比前几年好多了。

據調查現在一般人的經濟狀況比前幾年好多了。

According to a survey the financial situation of the general public at present is much better than that of several years ago.

(3)据我看他沒有朋友的原因是因为他太骄傲。

據我看他沒有朋友的原因是因爲他太驕傲。

In my opinion (as I see it) the reason that he doesn't have friends is due to his arrogance.

(4)据我所知那是一个很现代化的旅馆，什么都很方便。

據我所知那是一個很現代化的旅館，甚麼都很方便。

As far as I know (according to what I have learned) that is an up-to-date hotel. It is very convenient there.

一、常用词组练习：用本课的常用词组填空

　　1.我的同学和他的先生结婚三年了，有了一个孩子，最近因为（　　）离婚了。离婚后她的先生不肯（　　）孩子的教育费。

　　2.小张昨天在小赵的屋子里念书。小张念完了书走了以后，小赵的电视机就坏了，小赵说是小张把电视机弄坏的。虽然小张说不是他弄坏的，但是小赵不相信，每天给小张找麻烦。最后，小张为了（　　）给了小赵五十块钱。

　　3.他自从前年在一家电脑公司工作以后，（　　）比以前好得多了。

　　4.小王和小孙认识已经快两年了，到现在还不能结婚，因为两个人都分配不到住宅。住房问题（　　）他们婚姻的（　　）了。

二、猜测词组的意思（看本课课文，从上下文猜，不用字典）

　　1.私营业主是什么意思？

　　2.台胞是从什么地方回到什么地方去的中国人？

　　3.这辆车不是公司的，是我的私人财产。你用以前请先问问我。

　　　私人财产是什么意思？

　　4.现在在中国最热门的话题是个人投资，社会上大家都对这件事感兴趣，大家都想知道怎么投资最好。

　　　热门话题是什么意思？

　　5.离婚的夫妇如果有孩子，一般是父亲给赡养费。

　　　赡养费是什么钱？

三、语法练习：动宾语搭配(matching verb and object)

　　A.在下面的词组中，写出每个词组的主要动词(main verb)和主要受词(object, without its modifier)

　　1.公证婚前财产协议

　　2.有了"公证婚前财产协议"的新情况

　　3.占一定比例

　　4.成为婚姻关系间的障碍

5.怀疑对方的婚姻意图

6.选用"公证婚前财产协议"的办法

7.出现了第一个婚前财产公证的例子

8.重视长期以来形成的婚前财产婚后共有的婚姻观

9.有不少婚前有财产而婚后感情破裂的夫妇

10.是产生出公证婚前财产协议的原因

11.避免离婚时的财产纠纷

B.把上面的十一个动宾语词组翻译成英文

四、作文：《公证婚前财产协议》读后感 —— 用大约二百五十个字

五、阅读下面的短文：

独身女性

在一般中国人的心目中，"男大当婚，女大当嫁"这种传统观念仍然是人生应当走的道路，但是现在在中国有一些女性开始选择了另外的一条道路——独身。

她们选择了独身，一种是要自由。一位年轻的职业妇女说"当我看到一些父母从早到晚就是为子女忙碌，完全失去了自己的生活情趣时，我就决定不结婚了。对我来说，独身还有许多好处，例如：可以完全控制自己的时间；可以有自由培养我自己的兴趣，满足我自己的需要；不必忍受另外一个人的坏习惯；不必作什么事都得考虑到另外一个人的心情和喜好。"这种女性，她们重视的是"个人世界"，她们不愿意别人走进她们的"个人世界"。

还有一种是浪漫主义和理想主义者，她们也不愿意结婚。一位大学刚毕业的年轻姑娘说，她喜欢独身，她是一个浪漫主义者。她认为男性有三种。一种是以自我为中心的男人，她不能嫁给这种男人，因为她自己的个性太强。一种是把你当成他妹妹一样的男人，这种男人也不能嫁，因为在他面前女人不能有太多自己的意见，不能表现自己的个性。第三种是有才能，生活条件好的男人，但是他们一般比较自大。除了男性的这些问题以外，她觉得还有别的问题：浪漫的婚姻不稳定，稳定的婚姻不浪漫；平凡的丈夫没意思，有

意思的丈夫又找不到。这种种原因使她决定不结婚。这种女性，她们不是找不到对象，只要她们愿意很快就能结婚了，但是她们的要求太多，而且不愿意选择一种平凡的婚姻生活。

　　再有一种是受到实际情况的限制而找不到对象的。

　　不管是什么原因，这些女子都走出了中国传统的规范而去寻求自己喜爱的生活。

1.嫁	jià	(for a woman) marry
2.人生	rénshēng	life
3.职业妇女	zhíyè fùnǚ	a professional woman
4.忙碌	mánglù	be busy
5.失去	shīqù	to lose
6.生活情趣	shēnghuó qíngqù	interests in life
7.控制	kòngzhì	to control
8.满足需要	mǎnzú xūyào	to satisfy the need of
9.忍受	rěnshòu	to endure; to bear
10.心情	xīnqíng	state of mind; mood
11.浪漫主义者	làngmàn zhǔyì zhě	a person who is an incurable romantic
12.自我中心	zìwǒ zhōngxīn	be self-centered
13.个性	gèxìng	personality; individuality
14.强	qiáng	be strong
15.稳定	wěndìng	be stable; steady
16.平凡	píngfán	be ordinary; common
17.规范	guīfàn	norm
18.寻求	xúnqiú	to seek

一、常用辭組練習：用本課的常用辭組填空

　　1.我的同學和他的先生結婚三年了，有了一個孩子，最近因為（　　）離婚
　　　了。離婚後她的先生不肯（　　）孩子的教育費。

　　2.小張昨天在小趙的屋子裡念書。小張念完了書走了以後，小趙的電視機
　　　就壞了，小趙說是小張把電視機弄壞的。雖然小張說不是他弄壞的，但
　　　是小趙不相信，每天給小張找麻煩。最後，小張為了（　　）給了小趙五
　　　十塊錢。

　　3.他自從前年在一家電腦公司工作以後，（　　）比以前好得多了。

　　4.小王和小孫認識已經快兩年了，到現在還不能結婚，因為兩個人都分配
　　　不到住宅。住房問題（　　）他們婚姻的（　　）了。

二、猜測辭組的意思（看本課課文，從上下文猜，不用字典）

　　1.私營業主是甚麼意思？

　　2.臺胞是從甚麼地方回到什麼地方去的中國人？

　　3.這輛車不是公司的，是我的私人財產，你用以前請先問問我。
　　　私人財產是甚麼意思？

　　4.現在在中國最熱門的話題是個人投資，社會上大家都對這件事感興趣，
　　　都想知道怎麼投資最好。
　　　熱門話題是甚麼意思？

　　5.離婚的夫婦如果有孩子，一般是父親給贍養費。
　　　贍養費是甚麼錢？

三、語法練習：動賓語搭配(matching verb and object)

　　A.在下面的辭組中寫出每個辭組的主要動詞(main verb)和主要受詞
　　　(object, without its modifier)

　　　1.公證婚前財產協議

　　　2.有了“公證婚前財產協議”的新情況

　　　3.佔一定比例

　　　4.成為婚姻關係間的障礙

5.懷疑對方的婚姻意圖

6.選用"公證婚前財產協議"的辦法

7.出現了第一個婚前財產公證的例子

8.重視長期以來形成的婚前財產婚後共有的婚姻觀

9.有不少婚前有財產而婚後感情破裂的夫婦

10.是產生出公證婚前財產協議的原因

11.避免離婚時的財產糾紛

B.把上面的十一個動賓語辭組翻譯成英文

四、作文:《公證婚前財產協議》讀後感 —— 用大約二百五十個字

五、閱讀下面的短文:

獨身女性

在一般中國人的心目中,"男大當婚,女大當嫁"這種傳統觀念仍然是人生應當走的道路,但是現在在中國有一些女性開始選擇了另外的一條道路——獨身。

她們選擇了獨身,一種是要自由。一位年輕的職業婦女說"當我看到一些父母從早到晚就是為子女忙碌,完全失去了自己的生活情趣時,我就決定不結婚了。對我來說,獨身還有許多好處,例如:可以完全控制自己的時間;可以有自由培養我自己的興趣,滿足我自己的需要;不必忍受另外一個人的壞習慣;不必作甚麼事都得考慮到另外一個人的心情和喜好。"這種女性,她們重視的是"個人世界",她們不願意別人走進她們的"個人世界"。

還有一種是浪漫主義和理想主義者,她們也不願意結婚。一位大學剛畢業的年輕姑娘說,她喜歡獨身,她是一個浪漫主義者。她認為男性有三種。一種是以自我為中心的男人,她不能嫁給這種男人,因為她自己的個性太強。一種是把你當成他妹妹一樣的男人,這種男人也不能嫁,因為在他面前女人不能有太多自己的意見,不能表現自己的個性。第三種是有才能,生活條件好的男人,但是他們一般比較自大。除了男性的這些問題以外,她覺得還有別的問題:浪漫的婚姻不穩定,穩定的婚姻不浪漫;平凡的丈夫沒意思,有

意思的丈夫又找不到。這種種原因使她決定不結婚。這種女性，她們不是找不到對象，只要她們願意很快就能結婚了，但是她們的要求太多，而且不願意選擇一種平凡的婚姻生活。

再有一種是受到實際情況的限制而找不到對象的。

不管是什麼原因，這些女子都走出了中國傳統的規範而去尋求自己喜愛的生活。

1.嫁	jià	(for a woman) marry
2.人生	rénshēng	life
3.職業婦女	zhíyè fùnǚ	a professional woman
4.忙碌	mánglù	be busy
5.失去	shīqù	to lose
6.生活情趣	shēnghuó qíngqù	interests in life
7.控制	kòngzhì	to control
8.滿足需要	mǎnzú xūyào	to satisfy the need of
9.忍受	rěnshòu	to endure; to bear
10.心情	xīnqíng	state of mind; mood
11.浪漫主義者	làngmàn zhǔyì zhě	a person who is an incurable romantic
12.自我中心	zìwǒ zhōngxīn	be self-centered
13.個性	gèxìng	personality; individuality
14.強	qiáng	be strong
15.穩定	wěndìng	be stable; steady
16.平凡	píngfán	be ordinary; common
17.規範	guīfàn	norm
18.尋求	xúnqiú	to seek

Unit Four

4. 家庭 妇女 儿童

在中国，几辈人住在一起的大家庭存在了几千年。在这样的大家庭中，最长辈的人是家长，最有权力。他(她)掌握全家的钱财，决定儿子、女儿、孙子、孙女的婚事，也决定孩子们的前途。他(她)要儿子当商人，儿子就必须当商人。他(她)要女儿不读书，女儿就必须听话。在这样的大家庭里，晚辈的女人没有地位，只能服从长辈，服从丈夫。女人的责任是为大家庭生孩子、做饭…。哪个女人生的儿子多，她就对大家庭贡献大；哪个大家庭子女多、儿孙多，哪位家长就觉得高兴、自豪。

这种传统的家庭观念和家庭结构在几十年前开始发生了变化。家长不再有那么大的权力了。他们让孩子自由恋爱，让儿女自己选择前途。女人也有了地位，她们走出家门，去参加工作。到了八十年代，这种变化更大了。在城市里，大家庭都几乎不存在了。年轻人不再愿意和老年人住在一起，他们要独立，要自由地建立自己的小家庭。老年人也不再去维护自己的家长地位，而是去追求自己新的晚年生活。在新的小家庭中，不再是多子多女，而是一家一个"小皇帝"。"小皇帝"的妈妈们，地位也提高了，从没有权力到权力很大，有的妈妈甚至当上了"家长"。

新的家庭关系、妇女社会地位正在中国建立、发展。

4. 家庭 婦女 兒童

在中國，幾輩人住在一起的大家庭存在了幾千年。在這樣的大家庭中，最長輩的人是家長，最有權力。他(她)掌握全家的錢財，決定兒子、女兒、孫子、孫女的婚事，也決定孩子們的前途。他(她)要兒子當商人，兒子就必須當商人。他(她)要女兒不讀書，女兒就必須聽話。在這樣的大家庭裡，晚輩的女人沒有地位，只能服從長輩，服從丈夫。女人的責任是為大家庭生孩子、做飯…。哪個女人生的兒子多，她就對大家庭貢獻大；哪個大家庭子女多、兒孫多，哪位家長就覺得高興、自豪。

這種傳統的家庭觀念和家庭結構在幾十年前開始發生了變化。家長不再有那麼大的權力了。他們讓孩子自由戀愛，讓兒女自己選擇前途。女人也有了地位，她們走出家門，去參加工作。到了八十年代，這種變化更大了。在城市裡，大家庭都幾乎不存在了。年輕人不再願意和老年人住在一起，他們要獨立，要自由地建立自己的小家庭。老年人也不再去維護自己的家長地位，而是去追求自己新的晚年生活。在新的小家庭中，不再是多子多女，而是一家一個"小皇帝"。"小皇帝"的媽媽們，地位也提高了，從沒有權力到權力很大，有的媽媽甚至當上了"家長"。

新的家庭關係、婦女社會地位正在中國建立、發展。

生词　NEW WORDS

1.存在	存在	cúnzài	V. be in existence
2.幾輩人	几辈人	jǐbèirén	N. several generations
3.長輩	长辈	zhǎngbèi	N. elder member of a family
4.家長	家长	jiāzhǎng	N. the head of a family
5.權力	权力	quánlì	N. power
6.掌握	掌握	zhǎngwò	V. master; have in hand
7.錢財	钱财	qiáncái	N. wealth; money
8.前途	前途	qiántú	N. future; prospect
9.商人	商人	shāngrén	N. businessman
10.晚輩	晚辈	wǎnbèi	N. younger member of a family
11.服從	服从	fúcóng	V. submit (oneself) to ....
12.責任	责任	zérèn	N. duty; responsibility
13.貢獻	贡献	gòngxiàn	V/N. contribute; contribution
14.兒孫	儿孙	érsūn	N. children and grandchildren
15.自豪	自豪	zìháo	V. to pride oneself on...
16.結構	结构	jiégòu	N. structure
17.選擇	选择	xuǎnzé	V. select
18.幾乎	几乎	jīhū	Adv. almost; nearly
19.獨立	独立	dúlì	SV/N. independent; on one's own; independence
20.建立	建立	jiànlì	V. found; set up
21.維護	维护	wéihù	V. preserve; safeguard
22.晚年	晚年	wǎnnián	N. old age; one's later years; twilight years
23.皇帝	皇帝	huángdì	N. emperor

4.1　我和我老伴儿的拳舞之争

老伴儿近年来迷上了迪斯科，天一亮就往公园跑。从公园回来就对我说："你去公园看看，成百上千的人跳舞。过去打太极拳的人都改行了，只有你还打太极拳，打一早晨还不如我跳五分钟的活动量大……"跳迪斯科，那么快的节奏，我这两百来斤的身子怎么跟得上？

星期六，儿媳女儿聚在一起，欢迎老伴儿表演表演。老伴儿正在做饭，也不推辞，挥着一双沾满白面的手就舞了起来。大家不停地叫好，看完了还鼓掌。

但是，我还是觉得太极拳好，对老伴儿的迪斯科就是看不习惯。那音乐太吵，动作对老年人来说太轻浮。老伴儿则说迪斯科比太极拳好。我们的争论越来越大。她叫我"顽固派"，我就叫她"洋务派"。

最好笑的是我们的小孙女，才一岁多，刚学走路说话。奶奶一高兴就教她扭两下屁股；爷爷一喜欢就教她打几路拳。当她想跟奶奶去大街看汽车时，就扭两下屁股；想叫爷爷买巧克力时，就舞几下拳头。儿媳是老师，表扬孩子说："还是我们小红红聪明，中西结合。等长大了，就发明一套迪斯科式的太极拳，省得爷爷、奶奶吵架。"

4.1　我和我老伴兒的拳舞之爭

老伴兒近年來迷上了迪斯科，天一亮就往公園跑。從公園回來就對我說：“你去公園看看，成百上千的人跳舞。過去打太極拳的人都改行了，只有你還打太極拳，打一早晨還不如我跳五分鐘的活動量大……”跳迪斯科，那麼快的節奏，我這兩百來斤的身子怎麼跟得上？

星期六，兒媳女兒聚在一起，歡迎老伴兒表演表演。老伴兒正在做飯，也不推辭，揮着一雙沾滿白麵的手就舞了起來。大家不停地叫好，看完了還鼓掌。

但是，我還是覺得太極拳好，對老伴兒的迪斯科就是看不習慣。那音樂太吵，動作對老年人來說太輕浮。老伴兒則說迪斯科比太極拳好。我們的爭論越來越大。她叫我“頑固派”，我就叫她“洋務派”。

最好笑的是我們的小孫女，才一歲多，剛學走路說話。奶奶一高興就教她扭兩下屁股；爺爺一喜歡就教她打幾路拳。當她想跟奶奶去大街看汽車時，就扭兩下屁股；想叫爺爺買巧克力時，就舞幾下拳頭。兒媳是老師，表揚孩子說：“還是我們小紅紅聰明，中西結合。等長大了，就發明一套迪斯科式的太極拳，省得爺爺、奶奶吵架。”

生词 NEW WORDS

1.老伴	老伴	lǎobàn	N. (of an old married couple) husband or wife
2.打太極拳 打太极拳		dǎ tàijíquán	VO. do taiji (shadow boxing)
3.跳舞	跳舞	tiàowǔ	V. dance
4.迷上了	迷上了	míshànglě	RVC. infatuated with (person); obsessed with something
5.爭論	争论	zhēnglùn	N/V. debate; dispute; argue
6.改行	改行	gǎiháng	VO. change one's profession
7.活動量	活动量	huódòngliáng	N. capacity for exercise (to benefit one's health)
8.節奏	节奏	jiézòu	N. (musical) beat; tempo; pace
9.斤	斤	jīn	N. Chinese unit of weight=1/2 kilogram
10.身子	身子	shēnzǐ	N. body
11.聚	聚	jù	V. get together
12.推辭	推辞	tuīcí	V. decline(an appointment, invitation)
13.揮	挥	huì	V. wave
14.沾滿	沾满	zhānmǎn	RVC. (entirely) covered with
15.鼓掌	鼓掌	gǔzhǎng	VO. clap one's hands
16.頑固	顽固	wángù	SV. stubborn; bitterly opposed to change
17.音樂	音乐	yīnyuè	N. music
18.動作	动作	dòngzuò	N. movement; action
19.輕浮	轻浮	qīngfú	SV. frivolous
20.則	则	zé	Adv. however
21.派	派	pài	N. group; faction
22.洋務派	洋务派	yángwùpài	N. a group that acts ostentatiously in a foreign style
23.孫女	孙女	sūnnǚ	N. granddaughter
24..扭	扭	niǔ	V. (of body movement) sway from side to side
25.屁股	屁股	pìgǔ	N. buttocks; bottom

26.巧克力	巧克力	qiǎokèlì	N. chocolate
27.表揚	表扬	biǎoyáng	V. praise
28.結合	结合	jiéhé	V. integrate; combine
29.發明	发明	fāmíng	V. invent
30.省得	省得	shěngdé	V. so as to avoid(doing sth.); lest
31.吵架	吵架	chǎojià	VP. quarrel with someone

专用名词　PROPER NOUN

迪斯科	dísīkē	Disco

常用词组　STOCK PHRASES

1.迷上了那個人	迷上了那个人	be infatuated with that person
2.迷上了看電影	迷上了看电影	be obsessed with movies
3.迷上了看小说	迷上看了小说	be obsessed with novels
4.迷上了音樂	迷上了音乐	be obsessed with music
5.迷上了跳舞	迷上了跳舞	be obsessed with dancing
6.爭論問題	争论问题	argue an issue
7.節奏很快	节奏很快	the tempo(of the music) is fast; the pace(of one's life) is fast
8.生活節奏	生活节奏	the pace of (one's) life
9.動作輕浮	动作轻浮	behave frivolously
10.扭屁股	扭屁股	to shake one's buttocks
11.表揚孩子	表扬孩子	to praise a child
12.受到表揚	受到表扬	have been praised for... (have received praise)
13.中西結合	中西结合	to combine Chinese with Western... to integrate Chinese...with the Western

语法 GRAMMAR

1. 对 X 来说

Syntactically, the entire phrase can precede or follow the subject of the sentence. "X", in this condition, takes the form of a noun phrase. Semantically, this noun phrase identifies a certain person/group of people. In sentences having this phrase, the opinion or attitude taken by a person or a group of people towards some matter is expressed. It is a subjective opinion stating the attitude of a person or group; it is not stating a fact.

Examples:

(1)对我来说，你这几年的研究对社会的贡献很大。

對我來說，你這幾年的研究對社會的貢獻很大。

In my opinion (as far as I am concerned) your research of the last several years has made a great contribution to the society.

(2)对小孩子来说，世界上的一切都很新鲜。

對小孩子來說，世界上的一切都很新鮮。

To children, everything in the world is a novelty.

(3)对他来说，能在那个公司工作是一个很难得的机会。

對他來說，能在那個公司工作是一個很難得的機會。

As far as he is concerned, to be able to work in that company is a rare opportunity.

2. 则

"则" is mainly a cohesive tie which shows the logical relationships between the two clauses of a sentence. It is therefore, highly versatile in meaning. Its interpretation depends on the logical relationship of the two elements linked by it. In this lesson, we introduce the logical pattern of contrast in which the second unit contrasts with or works against the first in some way.

Examples:

(1)李老先生觉得打太极拳对身体很好，他老伴儿则认为迪斯科比太极拳还好。

154

李老先生覺得打太極拳對身體很好，他老伴兒則認爲迪斯科比太極拳還好。

Old Mr. Lǐ felt that tàijíquán was good for one's health; however, his wife considered that Disco was even better.

(2)她上课时不爱回答老师的问题，课后则话多得不得了。

她上課時不愛回答老師的問題，課後則話多得不得了。

In class, she doesn't like to answer teacher's questions, but she (certainly) has a lot to say after class.

(3)我们都只学了两年中文，而她则学了三年。

我們都只學了兩年中文，而她則學了三年。

We only studied Chinese for two years, but she studied for three.

3. 当 X (的) 时(候)

Appearing only in the written language, this time phrase is usually placed at the beginning of the sentence, before the subject. The X used in this phrase, i.e. between "当" and "时候" must either be a VP or a clause.

Semantically, this time phrase relates to the condition, in that an event will take/took place.

Examples:

(1)周末，当天气不好时，我们就待在家里看电视。

週末，當天氣不好時，我們就待在家裡看電視。

On weekends when the weather is bad, we stay home watching television.

At times, we may also put "每" before this time phrase to show emphasis.

(2)每当我觉得中文难，不想学时，老师就鼓励我。

每當我覺得中文難，不想學時，老師就鼓勵我。

Every time I felt that Chinese was difficult to learn and didn't want to learn it, my teacher would encourage me.

(3)当我十六岁时，就已经一米八五了。

當我十六歲時，就已經一米八五了。

When I was sixteen, I was already 1.85 meters tall.

4. 省得

"省得" is a cohesive tie which links two clauses together. Normally, it occurs at the beginning of the second clause. Semantically, it shows that one will do a certain thing(related in the first clause) in order to prevent an undesirable thing happening(related to the second clause).

Examples:

(1)他自己一个人搬行李，省得麻烦别人。

他自己一個人搬行李，省得麻煩別人。

He moves the luggage himself so as to avoid
putting someone else to trouble.

(2)你最好带上地图，省得迷路。

你最好帶上地圖，省得迷路。

You had better bring a map, lest you get lost.

(3)有事来个电话，省得你来回跑。

有事來個電話，省得你來回跑。

If something comes up just telephone me (meaning "no
need to come in person"). It will save you from running
back and forth.

(4)不要酒后开车，省得警察找你的麻烦。

不要酒後開車，省得警察找你的麻煩。

Don't drive after drinking, lest the police make trouble
for you.

(5)你最好提醒我一下，省得我忘了。

你最好提醒我一下，省得我忘了。

You had better remind me, lest I forget.

一、根据课文内容判断句子，对的在括号里写"T"，错的在括号里写"F"：

1. 太极拳是中国传统的体育运动。（　）

2. 打太极拳活动量大、节奏快，所以对身体非常有好处。（　）

3. 每天早上天一亮，成千上万的人去公园打太极拳。（　）

4. 中国现在跳迪斯科的人越来越多了。（　）

5. 小红红的妈妈认为，迪斯科的音乐太吵，动作轻浮，对老年人不合适。（　）

6. 小红红的奶奶改行跳迪斯科了，爷爷却仍然打太极拳。（　）

7. 小红红的爷爷奶奶经常为做饭的事情争吵。（　）

8. 小红红想长大以后发明一套迪斯科式的太极拳。（　）

二、造句

1. 对…来说　　2. 当…时　　3. 省得　　4. 迷上了　　5. 受到表扬

三、请用两百字左右，谈谈你对老年人跳迪斯科舞的看法。（你可以根据这
种方式写：1.跳迪斯科舞动作的样子，2.跳迪斯科舞对老人的好处，3.跳
迪斯科舞对老人的坏处，4.结论"conclusion"）

四、阅读下列短文：

我的家庭

　　我到三千里外的一个城市出差，收到老伴一封信，告诉我，儿子结婚了。
我的第一个想法就是，怎么事先没告诉我。可是又一想，孩子自己决定自己
的婚事，独立成家，这不正是我和老伴的希望吗？

　　老伴信上说，她在家，但事先也一点儿不知道。

　　儿子和这位刚结婚的儿媳——小丽是大学同学。大学毕业后，儿子上了
研究生，女朋友工作了，当了医生。

　　我出差后的一天晚上，儿子和小丽高高兴兴回家来，对妈妈说："让您
猜一件东西，贴了照片的。"妈妈猜了半天也没猜着，拿出来一看，竟是结
婚证书。

　　儿子长大了，恋爱了，早晚要结婚。结婚仪式怎么办？去大饭店？或者

在家里？我和老伴早商量了，也和儿子、小丽讨论过，一不请客，二不收礼物。至于他们自己的同学、朋友要不要在一起庆祝一下，由他们自己决定。

小俩口也认为没有必要举行任何结婚仪式。两个人从此生活到一起来了，这才是世界上最快乐最幸福的事！

于是，妈妈悄悄为他们准备了一些床上用品，替儿媳买了几件衣服。我们还存了一些钱，准备儿子结婚时为他们买一套新家具。

我们了解儿子，不会要求父母买这、买那，但没有想到，我们事先准备好的家具钱，他们也不肯收。

新屋里，除了一张床是新的，别的都是我们用过的旧家具——旧书桌、旧书架、旧沙发。

一对新人，生活在旧家具之中，却仍然那么幸福。

对儿子的恋爱、婚姻，我们一直是十分关心的。我们俩也常常讨论，但从不干预。孩子已经成年了，他有独立思想，我们相信他的能力。家长不应该掌握子女的命运、前途。决定他们命运的，是他们自己。

1.	出差	chūchāi	be on a business trip
2.	事先	shìxiān	in advance
3.	猜	cāi	to guess
4.	贴	tiē	mounted
5.	竟	jìng	unexpectedly
6.	仪式	yíshì	ceremony
7.	庆祝	qìngzhù	to celebrate
8.	悄悄	qiāoqiāo	quietly
9.	家具	jiājù	furniture
10.	干预	gānyù	to intervene

練習　EXERCISES

一、根據課文內容判斷句子，對的在括號裡寫 "T" ，錯的在括號裡寫 "F" ：
1. 太極拳是中國傳統的體育運動。（　）
2. 打太極拳活動量大、節奏快，所以對身體非常有好處。（　）
3. 每天早上天一亮，成千上萬的人去公園打太極拳。（　）
4. 中國現在跳迪斯科的人越來越多了。（　）
5. 小紅紅的媽媽認為，迪斯科的音樂太吵，動作輕浮，對老年人不合適。（　）
6. 小紅紅的奶奶改行跳迪斯科了，爺爺却仍然打太極拳。（　）
7. 小紅紅的爺爺奶奶經常為做飯的事情爭吵。（　）
8. 小紅紅想長大以後發明一套迪斯科式的太極拳。（　）

二、造句
1. 對...來說　　2. 當...時　　3. 省得　　4. 迷上了　　5. 受到表揚

三、請用兩百字左右，談談你對老年人跳迪斯科舞的看法。〔你可以根據這
　　種方式寫：1.跳迪斯科舞动作的样子，2.跳迪斯科舞对老人的好处，3.跳
　　迪斯科舞对老人的坏处，4.结论 "conclusion"〕

四、閱讀下列短文：

我的家庭

　　我到三千里外的一個城市出差，收到老伴一封信，告訴我，兒子結婚了。
我的第一個想法就是，怎麼事先沒告訴我。可是又一想，孩子自己決定自己
的婚事，獨立成家，這不正是我和老伴的希望嗎？

　　老伴信上說，她在家，但事先也一點兒不知道。

　　兒子和這位剛結婚的兒媳——小麗是大學同學。大學畢業後，兒子上了
研究生，女朋友工作了，當了醫生。

　　我出差後的一天晚上，兒子和小麗高高興興回家來，對媽媽說："讓您
猜一件東西，貼了照片的。"媽媽猜了半天也沒猜着，拿出來一看，竟是結
婚證書。

　　兒子長大了，戀愛了，早晚要結婚。結婚儀式怎麼辦？去大飯店？或者

159

在家裡？我和老伴早商量了，也和兒子、小麗討論過，一不請客，二不收禮物。至於他們自己的同學、朋友要不要在一起慶祝一下，由他們自己決定。

小倆口也認為沒有必要舉行任何結婚儀式。兩個人從此生活到一起來了，這才是世界上最快樂最幸福的事！

於是，媽媽悄悄為他們準備了一些床上用品，替兒媳買了幾件衣服。我們還存了一些錢，準備兒子結婚時為他們買一套新家具。

我們瞭解兒子，不會要求父母買這、買那，但沒有想到，我們事先準備好的家具錢，他們也不肯收。

新屋裡，除了一張床是新的，別的都是我們用過的舊家具——舊書桌、舊書架、舊沙發。

一對新人，生活在舊家具之中，却仍然那麼幸福。

對兒子的戀愛、婚姻，我們一直是十分關心的。我們倆也常常討論，但從不干預。孩子已經成年了，他有獨立思想，我們相信他的能力。家長不應該掌握子女的命運、前途。決定他們命運的，是他們自己。

1.	出差	chūchāi	be on a business trip
2.	事先	shìxiān	in advance
3.	猜	cāi	to guess
4.	貼	tiē	mounted
5.	竟	jìng	unexpectedly
6.	儀式	yíshì	ceremony
7.	慶祝	qìngzhù	to celebrate
8.	悄悄	qiāoqiāo	quietly
9.	家具	jiājù	furniture
10.	干預	gānyù	intervene

4.2　妻子下岗又上岗

妻子的单位，这两年一年不如一年。

一天，妻子的单位真的宣布破产了。妻子和他的同事，哭肿了眼睛，恋恋不舍地离开了她工作了 20 年的工厂，成了一个下岗女工。妻子下了岗，我倒舒服了几天：下班回家，可口的饭菜就已经做好了，这倒也挺不错的。可是没过几天，我发现妻子总也高兴不起来，尽管我说尽了安慰她的话。妻子总是说："我可不能在家呆着，女人 40 岁，孩子大了，正是工作的好时候，不管什么单位，只要要我，哪怕工作脏点累点我都愿意。"趁我上班不在家，她东奔西跑，终于找到了一个小工厂，又上岗了。

妻子重新上岗后，第一天就上夜班。尽管她为我和女儿准备好了晚饭才走，可是一到家，我还是觉得家里好像少了点儿什么。女儿也瞪大了眼睛问："爸爸，妈妈不上夜班不行吗？如果你不在，妈妈又上夜班，我怎么办呢？"。

如果说妻子的下岗，曾经给我们这个小家庭带来了一时的不安，那么，妻子重新就业，又给我们这个小家庭带来了什么新情况，新问题呢？以前，家里早上吃什么，我从来不用管，每天早上我到公园去跑一圈，回来吃完早饭就上班。现在不行了，得早早起床，为自己和女儿准备早饭，忙得一塌糊涂。以前下班后，我可以在办公室里和同事们聊聊天，不用考虑什么时候回家。现在不行了，想到妻子要上夜班，哪怕同事们说我"怕老婆"也得抓紧时间往家里跑，怕女儿一个人在家害怕。过去，妻子在工厂里工作很轻松，回到家能把家务全都干了，现在，妻子下班一到家，常常就倒在沙发上睡着了。看她累成那个样子，我也很心痛，就主动多干家务，不仅做饭、洗碗、收拾房间，连衣服我也全洗了。我劝她："别干了，再找个好点儿的单位吧！"她却坚持说："不行"。

　　一个月过去了，一天，妻子回家，拿着刚发的工资，高兴地说："怎么样，老公，比以前多一倍呢！"妻子下岗又上岗，情绪很快地稳定了下来，又重新找回了自己，也锻炼了我这个当丈夫的。

4.2 妻子下崗又上崗

妻子的單位，這兩年一年不如一年。

一天，妻子的單位真的宣布破產了。妻子和他的同事，哭腫了眼睛，戀戀不捨地離開了她工作了 20 年的工廠，成了一個下崗女工。妻子下了崗，我倒舒服了幾天：下班回家，可口的飯菜就已經做好了，這倒也挺不錯的。可是沒過幾天，我發現妻子總也高興不起來，儘管我說盡了安慰她的話。妻子總是說："我可不能在家呆着，女人 40 歲，孩子大了，正是工作的好時候，不管甚麼單位，只要要我，哪怕工作臟點累點我都願意。"趁我上班不在家，她東奔西跑，終於找到了一個小工廠，又上崗了。

妻子重新上崗後，第一天就上夜班。儘管她為我和女兒準備好了晚飯才走，可是一到家，我還是覺得家裡好像少了點兒甚麼。女兒也瞪大了眼睛問："爸爸，媽媽不上夜班不行嗎？如果你不在，媽媽又上夜班，我怎麼辦呢？"。

如果說妻子的下崗，曾經給我們這個小家庭帶來了一時的不安，那麼，妻子重新就業，又給我們這個小家庭帶來了甚麼新情況，新問題呢？以前，家裡早上吃什麼，我從來不用管，每天早上我到公園去跑一圈，回來吃完早飯就上班。現在不行了，得早早起床，為自己和女兒準備早飯，忙得一塌糊塗。以前下班後，我可以在辦公室里和同事們聊聊天，不用考慮甚麼時候回家。現在不行了，想到妻子要上夜班，哪怕同事們說我"怕老婆"也得抓緊時間往家裡跑，怕女兒一個人在家害怕。過去，妻子在工廠裡工作很輕鬆，回到家能把家務全都幹了，現在，妻子下班一到家，常常就倒在沙發上睡着了。看她累成那個樣子，我也很心痛，就主動多幹家務，不僅做飯、洗碗、收拾房間，連衣服我也全洗了。我勸她："別幹了，再找個好點兒的單位吧！"她却堅持説："不行"。

　　一個月過去了，一天，妻子回家，拿着剛發的工資，高興地説："怎麼樣，老公，比以前多一倍呢！"妻子下崗又上崗，情緒很快地穩定了下來，又重新找回了自己，也鍛煉了我這個當丈夫的。

生词 NEW WORDS

1. 妻子　　妻子　　qīzi　　　　　　　　N. wife
2. 下崗　　下岗　　xiàgǎng　　　　　VO. go off sentry duty (fig. to be laid off -

    only in mainland China)
3. 不如　　不如　　bùrú　　　　　　　VP. not as good as; not equal to
4. 宣布　　宣布　　xuānbù　　　　　　V. declare; proclaim
5. 破産　　破产　　pòchǎn　　　　　　VO. go bankrupt
6. 同事　　同事　　tóngshì　　　　　　N. coworker
7. 腫　　　肿　　　zhǒng　　　　　　SV. swollen; swelling
8. 戀戀不捨　恋恋不舍　liànliànbùshě　　VP. very unwilling to part with
9. 工廠　　工厂　　gōngchǎng　　　　N. factory; plant
10. 倒　　　倒　　　dǎo　　　　　　　V. fall; collapse
11. 倒　　　倒　　　dào　　　　　　　Adv. but actually; contrary to what you

    might think
12. 下班　　下班　　xiàbān　　　　　　VO. go off work
13. 可口　　可口　　kěkǒu　　　　　　SV. good to eat; tasty
14. 挺　　　挺　　　tǐng　　　　　　　Adv. very
15. 儘管　　尽管　　jǐnguǎn　　　　　Con. in spite of; despite
16. 盡　　　尽　　　jìn　　　　　　　　RVE. to exhaust all the possible means
17. 安慰　　安慰　　ānwèi　　　　　　V. comfort; console
18. 臟　　　脏　　　zāng　　　　　　　SV. be dirty
19. 趁　　　趁　　　chèn　　　　　　　Prop. while
20. 東奔西跑　东奔西跑　dōng-bēn-xī-pǎo　　VP. run around here and there
21. 終於　　终于　　zhōngyú　　　　　Adv. at last
22. 瞪大眼睛　瞪大眼睛　dèng dà yǎnjīng　　VP. open the eyes wide
23. 跑一圈　跑一圈　pǎo yīquān　　　VP. run a lap
24. 一塌糊塗　一塌糊涂　yī-tā-hú-tú　　Idiom. in a complete mess
25. 抓緊時間　抓紧时间　zhuājǐn shíjiān　　VP. make the best use of one's time
26. 害怕　　害怕　　hàipà　　　　　　SV. feel afraid
27. 輕鬆　　轻松　　qīngsōng　　　　　SV. relaxed
28. 沙發　　沙发　　shāfā　　　　　　N. sofa

29.	心痛	心痛	xīntòng	VP.(makes one's) heart ache (to see such...)
30.	不僅	不仅	bùjǐn	Con. not only
31.	勸	劝	quàn	V. urge; try to persuade
32.	堅持	坚持	jiānchí	Adv. insistently
33.	情緒	情绪	qíngxù	N. mood; state of mind
34.	穩定	稳定	wěndìng	SV. be calm; steady
35.	鍛煉	锻炼	duànliàn	V. train and form (character)

常用词组　STOCK PHRASES

1.	宣布破產	宣布破产	to declare bankruptcy
2.	東奔西跑	东奔西跑	to ruch about; run around here and there
3.	忙得一塌糊塗	忙得一塌糊涂	extremely busy (in a muddled manner)
4.	抓緊時間	抓紧时间	to make the best use of one's time

语法　GRAMMAR

1. 倒

倒 may be read in two different tones, "dǎo" and "dào." "dǎo" functions as a verb, as in the sentence 我倒在沙发上睡着了 "I fell (threw myself down) in the sofa and fell asleep immediately." "dào," on the other hand, is an adverb, which has various interpretations. Here, we introduce only one, indicating that something has turned out better than one would have expected.

Examples:

(1) 我弟弟没考上重点中学，现在在职业中学念书，念职业中学倒也不错。

我弟弟沒考上重點中學，現在在職業中學念書，念職業中學倒也不錯。

My younger brother did not pass the examination for a top-ranked high school. He is now studying at a vocational high school, but that actually is not too bad.

(implied: studying at a vocational school is not as bad as I might have thought)

(2) 离婚以后，她在心里上倒觉得轻松得多。

離婚以後，她在心裡上倒覺得輕鬆得多。

After the divorce, she actually felt much more relaxed in her mind.

(implied: Being divorced turns out to be better than she expected.)

(3) 他每天工作时间很长，钱倒挣得不少。

他每天工作時間很長，錢倒掙得不少。

His daily working hours are very long, but he makes good money.

(implied: "Working long hours" has its advantage.)

2. 尽管......就是/但是/还是

A. S1 + 尽管 + VP1, S2 + 可是 + VP2

In this pattern 尽管 may also be placed before S1. It is often used in conjunction with 可是，但是 or 还是. If S2 coincides with S1, S2 will be dropped. Semantically, 尽管 is used to imply a contrast between circumstances.

Examples:

(1)李健尽管已经八十多岁了，脑子还是很好。

李健儘管已經八十多歲了，腦子還是很好。

Lǐ Jiàn, in spite of being eighty some years old, is still mentally very alert.

(2)尽管广场上人山人海，可是我一看就看到他了。

儘管廣場上人山人海，可是我一看就看到他了。

Despite the fact that the public square was full of people, I saw him right away.

B.　S1 + VP1, 尽管 S2 + VP2

The position of the two clauses may be reversed, placing the 尽管 clause at the rear, as if to supply an additional comment. In such usage, 可是，但是，还是 will be excluded from the entire sentence.

Examples:

(1)这本书写得真不错，尽管写书的人才二十几岁。

這本書寫得真不錯，儘管寫書的人才二十幾歲。

This book is written well, despite the fact that the person who wrote it was only in his twenties.

(2)这个地区的文盲率很高，尽管政府已经实行了几十年的义务教育了。

這個地區的文盲率很高，儘管政府已經實行了幾十年的義務教育了。

The rate of illiteracy is rather high, in spite of the fact that the government has enforced compulsory education for several decades.

3. 不管.....都/也

不管 + (alternative question or question word question) + S + VP

This pattern expresses: 1) the determination of the main character, the "S," to take a certain action regardless of whatever else happens, 2) a certain situation or condition remains unchanged despite any interference. 不管 is used to introduce the cited event or interference. Syntactically, this element must be rendered in the form of a question, either as an "alternative question" or a "question word question," but not in the form of a regular question, signaled by "吗。" In other words, the immediate constituent following 不管 must include one of these elements: 谁，什么，怎么，哪儿，多么， or "positive VP + negative VP." Furthermore, 不管 is used in conjunction with 都 or 也 to indicate that there are no exceptions.

Examples:

(1) 文小红的父母不同意她跟王新结婚。可是，文小红和王新相爱已经两年了。他们决定，不管有多么大的障碍，他们都会在下个月结婚。

文小紅的父母不同意她跟王新結婚，可是，文小紅和王新相愛已經兩年了。他們決定，不管有多麼大的障礙，他們都會在下個月結婚。

Wén Xiǎo Hóng's parents would not consent to her marrying Wáng Xīn. However, Wén Xiǎo Hóng and Wáng Xīn have loved each other for two years. They decided that they would get married next month regardless of how many serious obstacles there might be.

(2) 我大概是把那本书丢了，不管我怎么找也找不着。

我大概是把那本書丟了，不管我怎麼找也找不着。

I have probably lost that book. I could not find it no matter how I looked for it.

(3) 不管你用什么方法让她注意你都沒用，她已经有对象了。

不管你用什麼方法讓她注意你都沒用，她已經有對象了。

It doesn't make any difference what methods you employ to attract her attention. She already has a serious boy friend (a marriage prospect.)

4. 如果.....那么.....   如果 + clause 1, 那么 , clause 2

如果.....那么..... is a pattern for hypothetical sentences. Either the entire sentence is a hypothesis of cause-effect relation; or clause 2 is a hypothesis based on the fact stated in clause 1. The interpretation has to be judged from the context.

Note that the function of 那么 in the pattern "如果.....那么....." differs from "那么，....." In the second case, 那么 may be interpreted as "in that case, (then)....." 那么 refers to the message in the preceding discourse. In this second usage, the message in the preceding discourse and that follows 那么 are both facts.

Examples:

(1)如果这些商品的价格不降低，那么，一定卖不出去。

如果這些商品的價格不降低，那麼，一定賣不出去。

If the prices of these goods were not lowered, they could not be sold.

(2)如果教育经费不增加，那么，学校的问题就会一天比一天严重。

如果教育經費不增加，那麼，學校的問題就會一天比一天嚴重。

In case educational funds were not increased, the problems in the schools would become more serious day by day.

(3)如果你能在那么大的电脑公司找到工作，那么，在小公司更没有问题了。

如果你能在那麼大的電腦公司找到工作，那麼，在小公司更沒有問題了。

If you could find a job in such a big computer company, you would surely not have any problem finding jobs in small companies.

(Clause 1 is a fact, while clause 2 is a speculation.)

5. 哪怕.....也/都.....   哪怕 + S1 + VP1, S2 + 也/都 + VP2

This pattern is used to state hyperbolically that nothing could change the mind of the person, S2, to do or not to do the thing that he or she wanted to do. 哪怕 is used to point out the extreme nature of the illustration.

Examples:

(1)哪怕把所有的存款都用了，我也要买那辆汽车。

哪怕把所有的存款都用了，我也要買那輛汽車。

I must buy that car even if I have to spend all my savings.

(2)哪怕晚饭已经放在桌子上，他也不愿意离开电视机。

哪怕晚飯已經放在桌子上，他也不願意離開電視機。

Even if his dinner is on the table, he won't leave the TV set.

(implied: He is addicted to watching television.)

(3)哪怕他是百万富翁，我妹妹都不要嫁给他。

哪怕他是百萬富翁，我妹妹都不要嫁給他。

Even if he were a millionaire, my younger sister wouldn't marry him.

练习　EXERCISES

一、常用词组练习：用本课的常用词组填空。

1.就要出国了，你的护照还没申请好，飞机票也还没买，赶快（　　）把这些事办好。不要每天就在外头玩儿。

2.王东的儿子上了一所很贵的私立中学。为了给儿子交学费，王东除了本来的工作以外，还兼了两份职。每天（　　）连吃饭的时间都有问题。

3.我朋友的公司主要是卖冰箱、彩电和别的现代化的电器。原来买卖很好，但自从前年对面开了一家新的电器公司以后，他的商品就卖得越来越少了。今年的情况更坏，现在甚至连工人的工资都发不出了，债务越来越多，上个月只好（　　），把公司、商品都卖了还债。

4.他申请公费留学没申请到，却申请到了自费留学，但他没有钱，得想办法弄钱，所以每天不在家，在外头（　　），跟亲戚朋友借钱。

二、猜测词组的意思（看本课课文的上下文，不用字典）。

1.他上个月到银行去申请借钱，但是没申请到，因为他在申请表上填的资料不够清楚。银行要他重新填申请表，再申请。
重新是什么意思？

2.他在单位里工作很主动，什么事都不必有人让他作才作。单位里的人都认为他是工作态度最好的一个。
主动是什么意思？

三、造句：用下面的语法点和常用词组造句，每项造一句。(Simple sentences will not be acceptable. Your sentences must provide context such as time, location, condition, personal opinion, etc.)

1.倒（dào）　　　4.如果......那么......　　7.忙得一塌糊涂

2.尽管　　　　　　5.哪怕　　　　　　　　8.宣布破产

3.不管　　　　　　6.东奔西跑　　　　　　9.抓紧时间

四、阅读理解：用本课的内容回答问题。

1.为什么"妻子"不在工厂工作了？她离开工厂的时候觉得怎么样？

2."丈夫"在"妻子"离开工作单位后的头几天觉得怎么样？为什么？

3.“妻子”为什么不愿意在家呆着？她准备怎么办？

4.“妻子”的第二份工作是什么情况？她每天上班前得做什么？

5.“丈夫”和“女儿”对“妻子“的第二份工作觉得怎么样？

6.“妻子”的第二份工作对“丈夫”的生活有什么影响？

（用你自己的话简单说明）

7.你认为“妻子”下岗又上岗的情况对他们夫妇的感情有什么影响？

8.用大约一百五十个字写出你念完这课书以后的感想（gǎnxiǎng "impressions"）。

五、阅读下面的短文：

女性走回厨房
是进步？　还是倒退？

从家庭走向社会，是妇女人格独立，经济地位和社会地位提高的表现。但是有意思的是，近年来一些妇女又走回家庭，走回厨房，“专职”的家庭妇女人数在不断增加：

这种现象在中国的出现，主要有两个原因：

一是职业妇女一方面要工作，另一方面又要干家务，在时间、精力上常常要作痛苦的选择。如今在社会上竞争越来越利害，女性想干好工作，就不能不在事业上化时间和精力，而回家后家务又不能不干。有的女性觉得这样太累，而且很可能结果是工作没干好，家里也搞得乱七八糟，所以不如呆在家里，专心干家务。今年三十岁的小王原来在一家工厂工作，每天上下班路上就要化两小时。这些年工厂情况不太好，她就办了手续，离开工厂，在家“专职”干家务。“我不工作在家以后，家里干净多了，生活也有秩序了，我也不用一心挂两头了。”她说。

另一个原因是从经济方面考虑的结果。你看，刚过了三十岁生日的小刘，自从生了个胖儿子，就不再工作了。她的理由是：“现在请个保姆，又得给她工资，又得给她吃饭，我一个人的工资都不够。而且自己的孩子自己照顾会好得多。”她打算等孩子上学后，再重新工作。这段时间里，她想多学习点儿新知识，以后可以找到更好的工作。

如今的“专职家庭妇女”跟以前所说的“家庭妇女”有很大的不同：她

们中有许多人具有高学历；她们原来一般都有固定工作；一般是孩子出生后才不工作；她们的丈夫大多数收入较高。你认为这种现象是进步，还是倒退呢？有人认为，长期以来，我们一直主张妇女从家庭中走出来，走进社会，如今妇女又重新回到厨房，这是一种倒退。但是也有人认为，应该尊重妇女自己的意愿，妇女有走出家庭的自由，也有返回厨房的自由，这才真正是妇女的解放。

1.倒退	dàotuì	to go backwards
2.人格独立	réngé dúlì	independence of character
3.专职	zhuānzhí	full-time
4.精力	jīnglì	energy (here: efforts)
5.竞争	jìngzhēng	competition
6.乱七八糟	luànqībāzāo	in a mess
7.办手续	bàn shǒuxù	to go through the procedures of
8.有秩序	yǒu zhìxù	orderly
9.保姆	bǎomǔ	housekeeper
10.照顾	zhàogù	to look after
11.知识	zhīshǐ	knowledge
12.尊重	zūnzhòng	to respect (a person's opinions, ideas - to express respect for a person, "尊敬 zūnjìng" must be used)
13.意愿	yìyuàn	wish; aspiration

練習　EXERCISES

一、常用辭組練習：用本課的常用辭組填空。
　　1.就要出國了，你的護照還沒申請好，飛機票也還沒買，趕快（　　）把這些事辦好。不要每天就在外頭玩兒。
　　2.王東的兒子上了一所很貴的私立中學。為了給兒子交學費，王東除了本來的工作以外，還兼了兩份職。每天（　　）連吃飯的時間都有問題。
　　3.我朋友的公司主要是賣冰箱、彩電和別的現代化的電器。原來買賣很好，但自從前年對面開了一家新的電器公司以後，他的商品就賣得越來越少了。今年的情況更壞，現在甚至連工人的工資都發不出了，債務越來越多，上個月只好（　　），把公司、商品都賣了還債。
　　4.他申請公費留學沒申請到，却申請到了自費留學，但他沒有錢，得想辦法弄錢，所以每天不在家，在外頭（　　），跟親戚朋友借錢。

二、猜測辭組的意思（看本課課文的上下文，不用字典）。
　　1.他上個月到銀行去申請借錢，但是沒申請到，因為他在申請表上填的資料不夠清楚。銀行要他重新填申請表，再申請。
　　重新是什麼意思？
　　2.他在單位裡工作很主動，什麼事都不必有人讓他作才作。單位裡的人都認為他是工作態度最好的一個。
　　主動是什麼意思？

三、造句：用下面的語法點和常用辭組造句，每項造一句。(Simple sentences will not be acceptable. Your sentences must provide context such as time, location, condition, personal opinion, etc.)
　　1.倒（dào）　　4.如果.....那麼......　　7.忙得一塌糊塗
　　2.儘管　　　　5.哪怕　　　　　　　8.宣布破產
　　3.不管　　　　6.東奔西跑　　　　　9.抓緊時間

四、閱讀理解：用本課的內容回答問題。
　　1.為甚麼"妻子"不在工廠工作了？她離開工廠的時候覺得怎麼樣？
　　2."丈夫"在"妻子"離開工作單位後的頭幾天覺得怎麼樣？為甚麼？

3. "妻子" 爲甚麼不願意在家呆着？她準備怎麼辦？
4. "妻子" 的第二份工作是甚麼情況？她每天上班前得做甚麼？
5. "丈夫" 和 "女兒" 對 "妻子" 的第二份工作覺得怎麼樣？
6. "妻子" 的第二份工作對 "丈夫" 的生活有甚麼影響？
   （用你自己的話簡單説明）
7. 你認爲 "妻子" 下崗又上崗的情況對他們夫婦的感情有什麼影響？
8. 用大約一百五十個字寫出你念完這課書以後的感想（gǎnxiǎng
   "impressions"）。

五、閱讀下面的短文：

女性走回廚房
是進步？ 還是倒退？

從家庭走向社會，是婦女人格獨立，經濟地位和社會地位提高的表現。
但是有意思的是，近年來一些婦女又走回家庭，走回廚房，"專職" 的家庭
婦女人數在不斷增加：

這種現象在中國的出現，主要有兩個原因：

一是職業婦女一方面要工作，另一方面又要幹家務，在時間、精力上常
常要作痛苦的選擇。如今在社會上競爭越來越利害，女性想幹好工作，就不
能不在事業上化時間和精力，而回家後家務又不能不幹。有的女性覺得這樣
太累，而且很可能結果是工作沒幹好，家裡也搞得亂七八糟，所以不如呆在
家裡，專心幹家務。今年三十歲的小王原來在一家工廠工作，每天上下班路
上就要化兩小時。這些年工廠情況不太好，她就辦了手續，離開工廠，在家
"專職" 幹家務。"我不工作在家以後，家裡乾淨多了，生活也有秩序了，
我也不用一心掛兩頭了。" 她説。

另一個原因是從經濟方面考慮的結果。你看，剛過了三十歲生日的小劉，
自從生了個胖兒子，就不再工作了。她的理由是："現在請個保姆，又得給
她工資，又得給她吃飯，我一個人的工資都不夠。而且自己的孩子自己照顧
會好得多。" 她打算等孩子上學後，再重新工作。這段時間裡，她想多學習
點兒新知識，以後可以找到更好的工作。

如今的 "專職家庭婦女" 跟以前所説的 "家庭婦女" 有很大的不同：她

們中有許多人具有高學歷；她們原來一般都有固定工作；一般是孩子出生後才不工作；她們的丈夫大多數收入較高。你認為這種現象是進步，還是倒退呢？有人認為，長期以來，我們一直主張婦女從家庭中走出來，走進社會，如今婦女又重新回到廚房，這是一種倒退。但是也有人認為，應該尊重婦女自己的意願，婦女有走出家庭的自由，也有返回廚房的自由，這才真正是婦女的解放。

1. 倒退　dàotuì　to go backwards
2. 人格獨立　réngé dúlì　independence of character
3. 專職　zhuānzhí　full-time
4. 精力　jīnglì　energy (here: efforts)
5. 競爭　jìngzhēng　competition
6. 亂七八糟　luànqībāzāo　in a mess
7. 辦手續　bàn shǒuxù　to go through the procedures of
8. 有秩序　yǒu zhìxù　orderly
9. 保姆　bǎomǔ　housekeeper
10. 照顧　zhàogù　to look after
11. 知識　zhīshǐ　knowledge
12. 尊重　zūnzhòng　to respect (a person's opinions, ideas - to express respect for a person, "尊敬 zūnjìng" must be used)
13. 意願　yìyuàn　wish; aspiration

4.3　贝贝进行曲

贝贝一岁。

那天，小俩口都领了工资。年轻的妈妈下班回来得特别晚，一到家，立刻抱起贝贝亲了好几口，便跌坐到椅子里，她精疲力尽了。

跑遍了半个城市，收获巨大。她一边喘气一边从大包里掏出许多东西来，满满地摆了半张床。

年轻的爸爸看了看，皱皱眉头："你真舍得，花了多少钱？"

"工资去了一半！"她一边说，一边逗着孩子满床抓。

"到时候没钱买饭票，又得每天带饭吃咸菜。"

"关键是他的营养得跟上啊，我怕什么呢？"她说，"我们这辈子反正不行了……"

"这倒是，"年轻的爸爸赞同，"我们这辈子已经完了，就得在他身上花本钱了！"

贝贝三岁。

"那件大衣多少钱？"年轻的妈妈问。

"三十二元。"营业员答。

"真漂亮。贝贝，"她又问儿子，"喜欢不喜欢？"

"喜欢！"儿子回答得脆响、特甜。

"买吧？"她再问丈夫。

"买吧！"他也很大方。

大衣买好了，他们又来到玩具柜。

贝贝一眼看上了那个大型的"变形金刚"，一问价钱，四十八元。

"太贵了，不能买。"爸爸说。

可是贝贝立刻大哭起来，"我要，我要买嘛！"

妈妈咬咬牙，对爸爸说："这是智力投资，给他买吧，我的毛衣不买了。"

"可是，你……"爸爸看着妈妈，无可奈何地说："好吧，给他买，我们这辈子已经完了，就看他了。"

贝贝五岁。

在动物园里，贝贝玩得可高兴了。他大开了眼界，增长了知识。

"贝贝，那是什么？"妈妈问。

"小鸟。"孩子迅速地回答。

"爸爸考考你，树上有五只鸟，打死了一只，还剩几只？"

"一只也没有了，全飞了。"

"贝贝真棒！真聪明，长大一定有出息。"爸爸满意地说。"来，给你巧克力，这是奖品。"

贝贝得意地接过巧克力吃起来。

"给妈妈一块吧，贝贝，我也有点儿饿。"妈妈说。

"不，不给，这是我的，不给你们吃！"

"为什么不给？是我们给你买的！"爸爸生气地说。

"爸爸妈妈说过，你们吃什么、穿什么都没有关系，关键是要让我高兴！"贝贝理直气壮地回答。

"唉！"妈妈深深地叹了一口气，"我们为他花了那么多心血，连一块巧克力也吃不到。"

爸爸也伤心地叹了口气，突然，他举起了右手，向贝贝打去……

4.3 貝貝進行曲

貝貝一歲。

那天，小倆口都領了工資。年輕的媽媽下班回來得特別晚，一到家，立刻抱起貝貝親了好幾口，便跌坐到椅子裡，她精疲力盡了。

跑遍了半個城市，收獲巨大。她一邊喘氣一邊從大包裡掏出許多東西來，滿滿地擺了半張床。

年輕的爸爸看了看，皺皺眉頭：“你真捨得，花了多少錢？”

“工資去了一半！”她一邊說，一邊逗著孩子滿床抓。

“到時候沒錢買飯票，又得每天帶飯吃鹹菜。”

“關鍵是他的營養得跟上啊，我怕甚麼呢？”她說，“我們這輩子反正不行了……”

“這倒是，”年輕的爸爸贊同，“我們這輩子已經完了，就得在他身上花本錢了！”

貝貝三歲。

“那件大衣多少錢？”年輕的媽媽問。

“三十二元。”營業員答。

“真漂亮。貝貝，”她又問兒子，“喜歡不喜歡？”

“喜歡！”兒子回答得脆響、特甜。

“買吧？”她再問丈夫。

“買吧！”他也很大方。

大衣買好了，他們又來到玩具櫃。

貝貝一眼看上了那個大型的“變形金剛”，一問價錢，四十八元。

"太貴了，不能買。"爸爸說。

可是貝貝立刻大哭起來，"我要，我要買嘛！"

媽媽咬咬牙，對爸爸說："這是智力投資，給他買吧，我的毛衣不買了。"

"可是，你......"爸爸看着媽媽，無可奈何地說："好吧，給他買，我們這輩子已經完了，就看他了。"

貝貝五歲。

在動物園裡，貝貝玩得可高興了。他大開了眼界，增長了知識。

"貝貝，那是甚麼？"媽媽問。

"小鳥。"孩子迅速地回答。

"爸爸考考你，樹上有五隻鳥，打死了一隻，還剩幾隻？"

"一隻也沒有了，全飛了。"

"貝貝真棒！真聰明，長大一定有出息。"爸爸滿意地說。"來，給你巧克力，這是獎品。"

貝貝得意地接過巧克力吃起來。

"給媽媽一塊吧，貝貝，我也有點兒餓。"媽媽說。

"不，不給，這是我的，不給你們吃！"

"爲甚麼不給？是我們給你買的！"爸爸生氣地說。

"爸爸媽媽說過，你們吃甚麼、穿甚麼都沒有關係，關鍵是要讓我高興！"貝貝理直氣壯地回答。

"唉！"媽媽深深地嘆了一口氣，"我們爲他花了那麼多心血，連一塊巧克力也吃不到。"

爸爸也傷心地嘆了口氣，突然，他舉起了右手，向貝貝打去

......

语法　GRAMMAR

1. 反正　　　　　anyway; anyhow

　　A. In a sentence of two chauses of which the first contains 无论 "regardless" or 不管"no matter what(the circumstances)", 反正 in the second clause indicates that the outcome would have been the same. [see sentences (1) and (2)]

　　B. A clause with 反正 indicates an irreversible situation, and the accompanying clause suggests an appropriate action. Either clause may come first. [see sentences (3) and (4)]

Examples:

(1)不管你去不去，反正我得去。

　　不管你去不去，反正我得去。

　　Whether you go or not, I'm going anyway.

(2)无论你说什么，反正我不相信。

　　無論你説什麼，反正我不相信。

　　No matter what you say, I don't believe it anyway.

(3)我们这辈子反正不行了，就看你们的了。

　　我們這輩子反正不行了，就看你們的了。

　　It's all up with our generation anyway, it will have

　　to depend on you.

(4)反正车票已经买来了，你就和我们一起去吧。

　　反正車票已經買來了，你就和我們一起去吧。

　　We have already bought the tickets anyway; you had

　　better go with us.

2.　一+V

This verb phrase indicates an action of a very short duration. Verbs commonly used this way are 看、听、学、想、说.

Examples:

(1)早上我打开窗户一看，外面下雪了。

　　早上我打開窗戶一看，外面下雪了。

This morning, when I opened the window I saw that it
was snowing.

(2)我打电话一问，才知道她已经回国了。

我打電話一問，才知道她已經回國了。

Only when I phoned and inquired did I know that she
had already come back to the country.

This adverb 一 can also be used with another adverb 就 to indicate
that the second event (the "就 VP") follows the first
(the "一VP") almost immediately in happening. The 一....就 also expresses
that, habitually, whenever event 1 happens, event 2 follows immediately.

Examples:

(3)我一听声音就知道是小王来了。

我一聽聲音就知道是小王來了。

As soon as I heard a voice, I knew that it was Xiǎo
Wáng who had come.

(4)老师一说我就明白了。

老師一説我就明白了。

I understood the moment the techer spoke.

(5)他一拿起书来，就想睡觉。

他一拿起書來，就想睡覺。

He feels sleepy whenever he picks up a book.

185

1. 進行曲　进行曲　jìnxíngqǔ　　N. march (music)
2. 領工資　领工资　lǐng gōngzī　　VO. get pay
3. 抱　　　抱　　　bào　　　　　V. hug; hold...in the arms
4. 親　　　亲　　　qīn　　　　　V. kiss
5. 跌　　　跌　　　diē　　　　　V. fall down
6. 精疲力盡　精疲力尽　jīngpí lìjìn　Ph. exhausted
7. 跑遍　　跑遍　　pǎobiàn　　RVC. running everywhere (here: exhausted all possibilities)
8. 收獲　　收获　　shōuhuò　　N. gains; results
9. 巨大　　巨大　　jùdà　　　SV. big; huge
10. 喘氣　　喘气　　chuǎnqì　　VO. breathe heavily
11. 大包　　大包　　dàbāo　　　N. big bag
12. 掏　　　掏　　　tāo　　　　V. pull out; draw out(from pocket, bag)
13. 擺　　　摆　　　bǎi　　　　V. put; place; arrange
14. 皺眉頭　皱眉头　zhòu méitóu　VO. knit one's brows; frown
15. 你真捨得
　　你真舍得　nǐ zhēn shědé　(here) How generous of you!
16. 逗　　　逗　　　dòu　　　　V. tease; play with
17. 抓　　　抓　　　zhuā　　　V. grab; clutch
18. 飯票　　饭票　　fànpiào　　N. food coupon; meal ticket
19. 鹹菜　　咸菜　　xiáncài　　N. pickles; salted vegetables
20. 關鍵　　关键　　guānjiàn　　N. key to situation; crucial importance
21. 營養　　营养　　yíngyǎng　　N. nutrition
22. 這輩子　这辈子　zhè bèizi　　N. this generation; this life-time
23. 反正　　反正　　fǎnzhèng　　Adv. anyway
24. 這倒是　这倒是　zhè dǎoshì　Ph. right; this actually is the case
25. 贊同　　赞同　　zàntóng　　V. agree with
26. 花本錢　花本钱　huā běnqián　VO. spend money(time,energy)on...

27.營業員	营业员	yíngyèyuán	N. salesperson
28.脆響	脆响	cuìxiǎng	Adv. crisply
29.玩具櫃	玩具柜	wánjùguì	N. toys case
30.智力	智力	zhìlì	N. intelligence
31.投資	投资	tóuzī	N. investment
32.無可奈何	无可奈何	wú kě nài hé	Ph. be utterly helpless; having no way out; reluctantly
33.動物園	动物园	dòngwùyuán	N. zoo
34.開眼界	开眼界	kāi yǎnjiè	VO. widen one's view; broaden one's mind
35.知識	知识	zhīshì	N. knowledge
36.剩	剩	shèng	V. be left
37.棒	棒	bàng	SV. excellent
38.有出息	有出息	yǒu chūxǐ	VO. promising
39.滿意	满意	mǎnyì	SV. be satisfied
40.獎品	奖品	jiǎngpǐn	N. award; prize
41.得意	得意	déyì	SV. complacent
42.理直氣壯	理直气壮	lǐzhí qìzhuàng	Ph. with perfect assurance; being bold and assured
43.嘆	叹	tàn	V. sigh
44.心血	心血	xīnxuè	N. painstaking care; painstaking labor
45.傷心	伤心	shāngxīn	SV. sad; grieved

常用词组

1.有營養	有营养	nutritious
2.營養豐富	营养丰富	rich in nourishment
3.智力投資	智力投资	to invest in the intellectual development of a child
4.國外投資	国外投资	foreign investment
5.知識份子	知识分子	an intellectual

练习　EXERCISES

一、选词填空：

　　大方、眼界、精疲力尽、皇帝、外国、增长、出息、
　　本钱、政策、迅速、工资、营养、智力、舍得、聪明

　　为了让人口(　　)得慢点儿，从70年代开始，中国的(　　)是一家一个孩子。不少孩子成了家庭中的小(　　)。年轻的父母们(　　)并不高，可是为了让孩子的(　　)跟得上，他们自己不(　　)吃，为了给孩子买漂亮的衣服，买(　　)玩具，他们非常(　　)，自己的衣服可以不买，还认为这是(　　)投资。下班以后，已经累得(　　)了，可是孩子要去公园玩，要去开(　　)，父母们会(　　)答应，立刻带"小皇帝"出去玩。每一家都盼望自己家的孩子(　　)，有(　　)，有所作为，所以愿意在孩子身上花(　　)。

二、用本课的五个常用词组造句：每个词组作一个句子

三、用约两百个字写出你对解决中国人口问题的建议：
　　可用这种方式写：1.中国人口过多造成的问题，2.你认为应该用什么方法解决这个问题，3.你的建议根据什么理由？4.结论〔conclusion〕

四、阅读下列短文：

开学第一天

　　九月一日是上海市中小学开学的第一天，也是大学新同学到校的日子。
　　在一所小学，许多家长站在自己孩子的教室门口。虽然老师已经走进教室，要上课了，但是还有一些家长进教室，有的从孩子嘴里拿下半个面包，有的帮助孩子从书包里拿书，进进出出，乱得很。老师一次次地请家长离开，但家长好像总是不放心自己的孩子，不愿意离开。后来有一些家长又来到教室旁边的操场上，等孩子放学，一些小学生从窗户看他们，不能好好上课。
　　中学又怎么样呢？在一所女子中学宿舍，你可以看到家长在为孩子整理床、挂窗帘、洗碗、洗衣服……一位老师说，以前有一位家长天天来帮女儿打

188

开水，说怕女儿烫伤。

在上海一所大学，首先引起你注意的是一辆辆送新同学的汽车；有的是出租汽车，但更多的是公家的汽车！有些学生的家长是干部，他们因为工作需要有汽车，于是就利用这个条件送自己的孩子。这些汽车有上海市的，别的城市的，哪儿的车都有。走进新同学宿舍，你会奇怪，学生坐在椅子上，家长们在双层床上爬上爬下，忙着整理床、挂蚊帐……问一位东北来的家长，为什么这么远还要送孩子来上学？他说孩子生活能力不强，自己不能照顾自己。

看看这些，真叫人担心，这些孩子离开父母、进入社会后怎么生活？

1.面包	miànbāo	bread
2.书包	shūbāo	schoolbag
3.操场	cāochǎng	playground; athletic field
4.整理	zhěnglǐ	to put in order
5.窗帘	chuānglián	window curtain
6.打开水	dǎ kāishuǐ	to fetch boiled water
7.烫伤	tàngshāng	to scald/to be scalded
8.出租汽车	chūzū qìchē	taxi
9.公家的	gōngjiā de	(something) not privately owned, belonging to the organization in which one works
10.干部	gànbù	cadre; originally a functionary in the Party, now referring to an administrative level worker (used in mainland China only)
11.双层床	shuāngcéngchuáng	double-decker bed
12.蚊帐	wénzhàng	mosquito net
13.担心	dānxīn	be worried

練習　EXERCISES

一、選詞填空：

　　大方、眼界、精疲力盡、皇帝、外國、增長、出息、
　　本錢、政策、迅速、工資、營養、智力、捨得、聰明

　　為了讓人口(　　)得慢點兒，從70年代開始，中國的(　　)是一家一個孩
子。不少孩子成了家庭中的小(　　)。年輕的父母們(　　)並不高，可是為了
讓孩子的(　　)跟得上，他們自己不(　　)吃，為了給孩子買漂亮的衣服，
買(　　)玩具，他們非常(　　)，自己的衣服可以不買，還認為這是(　　)投
資。下班以後，已經累得(　　)了，可是孩子要去公園玩，要去開(　　)，父
母們會(　　)答應，立刻帶"小皇帝"出去玩。每一家都盼望自己家的孩子
(　　)，有(　　)，有所作為，所以願意在孩子身上花(　　)。

二、用本課的五個常用詞組造句：每個詞組作一個句子

三、用約兩百個字寫出你對解決中國人口問題的建議：

　　可用這種方式寫：1.中國人口過多造成的問題；2.你認為應該用甚麼方法
解決這個問題，3.你的建議根據甚麼理由？4.結論（conclusion）

四、閱讀下列短文：

開學第一天

　　九月一日是上海市中小學開學的第一天，也是大學新同學到校的日子。

　　在一所小學，許多家長站在自己孩子的教室門口。雖然老師已經走進教
室，要上課了，但是還有一些家長進教室，有的從孩子嘴裡拿下半個麵包，
有的幫助孩子從書包裡拿書，進進出出，亂得很。老師一次次地請家長離開，
但家長好像總是不放心自己的孩子，不願意離開。後來有一些家長又來到教
室旁邊的操場上，等孩子放學，一些小學生從窗戶看他們，不能好好上課。

　　中學又怎麼樣呢？在一所女子中學宿舍，你可以看到家長在為孩子整理
床、掛窗簾、洗碗、洗衣服……一位老師說，以前有一位家長天天來幫女兒打
開水，說怕女兒燙傷。

　　在上海一所大學，首先引起你注意的是一輛輛送新同學的汽車；有的是

出租汽車，但更多的是公家的汽車！有些學生的家長是幹部，他們因為工作需要有汽車，於是就利用這個條件送自己的孩子。這些汽車有上海市的，別的城市的，哪兒的車都有。走進新同學宿舍，你會奇怪，學生坐在椅子上，家長們在雙層床上爬上爬下，忙着整理床、掛蚊帳……問一位東北來的家長，為甚麼這麼遠還要送孩子來上學？他說孩子生活能力不強，自己不能照顧自己。

看看這些，真叫人擔心，這些孩子離開父母、進入社會後怎麼生活？

1.麵包	miànbāo	bread
2.書包	shūbāo	schoolbag
3.操場	cāochǎng	playground; athletic field
4.整理	zhěnglǐ	to put in order
5.窗簾	chuānglián	window curtain
6.打開水	dǎ kāishuǐ	to fetch boiled water
7.燙傷	tàngshāng	to scald/to be scalded
8.出租汽車	chūzū qìchē	taxi
9.公家的	gōngjiā de	(something) not privately owned, belonging to the organization in which one works
10.幹部	gànbù	cadre; originally a functionary in the Party, now referring to an administrative level worker (used in mainland China only)
11.雙層床	shuāngcéngchuáng	double-decker bed
12.蚊帳	wénzhàng	mosquito net
13.擔心	dānxīn	be worried

Unit Five

5. 经济发展的动态

八十年代初的改革开放不但使中国的经济有了很大的进展，也使中国人在思想上有了很大的改变。

"万般皆下品，唯有读书高"，是长期以来深深地扎根在中国人头脑里的一种传统观念。中国人一向崇拜"读书人"，轻视商人。知识份子受人尊敬，而商人却让人看不起。但这种思想在九十年代的今天已经大大地改变了。商人的社会地位，由于经济发展的快速，提高到前所未有的地步。他们的生活水平比知识分子的高得多，而成为一般人羡慕的对象。中国人现在对"读书"与"从商"的传统观念也因此发生了改变。"经商"变成了一般人所追求的事业。

第二个思想上的变化是人们对"铁饭碗"看法的改变。在一九四九年到一九七零年底期间，中国人习惯于在固定的工作单位上端铁饭碗。没有了铁饭碗就是失业，就要挨饿。因此，"铁饭碗"是非常重要的。但是在今天的中国人心目中，"铁饭碗"已不再像当年那样神圣了。九十年代的中国，不但有了越来越多的中外合资企业，也有了更多的大型私人企业和个人经商。这种倾向于发展商品经济的情况，为人们提供了一个很大的人力市场，也带来了更高的工资。城镇的职工开始告别了终身为一个单位工作的谋生方式，农民也有了机会走出土地、走出家乡。现在就业不再仅仅是为了养家活口，更重要的是为了提高生活水平。因此，工资收入成了一般人民选择职业的第一考虑。

人们在思想上的解放，使现在的中国经济发展得五花八门。社会上也因此出现了各种各样的商业形态。本单元给各位介绍了几种九十年代末新发展出来的商业行为。这些都是中华人民共和国建国以来至八十年代所没有的。

5. 經濟發展的動態

八十年代初的改革開放不但使中國的經濟有了很大的進展，也使中國人在思想上有了很大的改變。

"萬般皆下品，唯有讀書高"，是長期以來深深地札根在中國人頭腦裡的一種傳統觀念。中國人一向崇拜"讀書人"，輕視商人。知識份子受人尊敬，而商人卻讓人看不起。但這種思想在九十年代的今天已經大大地改變了。商人的社會地位，由於經濟發展的快速，提高到前所未有的地步。他們的生活水平比知識分子的高得多，而成為一般人羨慕的對象。中國人現在對"讀書"與"從商"的傳統觀念也因此發生了改變。"經商"變成了一般人所追求的事業。

第二個思想上的變化是人們對"鐵飯碗"看法的改變。在一九四九年到一九七零年底期間，中國人習慣於在固定的工作單位上端鐵飯碗。沒有了鐵飯碗就是失業，就要挨餓。因此，"鐵飯碗"是非常重要的。但是在今天的中國人心目中，"鐵飯碗"已不再像當年那樣神聖了。九十年代的中國，不但有了越來越多的中外合資企業，也有了更多的大型私人企業和個人經商。這種傾向於發展商品經濟的情況，為人們提供了一個很大的人力市場，也帶來了更高的工資。城鎮的職工開始告別了終身為一個單位工作的謀生方式，農民也有了機會走出土地、走出家鄉。現在就業不再僅僅是為了養家活口，更重要的是為了提高生活水平。因此，工資收入成了一般人民選擇職業的第一考慮。

人們在思想上的解放，使現在的中國經濟發展得五花八門。社會上也因此出現了各種各樣的商業形態。本單元給各位介紹了幾種九十年代末新發展出來的商業行為。這些都是中華人民共和國建國以來至八十年代所沒有的。

生词 NEW WORDS

1. 拍賣	拍卖	pāimài	V/N. auction
2. 進展	进展	jìnzhǎn	N. progress

3. 萬般皆下品，唯有讀書高
万般皆下品，唯有读书高

wànbān jiē xiàpǐn, wéi yǒu dúshū gāo — Everything else is inferior, only study is superior.

4. 扎根在	扎根在	zhāgēn zài	VP. take root in
5. 頭腦	头脑	tóunǎo	N. head; brains
6. 崇拜	崇拜	chóngbài	V. worship
7. 輕視	轻视	qīngshì	V. look down on
8. 快速	快速	kuàisù	N. swiftness; rapidity
9. 地步	地步	dìbù	N. (raised to the)point (of); condition
10. 羨慕	羡慕	xiànmù	V. envy
11. 對象	对象	duìxiàng	N. object; target
12. 從商	从商	cóngshāng	VO. to engage in trade/business
13. 鐵飯碗	铁饭碗	tiě fànwǎn	N. (lit. iron rice bowl) guaranteed livelihood
14. 固定	固定	gùdìng	SV. fixed; permanent
15. 端	端	duān	V. hold sth. with both hands
16. 挨餓	挨饿	āi'è	VO. suffer from hunger

17. 在...心目中
在...心目中

zài…xīnmù zhōng — Ph. to sb's mind; in some people's view

18. 神聖	神圣	shénshèng	SV. sacred; holy
19. 大型	大型	dàxíng	SV. large-scale; large
20. 傾向於	倾向于	qīngxiàng	V. be inclined to
21. 提供	提供	tígōng	V. offer; provide
22. 城鎮	城镇	chéngzhèn	N. cities and towns
23. 告別	告别	gàobié	V. say good-bye to (here, figurative)
24. 終身	终身	zhōngshēn	N. all one's life

25. 謀生	谋生	móushēng	V. make a living
26. 僅僅	仅仅	jǐnjǐn	Adv. only; merely; barely
27. 廣大	广大	guǎngdà	SV. vast(number of); the broad masses of
28. 解放	解放	jiěfàng	N. liberation
29. 五花八門 五花八門	五花八门	wǔ huā bā mén	Ph. multifarious; of a rich variety
30. 形態	形态	xíngtài	N. pattern
31. 行為	行为	xíngwéi	N. behavior
32. 中華人民共和國 中华人民共和国		zhōnghuá rénmín gònghéguó	N. the People's Republic of China
33. 建國	建国	jiànguó	VO. to found a state

5.1 个人投资

买房子 —— 新的领域

随着商品经济的发展，"投资"成为一个新的社会热点，怎样投资是现在一般人脑子里经常考虑的问题。

老李的伯父住在香港，两年前回上海探亲。在一次饭后的闲谈中，伯父谈起香港的房地价，他说那真是"寸土如金"。普普通通的一套公寓都要上百万元。老李惊讶地说"那有一套公寓的人不就都是百万富翁了吗？""是啊"伯父说，"如果上海也像香港的话，凭你们现在的这套房子，没有百万，也有几十万了。"

伯父所说的话打动了老李的心。他想自己的工作业务是维修楼房，自己对房屋的空间很熟悉，对房屋装潢也有经验，何不试试看买一套房子呢，也许这个机会比其他的机会容易发财得多。于是，伯父一走，老李就说动了他的弟弟，两人一同将多年来积蓄下来的几万元买了两套二室一厅的市区住房，整理过以后租了给别人，自己做起房东来了。

两年多过去了，直线上升的房价到达了四千八百元一个平方米，老李决定将房子卖掉，然后或是再买大一点的房子，或是考虑别的投资。他和弟弟的两套普普通通的商品房，一下子价值倍增，几万元的投入，仅仅两年的时间就换回了四十万元的利润。

这种具有稳定性而利润又高的商业方式，使越来越多像老李一样的人，投资于房地产业。他们有的是筹资甚至借款买下他们认为将会升值的房产，有的学会了用较少的预付款买下还未造好的房子，等房价上升后再抛出盈利。更有的当起房地产经纪商来了。

房地产热的兴起使许多人开始考虑到长期投资的可能性。

5.1 個人投資
買房子 —— 新的領域

隨着商品經濟的發展，"投資"成為一個新的社會熱點，怎樣投資是現在一般人腦子裡經常考慮的問題。

老李的伯父住在香港，兩年前回上海探親。在一次飯後的閒談中，伯父談起香港的房地價，他說那真是"寸土如金"。普普通通的一套公寓都要上百萬元。老李驚訝地說"那有一套公寓的人不就都是百萬富翁了嗎？""是啊"伯父說，"如果上海也像香港的話，憑你們現在的這套房子，沒有百萬，也有幾十萬了。"

伯父所說的話打動了老李的心。他想自己的工作業務是維修樓房，自己對房屋的空間很熟悉，對房屋裝潢也有經驗，何不試試看買一套房子呢，也許這個機會比其他的機會容易發財得多。於是，伯父一走，老李就說動了他的弟弟，兩人一同將多年來積蓄下來的幾萬元買了兩套二室一廳的市區住房，整理過以後租了給別人，自己做起房東來了。

兩年多過去了，直線上升的房價到達了四千八百元一個平方米，老李決定將房子賣掉，然後或是再買大一點的房子，或是考慮別的投資。他和弟弟的兩套普普通通的商品房，一下子價值倍增，幾萬元的投入，僅僅兩年的時間就換回了四十萬元的利潤。

這種具有穩定性而利潤又高的商業方式，使越來越多像老李一樣的人，投資於房地產業。他們有的是籌資甚至借款買下他們認為將會升值的房產，有的學會了用較少的預付款買下還未造好的房子，等房價上升後再拋出盈利。更有的當起房地產經紀商來了。

房地產熱的興起使許多人開始考慮到長期投資的可能性。

生词　NEW WORDS

1.領域	领域	lǐngyù	N. dimension; domain
2.熱點	热点	rèdiǎn	N. craze (社会热点, social craze)
3.經常	经常	jīngcháng	Adv. constantly
4.探親	探亲	tànqīn	VO. go back home to visit one's family
5.閒談	闲谈	xiántán	V. chat; engage in chitchat
6.寸土如金			
寸土如金		cùn tǔ rú jīn	Ph. land as dear as gold
7.驚訝地	惊讶地	jīngyà dì	Adv. amazingly; surprisingly
8.套	套	tào	M. for an apartment
9.百萬富翁			
百万富翁		bǎiwàn fùwēng	N. millionaire
10.打動	打动	dǎdòng	RV. move; touch
X 打動 Y 的心			VP. X moves or touches Y's heart
11.維修	维修	wéixiū	V. keep in (good) repair; maintain
12.裝潢	装潢	zhuānghuáng	V. decorate
13.何不	何不	hébù	QW. why not... (何不+V)
14.發財	发财	fācái	VO. get rich; make big money
15.說動	说动	shuódòng	RVC. convince; persuade
16.積蓄	积蓄	jīxù	V. save; put aside
17.市區	市区	shìqū	N. city proper; urban district
18.房東	房东	fángdōng	N. the owner of the house or apartment one lives in
19.直線上升			
直线上升		zhíxiàn shàngshēng	Ph. sharp rise (lit. shoot up in a straight line)
20.倍增	倍增	bèizēng	VP. has doubled and redoubled
21.利潤	利润	lìrùn	N. profit
22.產業	产业	chǎnyè	N. estate; property
23.籌資	筹资	chóuzī	VO. raise money
24.借款	借款	jièkuǎn	VO. borrow money

25. 將	将	jiāng	Prep. same as 把
26. 預付款	预付款	yùfù kuǎn	N. down payment
27. 拋出	拋出	pāochū	RVC. sell off (a term used especially in the stock market)
28. 盈利	盈利	yínglì	VO. net the profits
29. 經紀商	经纪商	jīngjìshāng	N. broker
30. 興起	兴起	xīngqǐ	N. rise; upsurge

语法　GRAMMAR

1. 上 + Nu + (M+N)

The numbers following "上" can only be "百, 千, 万", etc. "上百" means "up to a hundred", "上千, up to a thousand", and "上万 , up to ten thousand." This is basically a noun phrase.

Examples:

(1)昨天一天我走了上百里路，到家后精疲力尽了。

　昨天一天我走了上百里路，到家後精疲力盡了。

　Yesterday I walked as far as a hundred miles(up to a

　hundred miles). I was totally exhausted when I got home.

(2)随着经济的好转，每年到了春暖花开的时候，就有上万的中国人到

　各地去旅游。

　隨着經濟的好轉，每年到了春暖花開的時候，就有上萬的中國人到各

　地去旅遊。

　Following the improvement of the economy, every year when

　the flowers bloom in the warmth of the spring, multitudes

　of Chinese(up to ten thousand Chinese) go on excursions

　everywhere.

(3)每天上下班的时候，街上来来去去的自行车上千上万。

　每天上下班的時候，街上來來去去的自行車上千上萬。

　Everyday going to and coming from work, thousands and

　thousands of bicycles come and go on the streets.

2. 何不……(呢)?

何不 occurs before the verb phrase of the clause. 呢 is optional. If 呢 is used, it must be placed at the end of the clause. This is a rhetorical sentence which is asked for the sake of effect, or for persuasion. The subject of the sentence, whether explicitly stated or not is either "you" or "we".

Examples;

(1)何不问问老王，他认识那个人，对他的情况很熟悉。

　何不問問老王，他認識那個人，對他的情況很熟悉。

Why don't you ask Lǎo Wáng? He knows that person, and he is very familiar with his situation.

(2)既然你没错，何不理直气壮地跟他争论一下呢？

既然你沒錯，何不理直氣壯地跟他爭論一下呢？

Since(it is the case that) you are not wrong, why don't you argue it with him outright?

(3)小王下个月要去香港，我们何不请他把这个礼物带去呢？

小王下個月要去香港，我們何不請他把這個禮物帶去呢？

Xiǎo Wáng is going to Hong Kong next month, why don't we ask him to take this gift with him(for us)?

3. 将

It is imperative that not to confuse 将 with 将来. While 将来,"future" or "in the future," functions either as a noun or a time word, 将 is an adverb or a preposition.

One should further distinguish the two functions of 将. When 将 is followed by a verb, it is an adverb, meaning "will."
将, when followed by a noun, is the equivalent of 把. The difference between 将 and 把 is that the former is literary, the latter colloquial.
Examples:

(1)申请到奖学金后，我将去中国留学。

申請到獎學金後，我將去中國留學。

After I get this scholarship, I will go to China to study.

(2)他两年前就将硕士学位念完了。

他兩年前就將碩士學位念完了。

Two years ago he completed his studies for the Master's degree.

(3)我们需要将这个文盲问题再好好地研究一下。

我們需要將這個文盲問題再好好地研究一下。

We need to do a careful study of the problem of illiteracy.

4. (就是)没有...也有...　　就是 + VP1, ...也 + neg + VP2　　"even if...."

The first part of the pattern, 就是..., expresses a supposition while the second part, 也..., states an unconditional fact. In forms, if V1 is positive, V2 must be negative, and vice versa. (Note that in this lesson, 没有 and 有 are the main verbs.) Notice also that, in English, the "even if" clause can be either the first or the second clause. In Chinese, however, the order is fixed. The unconditional clause has to be the second clause.

Examples:

(1)今天晚上的表演就是好得不得了，我也不能去看，我太忙了。

今天晚上的表演就是好得不得了，我也不能去看，我太忙了。

I can't go to see tonight's performance even if it is excellent. I am too busy.

(2)就是我不在，也会有人接待你。

就是我不在，也會有人接待你。

Even if I am not there, there will be someone to greet you.

(3)他发大财了，现在就是没有百万也有几十万了。

他發大財了，現在就是沒有百萬也有幾十萬了。

He has made a lot of money. Now even if he doesn't have millions, he still has several hundred thousands.

5. V + 于 + NP

Used only in written language. 于 is a highly versatile function word (虚词 xūcí) which has no meaning of its own. It links two components in a sentence to show that they relate to each other in a particular way. One condition in using this construction is that the first component is a verb and the second, in most cases, a NP which tells the source or the scope of the verb. The English translation of 于 must vary according to the preposition that the verb normally takes.

Examples:

(1)王中一九九零年毕业于哥伦比亚大学。

王中一九九零年畢業於哥倫比亞大學。

Wáng Zhōng graduated from Columbia University in 1990.

204

(2)我不习惯于这种生活方式。

  我不習慣於這種生活方式。

  I am not accustomed to this style of living.

(3)中国现时倾向于发展商品经济。

  中國現時傾向於發展商品經濟。

  China is, at present, tending foward the development of a
  commercial economy.

(4)大城市我都可以住，不限于纽约市。

  大城市我都可以住，不限於紐約市。

  I can live in any big city, not only (limited to) New York.

(5)许多人投资于房地产业，因为比较稳定。

  許多人投資於房地產業，因為比較穩定。

  Many people invest in real estate because it is relatively
  stable.

一、选词填空：

打动、发财、投资、积蓄、维修、兴趣、最好、经纪商、房东、
借款、筹资、一套、盈利

老李这几年辛辛苦苦地（　　）了两万余元。近来，房产热的兴起，（
　）了他的心。他觉得可以（　　）的时候到了，可以把钱（　　）在房产上，赚
点利润。于是就各处（　　），在市区热闹的地方买了（　　）一房一厅的公
寓，自己作（　　），租给别人住。没想到，一年后他不但没有（　　），反
而经常要（　　）来维持他的公寓。他的公寓是旧的，常常出问题，而他自己
又不会（　　），一有问题就得找工人来弄。考虑了很久，决定（　　）还是
把公寓卖了，要是他还是对房产业有（　　），可以作房地产（　　）的业务。

二、用本课和前几课的生词写出十五个与投资最有关系的词组：

三、根据本课内容回答下面的问题：
　　1.用汉语解释下面的词组：
　　　　　a.寸土如金　b.百万富翁　c.抛出盈利　d.直线上升
　　2.可以用什么成语来形容香港和东京地价特别高的情况？
　　3.是哪两个条件使老李认为他可以把钱投资在房产上？
　　4.什么情况使老李的投资成功了？他得到了什么好处？
　　5.一般人认为投资于房地产的好处是什么？（举出两点）
　　6.投资于房地产最普通的两个方法是什么？—用你自己的话写出来，不
　　　要抄书（抄书 "copy from the text word for word）

四、阅读下面的两段短文：

A. 房地产业和房地产市场

房地（房屋和土地）产业是改革开放以后发展出来的新型产业；房地产市场是指各种方式的房地产交易活动。这些活动包括房产、地产使用权的买卖与租赁、转让等。

中国土地实行的是社会主义公有制，"买卖土地"在中国是指国有土地使用权的出让，转让，出租和抵押等。《中华人民共和国宪法修正案》第二条说："所有的组织或者个人都不能侵占，买卖或者以其他方式非法转让土地。土地的使用权可以根据法律的规定转让。

1.使用权	shǐyòng quán	right of use
2.租赁	zūlìn	to lease; rent
3.转让	zhuǎnràng	to transfer the possession of
4.社会主义	shèhuìzhǔyì	socialism
5.抵押	dǐyā	to offer as collateral
6.宪法	xiànfǎ	constitution
7.修正案	xiūzhèng àn	amendment
8.组织	zǔzhī	organization
9.侵占	qīnzhàn	to seize; occupy
10.非法	fēifǎ	illegal; unlawful
11.法律	fǎlǜ	law

B. 恒生房地产———聘请

恒生房地产公司已批租到中山路71号街坊23850平方米土地，建造广州"中山村"。经羊城区劳动局、人事局批准，向社会征聘有理想，踏实，努力，具有大专以上学历人才。

1.工程师：10名，具工程现场5年以上专业工作经验。

2.各部门干部：6名，具五年以上工作经验，2年干部经验。

3.总经理秘书：1名，女，具5年以上经验，有较强的公关能力，能用电脑能速记。

英语流利、积极进取、具有广州市区常住户口者，自见报起5日内，将本人简历、最高学历证书和工作证复印件、联系地址、电话号码、近期1寸照片一张寄：广州中山路666号广州恒生房地产公司管理部（邮编200001）。本公司在2星期内通知面试。一经录用，享受中外合资企业待遇。人情所托，概不录用。谢绝来访来电。

广州恒生房地产公司

1.聘请	pìnqǐng	to invite (someone to take a position)
2.街坊	jiēfāng	neighborhood
3.劳动局	láodòngjú	labor department
4.人事局	rénshìjú	personnel department
5.批准	pīzhǔn	to approve
6.有理想	yǒulǐxiǎng	be goal oriented
7.踏实	tāshí	be steadfast in one's work
8.大专	dàzhuān	colleges and universities
9.学历	xuélì	educational background
10.现场	xiànchǎng	site
11.速记	sùjì	shorthand
12.进取	jìnqǔ	be eager to make progress; be enterprising
13.户口	hùkǒu	registered permanent residence
14.简历	jiǎnlì	résumé
15.证书	zhèngshū	certificate
16.复印件	fùyìn jiàn	Xerox copy
17.享受	xiǎngshòu	to enjoy
18.联系地址	liánxì dìzhǐ	address (for making personal contact) (a term used in mainland China)
19.录用	lùyòng	to be hired; to be employed
20.托人情	tuō rénqíng	to ask an influential person to help arrange something; gain one's end through pull
21.(一)概	(yī)gài	without exception; totally
22.谢绝	xièjué	decline

練習 EXERCISES

一、選詞填空：

打動、發財、投資、積蓄、維修、興趣、最好、經紀商、房東、
借款、籌資、一套、盈利

老李這幾年辛辛苦苦地〔　　〕了兩萬餘元。近來，房產熱的興起，〔
　〕了他的心。他覺得可以〔　　〕的時候到了，可以把錢〔　　〕在房產上，賺
點利潤。於是就各處〔　　〕，在市區熱鬧的地方買了〔　　〕一房一廳的公
寓，自己作〔　　〕，租給別人住。沒想到，一年後他不但沒有〔　　〕，反
而經常要〔　　〕來維持他的公寓。他的公寓是舊的，常常出問題，而他自己
又不會〔　　〕，一有問題就得找工人來弄。考慮了很久，決定〔　　〕還是
把公寓賣了，要是他還是對房產業有〔　　〕，可以作房地產〔　　〕的業務。

二、用本課和前幾課的生辭寫出十五個與投資最有關係的辭組：

三、根據本課內容回答下面的問題：
　　1.用漢語解釋下面的辭組：
　　　　a.寸土如金　b.百萬富翁　c.拋出盈利　d.直線上升
　　2.可以用甚麼成語來形容香港和東京地價特別高的情況？
　　3.是哪兩個條件使老李認為他可以把錢投資在房產上？
　　4.甚麼情況使老李的投資成功了？他得到了甚麼好處？
　　5.一般人認為投資於房地產的好處是甚麼？（舉出兩點）
　　6.投資於房地產最普通的兩個方法是甚麼？──用你自己的話寫出來，不
　　　要抄書（抄書 "copy from the text word for word）

四、閱讀下面的兩段短文：

A. 房地產業和房地產市場

房地（房屋和土地）產業是改革開放以後發展出來的新型產業；房地產市場是指各種方式的房地產交易活動。這些活動包括房產、地產使用權的買賣與租賃、轉讓等。

中國土地實行的是社會主義公有制，"買賣土地"在中國是指國有土地使用權的出讓、轉讓、出租和抵押等。《中華人民共和國憲法修正案》第二條說："所有的組織或者個人都不能侵佔、買賣或者以其他方式非法轉讓土地。土地的使用權可以根據法律的規定轉讓。

1.使用權	shǐyòng quán	right of use
2.租賃	zūlìn	to lease; rent
3.轉讓	zhuǎnràng	to transfer the possession of
4.社會主義	shèhuìzhǔyì	socialism
5.抵押	dǐyā	to offer as collateral
6.憲法	xiànfǎ	constitution
7.修正案	xiūzhèng àn	amendment
8.組織	zǔzhī	organization
9.侵佔	qīnzhàn	to seize; occupy
10.非法	fēifǎ	illegal; unlawful
11.法律	fǎlǜ	law

B. 恆生房地產————聘請

恆生房地產公司已批租到中山路71號街坊23850平方米土地，建造廣州"中山村"。經羊城區勞動局、人事局批準，向社會徵聘有理想，踏實，努力，具有大專以上學歷人才。

1.工程師：10名，具工程現場5年以上專業工作經驗。

2.各部門幹部：6名，具五年以上工作經驗，2年幹部經驗。

3.總經理祕書：1名，女，具5年以上經驗，有較強的公關能力，能用電腦能速記。

英語流利、積極進取、具有廣州市區常住戶口者，自見報起5日內，將本人簡歷、最高學歷證書和工作證複印件、聯繫地址、電話號碼、近期1寸照片一張寄：廣州中山路666號廣州恆生房地產公司管理部〔郵編200001〕。本公司在2星期內通知面試。一經錄用，享受中外合資企業待遇。人情所託，概不錄用。謝絕來訪來電。

廣州恆生房地產公司

1. 聘請	pìnqǐng	to invite (someone to take a position)
2. 街坊	jiēfāng	neighborhood
3. 勞動局	láodòngjú	labor department
4. 人事局	rénshìjú	personnel department
5. 批準	pīzhǔn	to approve
6. 有理想	yǒulǐxiǎng	be goal oriented
7. 踏實	tāshí	be steadfast in one's work
8. 大專	dàzhuān	colleges and universities
9. 學歷	xuélì	educational background
10. 現場	xiànchǎng	site
11. 速記	sùjì	shorthand
12. 進取	jìnqǔ	be eager to make progress; be enterprising
13. 戶口	hùkǒu	registered permanent residence
14. 簡歷	jiǎnlì	résumé
15. 證書	zhèngshū	certificate
16. 複印件	fùyìn jiàn	Xerox copy
17. 享受	xiǎngshòu	to enjoy
18. 聯繫地址	liánxì dìzhǐ	address (for making personal contact)
		(a term used in mainland China)
19. 錄用	lùyòng	to be hired; to be employed
20. 托人情	tuō rénqíng	to ask an influential person to help arrange something; gain one's end through pull
21. (一)概	(yī)gài	without exception; totally
22. 謝絕	xièjué	decline

5.2 企业破产在中国

中国一向没有"破产"这个观念，但近年来，开始实行破产法。虽然破产法现在并不完善，还有许多需要改进的地方，但，却为许多经营不好的企业解决了一些问题。关于破产法早期实行的情况，请看下面的两个例子：

1992年四川省重庆市中级人民法院判决了中国第一起最大的国有企业破产案。跟这个案件直接有关的是重庆针织厂。该厂原来是西南地区最大的一家国营针织厂。由于长期管理很乱，经营不好，产品卖不出去。从1986年起一直亏损。到1992年5月，经营亏损一共2097万元。资产负债率为191%。在资产中有固定资产2328万元，其中大部分已作为银行贷款的抵押品。

这家企业从1991年年底到1992年10月，在短短的一年间，已拖欠职工工资和职工的集资款等个人财产大约300万元。在无法再经营下去的情况下，得到了有关部门的同意，于1992年6月8日向法院提出破产申请。

从法院审理过程到1992年10月4日债权申请结束时，这家企业共有57个债权人申请债权，总额达到8250万元。在这样严重的情况下，法院为了保护债权人和债务人的合法经济权益，在1992年11月3日宣布重庆针织总厂破产。

重庆市中级人民法院在宣布这家企业破产的同时，还宣布成立一个由十二个有关部门的人员组成的清算组，半个月内进厂对破产后的财产进行清算整理。

另外还有一个例子是，对一个救活无望的企业，最后按照《企业破产法》的规定，宣布破产。

广东省广州市有一家公司，亏损达312万多元。总债务166

万元。1992 年 3 月，这家公司向法院申请破产还债。广州市中级人民法院受理了此案。法院希望通过拍卖底价为 78 万多元的生产设备，使这家公司的大部分债务得到解决。但是，拍卖的结果不理想，最后，拍卖成交额只有 36 万元，是拍卖底价的一半。

随着经济体制的改革和市场经济在中国的发展，破产法将会逐步变得完善。

5.2 企業破產在中國

中國一向沒有"破產"這個觀念，但近年來，開始實行破產法。雖然破產法現在並不完善，還有許多需要改進的地方，但，却為許多經營不好的企業解決了一些問題。關於破產法早期實行的情況，請看下面的兩個例子：

1992 年四川省重慶市中級人民法院判決了中國第一起最大的國有企業破產案。跟這個案件直接有關的是重慶針織廠。該廠原來是西南地區最大的一家國營針織廠。由於長期管理很亂，經營不好，產品賣不出去。從 1986 年起一直虧損。到 1992 年 5 月，經營虧損一共 2097 萬元。資產負債率為 191%。在資產中有固定資產 2328 萬元，其中大部分已作為銀行貸款的抵押品。

這家企業從 1991 年年底到 1992 年 10 月，在短短的一年間，已拖欠職工工資和職工的集資款等個人財產大約 300 萬元。在無法再經營下去的情況下，得到了有關部門的同意，於 1992 年 6 月 8 日向法院提出破產申請。

從法院審理過程到 1992 年 10 月 4 日債權申請結束時，這家企業共有 57 個債權人申請債權，總額達到 8250 萬元。在這樣嚴重的情況下，法院為了保護債權人和債務人的合法經濟權益，在 1992 年 11 月 3 日宣布重慶針織總廠破產。

重慶市中級人民法院在宣布這家企業破產的同時，還宣布成立一個由十二個有關部門的人員組成的清算組，半個月內進廠對破產後的財產進行清算整理。

另外還有一個例子是，對一個救活無望的企業，最後按照《企業破產法》的規定，宣布破產。

廣東省廣州市有一家公司，虧損達 312 萬多元。總債務 166

萬元。1992 年 3 月，這家公司向法院申請破產還債。廣州市中級人民法院受理了此案。法院希望通過拍賣底價為 78 萬多元的生產設備，使這家公司的大部分債務得到解決。但是，拍賣的結果不理想，最後，拍賣成交額只有 36 萬元，是拍賣底價的一半。

隨着經濟體制的改革和市場經濟在中國的發展，破產法將會逐步變得完善。

生词 NEW WORDS

1. 一向	一向	yīxiàng	Adv. all along; always
2. 完善	完善	wánshàn	SV. perfect; excellent
3. 改進	改进	gǎijìn	V. improve
4. 經營	经营	jīngyíng	V. manage; run
5. 關於	关于	guānyú	Prep. concerning; regarding
6. 法院	法院	fǎyuàn	N. court (of law)
7. 判決	判决	pànjué	V. make (court's) decision
8. 國有企業	国有企业	guóyǒu qǐyè	NP. state-owned enterprise
9. 案	案	àn	N. (law) case
10. 直接	直接	zhíjiē	Adv. directly
11. 針織廠	针织厂	zhēnzhī chǎng	N. knitting mill
12. 管理	管理	guǎnlǐ	N/V. manage; management
13. 經營	经营	jīngyíng	V. manage; run
14. 產品	产品	chǎnpǐn	N. product
15. 虧損	亏损	kuīsǔn	N/V. loss (in business); lose; deficit
16. 資產	资产	zīchǎn	N. assets (in accounting)
17. 資產負債率	资产负债率	zīchǎn fùzhài lǜ	NP. ratio of liabilities to assets
18. 為	为	wéi	V. to be (literary usage)
19. 貸款	贷款	dàikuǎn	N. (bank) loan
20. 抵押品	抵押品	dǐyā pǐn	N. collateral for a loan
21. 拖欠	拖欠	tuōqiàn	V. be behind in payment
22. 職工	职工	zhígōng	N. staff and workers
23. 於	于	yú	Part. in; on; at; to; by; from
24. 審理	审理	shěnlǐ	V. try; hear (a case)
25. 債權	债权	zhàiquán	N. creditor's rights
26. 總額	总额	zǒng'é	N. total (amount)
27. 債務	债务	zhàiwù	N. debt; liabilities
28. 債務人	债务人	zhàiwùrén	N. debtor
29. 過程	过程	guòchéng	N. process; course

30.結束	结束	jiéshù	V. end; conclude
31.保護	保护	bǎohù	V. protect; safeguard
32.合法	合法	héfǎ	SV. legal; lawful
33.權益	权益	quányì	N. rights and interests
34.組成	组成	zǔchéng	V. make up; compose
35.清算	清算	qīngsuàn	V. clear; settle (accounts)
36.整理	整理	zhěnglǐ	V. put in order; straighten out
37.救活無望	救活无望	jiùhuó wúwàng	VP. beyond hope of saving
38.還	还	huán	V. pay back
39.受理	受理	shòulǐ	V. accept and hear (a case)
40.底價	底价	dǐjià	NP. the floor or minimum price
41.成交額	成交额	chéngjiāo'é	NP. volume of business; amount of deals struck
42.體制	体制	tǐzhì	N. system; system of organization
43.逐步	逐步	zhúbù	Adv. step by step; progressively

地名　Place Names

1.四川省	四川省	Sìchuān shěng	Szechwan province
2.重慶市	重庆市	Chóngqìng shì	Chungking
3.廣東省	广东省	Guǎngdōng shěng	Kwangtung province
4.廣州市	广州市	Guǎngzhōu shì	Canton

常用词组　STOCK PHRASES

1.關於……情況	关于……情况	concerning the situation of
2.在……情況下	在……情况下	under the circumstances
3.按照規定	按照规定	according to rules
4.經營虧損	经营亏损	operating deficit
5.資產負債率	资产负债率	ratio of liabilities to assets
6.銀行貸款	银行贷款	bank loan
7.宣布破產	宣布破产	to declare bankruptcy
8.受理……案	受理……案	accept and hear the case of
9.判決……案	判决……案	(the court) decides the case of

语法　GRAMMAR

1. 关于　　　　(关于+X) + S + VP

　　As a prepositional phrase, 关于 and its object, differs from many other prepositional phrases in that it can only occur at the initial position of a sentence. Semantically, 关于 is a topic marker. It singles out the subject matter to be discussed, the "X." The remaining elements of the sentence, "S+VP," are the comment offered about the topic. Syntatically, the "X" although mostly NP's, may also be a VP.

　　A. Examples:

　　(1) 关于破产法我知道得很少。

　　　　關於破產法我知道得很少。

　　　　I don't know much about the law of bankruptcy.

　　(2) 关于研究生出国留学的政策，政府常常作不同的改动

　　　　關於研究生出國留學的政策，政府常常作不同的改動。

　　　　Concerning the policy of graduate students studying abroad, the government has made constant changes.

　　(3) 他生病以后变得很弱。关于他要怎么锻炼才能使身体再好起来的问题，我们应当问医生，不能随便作。

　　　　他生病以後變得很弱。關於他要怎麼鍛煉才能使身體再好起來的問題，我們應當問醫生，不能隨便作。

　　　　He became very weak after his illness. Regarding the question of how he should go through physical training to regain his health, we must consult a doctor. We just can't carry out whatever plans that we assume to be appropriate.

　　B. "关于+X" phrase may also be used as a modifier. In such usage, it will appear where it belongs: (关于+X)+的NP.

　　Examples:

　　(1) 我最近看了一些关于国际问题的书。

　　　　我最近看了一些關於國際問題的書。

　　　　Recently, I have read some books concerning international questions.

218

(2)公司今天早晨开了一个关于改进产品的会。

公司今天早晨開了一個關於改進產品的會。

This morning, our company held a meeting which concerned product improvement.

2. 该 + NP

该+NP is used to refer to something previously stated. It may be interpreted as "the said ..., this ..., that ..., or the above mentioned ...." In other words, 该 cannot be used without an explicit or implicit reference.

Examples:

(1)该校	該校	that/the above mentioned school
(2)该项工作	該項工作	the job/work in question
(3)该政策	該政策	this/the said policy

(4)该地交通方便。

該地交通方便。

That place (mentioned previously) is very convenient in terms of transport facilities.

3. 为   NP1 + 为 + NP2

In previous lessons, we learned that 为 was a preposition. We also learned that 为 together with 了, 为了, marked the purpose or cause of an action. In this lesson, 为 functions as a verb. Although it was originally used in classical Chinese, it is also used in modern times in formal writing. It is the equivalent of 是 in colloquial Chinese. When 为 functions as a verb, it should be read as "wéi".

Examples:

(1)东京为日本首都。

東京為日本首都。

Tokyo is the capital of Japan.

(2)该厂今年年初资产负债率为 191%。

該廠今年年初資產負債率為 191%。

Early this year the ratio of liabilities to assets of this factory was

191%.+

(3)他的单位要派他到德国去学习，期限为三年。

他的單位要派他到德國去學習，期限爲三年。

His work unit will send him to Germany to study. The time limit is three years.

3. 在.....下　　(在......下) + S + VP

在.....下 is a prepositional phrase which may occur before or after the subject. It is used mostly in discussing formal matters.

Examples:

(1)在这种情况下，我要重新考虑去不去中国的问题。

在這種情況下，我要重新考慮去不去中國的問題。

Under such circumstances, I must again consider the question of whether or not go to China.

(2)在马工程师管理下，那所大楼早盖好了半年。

在馬工程師管理下，那所大樓早蓋好了半年。

Under the supervision of Mr. Ma, the engineer, the building has been finished six months ahead of schedule.

(3)在孙校长指导下，该校学生的水平，跟两年前的相比，提高了很多。

在孫校長指導下，該校學生的水平，跟兩年前的相比，提高了很多。

Under the guidance of President Sūn, the standard of the students, when compared with that of two years ago, has been raised to be much higher.

一、常用词组练习：用本课的常用词组填空

1.〔　　〕中国近年来房地产经纪商兴起的资料，可以在 1998 年 5 月的《经济月刊》上找到。

2.美国一些有名的私立大学学费非常贵，许多学生为了交学费都要向银行〔　　〕。

3.虽然你的学历很高能力也很强，但是〔　　〕公司四年前的规定，你的工资不能超过五万元。如果你觉得不满意，我们只好请你到去的单位找工作了。

4.到今年三月，工厂〔　　〕已经达到六百万元，〔　　〕我们无法再经营下去的情况下只好宣布破产。

5.我同事和她丈夫的离婚案法院半年前已经〔　　〕了，现在在审理过程中，等到所有的资料都得到证明后，就会〔　　〕这个案子。

二、造句：用下面的语法点和常用词组造句，每项造一句。(Simple sentences will not be acceptable. Your sentences must provide context such as time, location, condition, personal opinions, etc.)

1.关于(as a topic marker)　　　　4.按照规定

2.该　　　　　　　　　　　　　　5.银行贷款

3.在.....情况下

三、语法练习：动宾语搭配(matching verb and object)

A.在下面的词组中，写出每个词组的主要动词(main verb)和主要受词(object, without modifier)。

1.判决了中国第一起最大的国有企业破产案

2.作为银行贷款的抵押品

3.拖欠职工工资和职工的集资款等个人财产大约 300 万元

4.得到了有关部门的同意

5.保护债权人和债务人的合法经济权益

6.成立一个由十二个有关部门的人员组成的清算组

7.拍卖底价为 78 万多元的生产设备

B.把上面的七个动宾语词组翻译成英文

四、把下面的两个时间性词组翻译成英文
1.从法院审理过程到 1992 年 10 月 4 日债权申请结束时
2.在宣布这家企业破产的同时

五、阅读理解（根据本课内容回答问题）
1.中国现在开始实行"破产法"的原因是什么？
2.四川省重庆市针织厂在中国实行破产法上有什么重要性？
3.按照时间的发展列出(to list)重庆市针织厂的问题：
　　(1) 1986 年到 1992 年 5 月
　　　　a.
　　　　b.
　　　　c.
　　(2) 1991 年底到 1992 年 10 月
　　　　a. 1992 年 6 月 8 日
　　　　b. 1992 年 10 月 4 日
　　(3) 1992 年 11 月 3 日
4.重庆市中级人民法院怎么处理(to handle)重庆市针织厂的案子？
5.广州市的一家公司为什么要申请破产？
6.广州市的中级人民法院怎么处理这个案子？
7.本课主要的目的是说明什么？（用三到五句话说明）
8.你认为为什么中国从 1949 年到 1990 年初都没有实行过"破产法"？现在有实行"破产法"的需要吗？为什么？

六、阅读下面的短文：

她的新选择

　　一九八五年，小李三十五岁。她和丈夫带着孩子从农村来到了城市。小李是个很有能力的人，一到了城市就在一个饭店里找到了一份工作，每个月工资是一百三十元，而且是铁饭碗，比在农村工作好得多了。当时她心里很高兴。因为有了铁饭碗，就不用担心没有工作，而且饭店里的工作不太忙，下班后除了照顾孩子以外还会有些空闲时间。小李太需要时间了。从小，她就羡慕读书人、文化人；从小，她就希望上大学，当作家。现在，她决定报考业余大学，实现自己的理想。

她在饭店工作了一年以后什么都变了。她交给饭店领导一份辞职报告，说要离开饭店去开个个体户。饭店的领导觉得很惊讶，因为大家都知道小李很喜欢饭店里的工作而且很努力。领导也觉得小李是个很难得的人才，希望可以把她留下来，甚至要给她把工资提高到二百元一个月。但是她说："我有一个孩子，我现在最大的问题就是穷。就是挣两百元一个月也还是太少了。饭店每个月交给政府一万多元。要是我自己有一个饭店，也许一个月挣不到一万，但是一年一定可以挣到一万。我相信，政策十年不会变，十年就是十万元，我为什么不去挣。"

就在她的新饭店开门的前一天，她收到了业余大学的通知书。她笑着对丈夫说："一辈子都想当文化人，学学写小说。现在机会来了，又要挣钱去了。"

六年过去了，小李的存款已经超过十万了。一家的生活也富裕起来了，孩子也上了重点中学了。现在她还喜欢读书，还关心文学。不过，当"读书人，文化人"已经是一个过去的梦了。

1. 担心	dānxīn	to feel anxious
2. 空闲时间	kōngxián shíjiān	spare time; free time
3. 文化人	wénhuà rén	a person working in literary or artistic fields
4. 作家	zuòjiā	a writer
5. 实现	shíxiàn	to realize
6. 领导	lǐngdǎo	the head (lit. leader)
7. 辞职	cízhí	to resign from one's work
8. 挣	zhèng	to earn
9. 通知书	tōngzhī shū	a letter of acceptance
10. 一辈子	yībèizi	all one's life
11. 文学	wénxué	literature
12. 梦	mèng	a dream

練習　EXERCISES

一、常用辭組練習：用本課的常用辭組填空

　1.（　　）中國近年來房地產經紀商興起的資料，可以在 1998 年 5 月的
　　《經濟月刊》上找到。

　2.美國一些有名的私立大學學費非常貴，許多學生為了交學費都要向銀
　　行（　　）。

　3.雖然你的學歷很高能力也很強，但是（　　）公司四年前的規定，你的
　　工資不能超過五萬元。如果你覺得不滿意，我們只好請你到去的單位找
　　工作了。

　4.到今年三月，工廠（　　）已經達到六百萬元，（　　）我們無法再經營
　　下去的情況下只好宣布破產。

　5.我同事和她丈夫的離婚案法院半年前已經（　　）了，現在在審理過程
　　中，等到所有的資料都得到證明後，就會（　　）這個案子。

二、造句：用下面的語法點和常用辭組造句，每項造一句。(Simple sentences
　　will not be acceptable. Your sentences must provide context such as
　　time, location, condition, personal opinions, etc.)

　1.關於(as a topic marker)　　4.按照規定
　2.該　　　　　　　　　　　　5.銀行貸款
　3.在⋯⋯情況下

三、語法練習：動賓語搭配(matching verb and object)

　A.在下面的辭組中，寫出每個辭組的主要動詞(main verb)和主要受詞
　　(object, without modifier)。

　1.判決了中國第一起最大的國有企業破產案
　2.作為銀行貸款的抵押品
　3.拖欠職工工資和職工的集資款等個人財產大約 300 萬元
　4.得到了有關部門的同意
　5.保護債權人和債務人的合法經濟權益
　6.成立一個由十二個有關部門的人員組成的清算組
　7.拍賣底價為 78 萬多元的生產設備

B.把上面的七個動賓語辭組翻譯成英文

四、把下面的兩個時間性辭組翻譯成英文
  1.從法院審理過程到 1992 年 10 月 4 日債權申請結束時
  2.在宣布這家企業破產的同時

五、閱讀理解（根據本課內容回答問題）
  1.中國現在開始實行"破產法"的原因是甚麼？
  2.四川省重慶市針織廠在中國實行破產法上有甚麼重要性？
  3.按照時間的發展列出(to list)重慶市針織廠的問題：
      (1) 1986 年到 1992 年 5 月
          a.
          b.
          c.
      (2) 1991 年底到 1992 年 10 月
          a. 1992 年 6 月 8 日
          b. 1992 年 10 月 4 日
      (3) 1992 年 11 月 3 日
  4.重慶市中級人民法院怎麼處理(to handle)重慶市針織廠的案子？
  5.廣州市的一家公司為甚麼要申請破產？
  6.廣州市的中級人民法院怎麼處理這個案子？
  7.本課主要的目的是說明甚麼？（用三到五句話說明）
  8.你認為為甚麼中國從 1949 年到 1990 年初都沒有實行過"破產法"？現
    在有實行"破產法"的需要嗎？為甚麼？

六、閱讀下面的短文：

她的新選擇

  一九八五年，小李三十五歲。她和丈夫帶着孩子從農村來到了城市。小
李是個很有能力的人，一到了城市就在一個飯店裡找到了一份工作，每個月
工資是一百三十元，而且是鐵飯碗，比在農村工作好得多了。當時她心裡很

225

高興。因為有了鐵飯碗，就不用擔心沒有工作，而且飯店裡的工作不太忙，下班後除了照顧孩子以外還會有些空閑時間。小李太需要時間了。從小，她就羨慕讀書人、文化人；從小，她就希望上大學，當作家。現在，她決定報考業餘大學，實現自己的理想。

她在飯店工作了一年以後什麼都變了。她交給飯店領導一份辭職報告，說要離開飯店去開個個體戶。飯店的領導覺得很驚訝，因為大家都知道小李很喜歡飯店裡的工作而且很努力。領導也覺得小李是個很難得的人才，希望可以把她留下來，甚至要給她把工資提高到二百元一個月。但是她說："我有一個孩子，我現在最大的問題就是窮。就是掙兩百元一個月也還是太少了。飯店每個月交給政府一萬多元。要是我自己有一個飯店，也許一個月掙不到一萬，但是一年一定可以掙到一萬。我相信，政策十年不會變，十年就是十萬元，我為什麼不去掙。"

就在她的新飯店開門的前一天，她收到了業餘大學的通知書。她笑着對丈夫說："一輩子都想當文化人，學學寫小說。現在機會來了，又要掙錢去了。"

六年過去了，小李的存款已經超過十萬了。一家的生活也富裕起來了，孩子也上了重點中學了。現在她還喜歡讀書，還關心文學。不過，當"讀書人，文化人"已經是一個過去的夢了。

1.	擔心	dānxīn	to feel anxious
2.	空閑時間	kōngxián shíjiān	spare time; free time
3.	文化人	wénhuà rén	a person working in literary or artistic fields
4.	作家	zuòjiā	a writer
5.	實現	shíxiàn	to realize
6.	領導	lǐngdǎo	the head (lit. leader)
7.	辭職	cízhí	to resign from one's work
8.	掙	zhèng	to earn
9.	通知書	tōngzhī shū	a letter of acceptance
10.	一輩子	yībèizi	all one's life
11.	文學	wénxué	literature
12.	夢	mèng	a dream

5.3 都市消费面面观

中国的消费市场越来越丰富多彩，如今的都市消费有哪些新特点呢？请看下面生活的几方面：

一、 吃"好"、吃"鲜"、吃"快"

过去，中国人对饮食的要求是：能吃饱，现在的要求是要吃好，要有营养。近年来，高粱、玉米、豆子等又变得热门起来，这反映了老百姓对食品营养的重视。

追求"鲜"是近年来中国人餐桌上的另一个特色。过去，受季节的影响，中国北方居民往往要靠土豆、萝卜和白菜过整个冬天；现在呢，每个城市每天都有大量新鲜蔬菜出现在市场上，红西红柿、紫茄子、黄瓜、青菜……，要什么有什么。即使冬天也不例外，人们每天都能吃到新鲜的蔬菜。

随着生活节奏的加快，中国人日常的饮食变得越来越简便了。原来居民花很长时间做饭的现象有了很大的改变，速冻饺子、方便面、包子、盒饭……这些中国式快餐已成为许多居民家中餐桌上的"常客"，而且，随着生活水平的不断提高，出去吃饭已很平常了。

与此同时，中国孩子对"洋快餐"也很感兴趣，但多数儿童不是为吃走进"洋"快餐店，而是更想得到一份有趣的小礼物。

二、 穿出不同

在北京的王府井百货大楼，当记者问一位正在选购服装的小姐"现在什么服装最流行"时，她说："想穿什么，什么就是流行"。这就是现在的年轻人对服装的追求。前些年满街飘起红裙子或黄裙子的现象已不见了，取而代之的是既有个性又得体的装扮。一位打扮入时的女士说："如果发现街上有人打扮得和我一样，第二天我一定会让自己换一种装扮。为了避免这种情况，我现在只定做服装，而不去商店买衣服了。穿着自己选定的服装，感觉特别好。"

的确，这些年来，中国人的外表发生了很大的变化。每个人根据自己不同的性格、职业、爱好，选择最合适自己的服装穿在身上，走在大街上。在大街上，你看吧，男男女女、老老少少，很少有哪两个人的衣服是完全一样的。穿出不同，追求个性美，已逐渐成为中国人的服装观念。

三、 休闲 旅游

1994 年 3 月以前，中国人每周只有一个休息日：星期日。此后，有一段时间实行隔周双休：这一周休息一天，下一周休息两天。从 1995 年 5 月开始，中国人终于可以每周休息两天了。

实行"双休制"后，人们都感觉到，在工作和家务之外，有了更多属于自己的自由时间。一个新的热门话题：休闲，也随之出现。

据调查：一般城市人外出休闲的选择是：逛街购物；走亲访友；游览参观；去歌舞厅、健身中心；看电影。在家休闲的人主要是看电视、听音乐、玩麻将牌。

商店利用双休日这个好机会，开展各种活动，促使人们在购物上花更多的钱。

双休日不仅促进了商业的发展，还带动了旅游业的迅速发展。如今，周末休闲旅游已经成为热门的旅游项目。旅游的人们多数参加旅游公司组织的一日游或两日游，而且常常是一家人亲朋友好一块儿去，既方便又热闹。

随着消费市场的发展，中国人的生活水平也在不断地提高。

5.3　都市消費面面觀

中國的消費市場越來越豐富多彩，如今的都市消費有哪些新特點呢？請看下面生活的幾方面：

一、 吃"好"、吃"鮮"、吃"快"

過去，中國人對飲食的要求是：能吃飽，現在的要求是要吃好，要有營養。近年來，高粱、玉米、豆子等又變得熱門起來，這反映了老百姓對食品營養的重視。

追求"鮮"是近年來中國人餐桌上的另一個特色。過去，受季節的影響，中國北方居民往往要靠土豆、蘿蔔和白菜過整個冬天；現在呢，每個城市每天都有大量新鮮蔬菜出現在市場上，紅西紅柿、紫茄子、黃瓜、青菜……，要什麼有什麼。即使冬天也不例外，人們每天都能吃到新鮮的蔬菜。

隨着生活節奏的加快，中國人日常的飲食變得越來越簡便了。原來居民花很長時間做飯的現象有了很大的改變，速凍餃子、方便面、包子、盒飯……這些中國式快餐已成為許多居民家中餐桌上的"常客"，而且，隨着生活水平的不斷提高，出去吃飯已很平常了。

與此同時，中國孩子對"洋快餐"也很感興趣，但多數兒童不是為吃走進"洋"快餐店，而是更想得到一份有趣的小禮物。

二、 穿出不同

在北京的王府井百貨大樓，當記者問一位正在選購服裝的小姐"現在什麼服裝最流行"時，她說："想穿什麼，什麼就是流行"。這就是現在的年輕人對服裝的追求。前些年滿街飄起紅裙子或黃裙子的現象已不見了，取而代之的是既有個性又得體的裝扮。一位打扮入時的女士說："如果發現街上有人打扮得和我一樣，第二天我一定會讓自己換一種裝扮。為了避免這種情況，我現在只定做服裝，而不去商店買衣服了。穿着自己選定的服裝，感覺特別好。"

的確，這些年來，中國人的外表發生了很大的變化。每個人根據自己不同的性格、職業、愛好，選擇最合適自己的服裝穿在身上，走在大街上。在大街上，你看吧，男男女女、老老少少，很少有哪兩個人的衣服是完全一樣的。穿出不同，追求個性美，已逐漸成爲中國人的服裝觀念。

三、 休閒　旅遊

1994 年 3 月以前，中國人每週只有一個休息日：星期日。此後，有一段時間實行隔週雙休：這一週休息一天，下一週休息兩天。從 1995 年 5 月開始，中國人終於可以每週休息兩天了。

實行"雙休制"後，人們都感覺到，在工作和家務之外，有了更多屬於自己的自由時間。一個新的熱門話題：休閒，也隨之出現。

據調查：一般城市人外出休閒的選擇是：逛街購物；走親訪友；遊覽參觀；去歌舞廳、健身中心；看電影。在家休閒的人主要是看電視、聽音樂、玩麻將牌。

商店利用雙休日這個好機會，開展各種活動，促使人們在購物上花更多的錢。

雙休日不僅促進了商業的發展，還帶動了旅遊業的迅速發展。如今，週末休閒旅遊已經成爲熱門的旅遊項目。旅遊的人們多數參加旅遊公司組織的一日游或兩日游，而且常常是一家人親朋友好一塊兒去，既方便又熱鬧。

隨着消費市場的發展，中國人的生活水平也在不斷的提高。

生词 NEW WORDS

蔬菜类 (shūcài lèi) VEGETABLES

1.高粱	高粱	gāoliáng	N. Chinese sorghum
2.玉米	玉米	yùmǐ	N. corn; maize
3.豆子	豆子	dòuzǐ	N. bean; legume
4.土豆	土豆	tǔdòu	N. potato (coll.)
5.蘿蔔	萝卜	luóbǒ	N. turnip
6.白菜	白菜	báicài	N. Chinese cabbage
7.西紅柿	西红柿	xīhóngshì	N. tomato
8.紫茄子	紫茄子	zǐ qiézǐ	N. (purple) eggplant
9.黃瓜	黄瓜	huángguā	N. cucumber
10.青菜	青菜	qīngcài	N. fresh vegetables in gen.; greens

快餐类 (kuàicān lèi) FAST FOOD

1.速凍餃子	速冻饺子	sùdòng jiǎozǐ	N. quick-frozen dumpling
2.方便麵	方便面	fāngbiàn miàn	N. instant noodles
3.包子	包子	bāozǐ	N. steamed stuffed bun
4.盒飯	盒饭	héfàn	N. box lunch

休闲的活动 (xiūxián de huódòng) LEISURE ACTIVITIES

1.逛街	逛街	guàngjiē	VP. strolling; window-shopping
2.走親訪友	走亲访友	zǒu-qīn-fǎng-yǒu	VP. calling on friends and relatives
3.遊覽參觀	游览参观	yóulǎn cānguān	VP. sightseeing; touring famous places
4.去歌舞廳	去歌舞厅	qù gēwǔtīng	VP. going to song and dance halls
5.去健身中心	去健身中心	qù jiànshēn zhōngxīn	VP. going to fitness centers
6.看電影	看电影	kàn diànyǐng	VO. seeing movies
7.看電視	看电视	kàn diànshì	VO. watching television
8.聽音樂	听音乐	tīng yīnyuè	VO. listening to music

9.玩麻將牌　　玩麻将牌　　wán májiàngpái　　VO. playing mahjong

1.都市　　都市　　dūshì　　N. city; metropolis
2.消費　　消费　　xiāofèi　　V. consume
3.豐富　　丰富　　fēngfù　　SV. rich
4.多彩　　多彩　　duōcǎi　　SV. varied; many-splendored
5.鮮　　鮮　　xiān　　SV. fresh
6.飲食　　饮食　　yǐnshí　　N. food and drink
7.餐桌　　餐桌　　cānzhuō　　N. dining table
8.季節　　季节　　jìjié　　N. season
9.靠　　靠　　kào　　Prep. depend on; rely on
10.即使....也　即使....也　jíshǐ....yě　　Con. even if
11.日常　　日常　　rìcháng　　Attr. daily; day-to-day
12.平常　　平常　　píngcháng　　SV. ordinary; common
13.有趣　　有趣　　yǒuqù　　SV. interesting
14.禮物　　礼物　　lǐwù　　N. gift; present
15.流行　　流行　　liúxíng　　SV. fashionable; in vogue
16.年輕人　年轻人　niánqīngrén N. young people
17.飄　　飘　　piāo　　V. flutter; wave
18.裙子　　裙子　　qúnzǐ　　N. skirt
19.取而代之　取而代之　qǔ ér dài zhī VP. take its place (lit. to take it and
　　　　　　　　　　　　　　replace it)
20.既....又....　既....又....　jì.... yòu....　Con. both...and
21.個性　　个性　　gèxìng　　N. individuality
22.得體　　得体　　détǐ　　SV. suitable; befitting
23.裝扮　　裝扮　　zhuāngbàn　N. attire; costume
24.打扮　　打扮　　dǎbàn　　V. make up; dress up
25.讓　　让　　ràng　　V. let or allow (someone do something)
26.定做　　定做　　dìngzuò　　VP. have something made to order
27.的確　　的确　　dìquè　　Adv. really; indeed
28.外表　　外表　　wàibiǎo　　N. exterior appearance

29.性格	性格	xìnggé	N. temperament; character
30.隔週	隔周	gézhōu	NP. every other week
31.促使	促使	cùshǐ	V. impel; spur
32.家務	家务	jiāwù	N. household duties

常用词组　STOCK PHRASES

1.與此同時	与此同时	at the same time as this
2.取而代之	取而代之	to replace somebody or something
3.開展活動	开展活动	to launch activities
4.豐富多彩	丰富多彩	be rich and colorful; be rich and varied
5.有營養	有营养	be nourishing; be nutritious
6.有個性	有个性	has individuality; has individual character
7.打扮入時	打扮入时	to dress fashionably

语法　GRAMMAR

1. 受 + NP　　　　S + 受 + NP

受 is the main verb in this pattern. It has the general meaning of
"receive," in the sense of "to receive, to be afflicted with, to be burdened
with, to suffer, etc." The NP, the object of 受, belongs to a closed list of
words of abstraction. Syntactically, the objective NPs of 受 may also
function as verbs. For example, 表扬 biǎoyáng "praise"; 限制 xiànzhì "to
restrict, restriction,"; 欢迎 huānyíng "welcome"; 影响 yǐngxiǎng "to affect,
to influence, effect"; 威胁 wēixié "to threaten, threat"; 伤害 shānghài "to
harm, to injure, injury," etc. One thing to remember is that while 受 is
constantly translated as "by," which is an English marker to mark passive
voice sentences, 受 in Chinese is not a passive marker, but an active verb in
an active sentence. This is one example that illustrates well that one can
never find a complete match of structure or terms between any two
languages. In fact, depending on contexts, 受 may be translated as "by" or
"to receive."

Examples:

(1) 他的著作很受欢迎。

他的著作很受歡迎。

His writings are very popular (lit., His writings receive much
welcome.)

(2) 常小英昨天上课的时候受到老师的表扬。

常小英昨天上課的時候受到老師的表揚。

Cháng Xiǎo Yīng was praised in class by the teacher yesterday.
(lit., Cháng Xiǎo Yīng received the teacher's praise in class
yesterday.)

(3) 过去中国北方居民所能吃到蔬菜的种类常受季节的限制。

過去中國北方居民所能吃到蔬菜的種類常受季節的限制。

Previously in China, the kinds of vegetables that were available to
the people who live in the north were restricted by the season.
(implied: winter.)

235

2. 不是 + A + 而是 + B

This pattern implies a contrast. It may be interpreted as "not A but B." Syntactically, both A and B can be a noun phrase, a verb phrase or even a clause.

Examples:

(1)你有问题的时候不能靠他，他不是一个勇敢的人，而是一个什么事都
怕的人。

你有問題的時候不能靠他，他不是一個勇敢的人，而是一個什麼事都
怕的人。

You can't rely on him (for help) when you have problems. He is not a brave man, but a coward (he is afraid of everything).

(2)他离开了那个公司，不是因为工资太低，而是觉得工作太单调。

他離開了那個公司，不是因為工資太低，而是覺得工作太單調。

He left that company. It is not because the salary was too low; he felt that the job was monotonous.

(3)他现在的生活不错，不是因为他家一直很富裕，而是他这二十年来积
蓄的结果。

他現在的生活不錯，不是因為他家一直很富裕，而是他這二十年來積
蓄的結果。

He now lives a good life. It is not because his family has always been well off; it was the outcome of his putting aside money for the last twenty years.

3. 促使　　　　S + (促使 + NP) + V + O

Semantically, 促使 conveys the idea that a particular situation, the "S" of the pattern, impels or spurs someone, the "NP," to do something, the "V+O."

Examples:

(1)工厂破产促使他各处去找工作。

工廠破產促使他各處去找工作。

The bankruptcy of the factory spurs him to go everywhere looking

236

for a job.

(2)他想发财的意图促使他筹款开了一个大的百货商店。

他想發財的意圖促使他籌款開了一個大的百貨商店。

His intention of becoming rich impelled him to raise money to open up a large department store.

(3)他再念一年就可以拿到硕士学位了，但是他的钱不够，这促使他向他 哥哥借钱。

他再念一年就可以拿到碩士學位了，但是他的錢不夠，這促使他向他 哥哥借錢。

He will receive his Master's degree in one more year. However, he doesn't have enough money. That impelled him to borrow money from his older brother.

4. 既......又......

既......又...... indicates that two conditions or two states of affairs of the same nature exist simultaneously.

Examples:

(1)张健既能干又努力，是个很好的工人。

張健既能幹又努力，是個很好的工人。

Zhāng Jiàn is both capable and diligent. He is a very good worker.

(2)赵文理既保守又顽固，所以朋友很少。

趙文理既保守又頑固，所以朋友很少。

Zhào Wén Lǐ is both conservative and stubborn. As a result, he has few friends.

(3)他想下个月搬到法国去住两年，但是他既不会说法文，又不懂法国 人的生活习惯。考虑过以后决定先学习一点儿法文再去。

他想下個月搬到法國去住兩年，但是他既不會說法文，又不懂法國人 的生活習慣。考慮過以後決定先學習一點兒法文再去。

He planned to move to France next month to live for two years. However, he could neither speak the language nor understand the people's habits and customs. After consideration, he decided that he would learn some French first and then go.

5. V + 之

"V+之," originally used in classical Chinese, is still used today in formal written Chinese. Syntactically speaking, 之 in this context can be identified as a third person pronoun, "it, her, him, them." The reference for 之 must be established in previous discourse. Note that this 之 can never be used as a subject of a sentence, only as an object.

Examples:

(1) 学而时习之　to study with constant perseverance and application
　　學而時習之　(lit., to study and practise it constantly)

(2) 怒目视之　　to stare at him with angry looks
　　怒目視之

(3) 取而代之　　to replace it (lit., to take it and replace it)
　　取而代之

(4) 易地而居之　to move to another place and live there
　　易地而居之

(5) 广州的汽车太多，交通常常出问题，空气污染也随之出现。
　　廣州的汽車太多，交通常常出問題，空氣污染也隨之出現。

There are too many cars in Guangzhou, often causing traffic problems; (along with traffic problems) air pollution has emerged.

一、常用词组练习：用本课的常用词组填空。

1.以前大家都认为高粱，玉米这些东西是不好的食物，但是现在都觉得应该多吃，因为现在大家都知道这些是（　　）的食物。

2.万里百货商店的商品五花八门（　　），有从各国来的日常生活用品，也有各种各样流行的女装，而且价格便宜，所以每天顾客很多。

3.小周每个月的工资差不多都化在买衣服、鞋子上。她希望自己是个穿得最得体，（　　）最入时的姑娘。

4.我们单位这两年在管理上作了许多改革，（　　）也大量提高了工人的工资。

5.夏天到了，学校都放假了。教育部门下星期起将要（　　）各种（　　）让学生们暑假中有事情作。

6.万青这个人长得很不好看，但是很多姑娘喜欢他，认为他（　　），他的样子、穿的衣服、对事情的看法都跟一般人不同。

7.该工厂领导腐败无能，他只重视建立公共关系，不重视实际的管理和生产，如果想办得好，该工厂得（　　），找一个既能干又负责的人。

二、造句：用下面的语法点和常用词组造句，每项造一句。(Simple sentences will not be acceptable. Your sentences must provide context such as time, location, condition, personal opinion, etc.)

1.受　　　　　　6.开展活动

2.不是....而是　　7.有营养

3.促使　　　　　8.有个性

4.既.....又　　　9.打扮入时

5.与此同时　　　10.丰富多彩

三、阅读理解（根据本课内容回答问题）

1.从哪些方面可以看出中国现在的消费市场发展得一天比一天繁荣？（简单说明）

2.从本课列出(listed)的蔬菜类中，写出

　a.你喜欢吃的蔬菜，

b.你不喜欢吃的蔬菜，

　　c.你认为是营养价值比较低的蔬菜。

3.写出两种你比较喜欢吃的中国快餐。

4.你认为中国的快餐和美国的有什么不同？

5.在你休闲的活动中最常作的是什么？

6.在本课的休闲活动中你不会去作的是什么？

7.简单说明中国人对饮食的要求，过去和现在有什么不同？

8.你认为，为什么现在中国北方居民在吃蔬菜上不再受到季节的限制？

9.中国人以前没有"快餐"的观念，现在"快餐"却成为一种平常的生活方式，这是为什么？你认为这是不是一种好的现象？

10.简单说明现在的中国姑娘对服装的看法：

　　a.什么是流行的服装？

　　b.什么是得体的装扮？

　　c.应该怎么选择自己的服装？

11.什么是"双修制"？是什么时候才实际开始实行的？

12."双修制"对经济发展有什么影响？对人民的生活有什么影响？

13.以前到中国各地去旅游的差不多都是外国人，现在去旅游的是中国人比外国人多。这是什么原因？

14.你认为本课的目的是什么？

四、阅读下面的短文：

"荣华鸡"大战"肯德基"

　　北京的快餐业近几年来几乎被"洋快餐"垄断了。主要原因是"洋快餐"已形成了一套完整的制作服务体系，而且店里装潢漂亮，干净卫生，而传统的中式快餐还停在路边摆摊的水平。"洋快餐"在中国的大发展，一方面对中国的饮食业冲击很大，另一方面又为他们提供了很好的经验。这些情况，使具有中国特别风味的中式快餐鸡——上海"荣华鸡"，1989年底在上海出现了。

　　上海荣华鸡快餐公司从成立那天起，就把"肯德基"作为自己的竞争对手。他们既学习"肯德基"服务和管理上的长处，又利用比较便宜的价格和中国人喜欢的口味跟"肯德基"竞争市场，一场"荣华鸡"和"肯德基"的大战就从此开始了。这场"斗鸡"首先是从上海的南京路上开始的。在南京路上有一家肯德基炸鸡店。"荣华鸡"也把快餐店开在那里。两种鸡斗了起来。在短短的三年间，"荣华鸡"就在上海开了九家连锁店，跟"肯德基"斗了个旗鼓相当。"荣华鸡"从那个时候起就开始有名起来了，上海人都把它叫做"上海第一炸鸡"。

勇敢的"荣华鸡"，不仅在上海跟"肯德基"斗，而且跑到北京去跟"肯德基"竞争市场。1992年10月8日上午，北京"上海荣华鸡"快餐厅开业了。它的店就开在"肯德基"东四分店的对面。

北京"上海荣华鸡"快餐厅是上海和北京两家公司合作，投资150万元盖成的有100平方米营业面积的快餐厅。店里装潢漂亮，几名穿着统一工作服的服务员在紧张地工作着。他们态度热情，服务周到，所以每天顾客都很多，而且常常会有几十位顾客在大门口外等着。据统计，从1992年10月8日开业以来，日平均营业额为1.6万元，最高时达2.1万元。

在热闹的"荣华鸡"对面，是"肯德基"东四分店。店里的那位"老先生"，好像对竞争对手不太在乎。"肯德基"的经理说欢迎有竞争对手，店里职工也认为顾客并没有因为"荣华鸡"而减少。

"荣华鸡"和"肯德基"的大战还在继续。两鸡相斗，谁最后能牲还不知道。不过人们都很关心这场大战。

在快节奏的现代生活中，人们希望有更多的快餐来竞争。

1.大战	dàzhàn	to battle
2.荣华鸡	Rónghuájī	Ronghua Fried Chicken
3.肯德基	Kěndéjī	Kentucky Fried Chicken
4.垄断	lǒngduàn	to monopolize
5.一套完整的体系	yī tào wánzhěng dě tǐxì	a complete system
6.制作	zhìzuò	operating
7.摆摊	bǎitān	to set up a stall
8.冲击	chōngjī	impact
9.竞争	jìngzhēng	to compete
10.竞争对手	jìngzhēng duìshǒu	competitor

11.	长处	chángchù	strong points
12.	口味	kǒuwèi	a person's taste
13.	斗鸡	dòujī	cockfighting
14.	炸鸡	zhájī	fried chicken
15.	连锁店	lián-suǒ-diàn	chain stores
16.	旗鼓相当	qí gǔ xiāngdāng	be well-matched
17.	东四分店	dōng sì fēndiàn	the Dōng-sì branch
18.	合作	hézuò	to work together
19.	服务周到	fúwù zhōudào	to provide good services
20.	不在乎	bù zàihū	not mind; to take no notice

練習 EXERCISES

一、常用辭組練習：用本課的常用辭組填空。

1. 以前大家都認爲高粱，玉米這些東西是不好的食物，但是現在都覺得應該多吃，因爲現在大家都知道這些是（　　）的食物。

2. 萬里百貨商店的商品五花八門（　　），有從各國來的日常生活用品，也有各種各樣流行的女裝，而且價格便宜，所以每天顧客很多。

3. 小周每個月的工資差不多都化在買衣服、鞋子上。她希望自己是個穿得最得體，（　　）最入時的姑娘。

4. 我們單位這兩年在管理上作了許多改革，（　　）也大量提高了工人的工資。

5. 夏天到了，學校都放假了。教育部門下星期起將要（　　）各種（　　）讓學生們暑假中有事情作。

6. 萬青這個人長得很不好看，但是很多姑娘喜歡他，認爲他（　　），他的樣子、穿的衣服、對事情的看法都跟一般人不同。

7. 該工廠領導腐敗無能，他只重視建立公共關係，不重視實際的管理和生產，如果想辦得好，該工廠得（　　），找一個既能幹又負責的人。

二、造句：用下面的語法點和常用辭組造句，每項造一句。(Simple sentences will not be acceptable. Your sentences must provide context such as time, location, condition, personal opinion, etc.)

1. 受　　　　　　6. 開展活動
2. 不是....而是　　7. 有營養
3. 促使　　　　　8. 有個性
4. 既.....又　　　9. 打扮入時
5. 與此同時　　　10. 豐富多彩

三、閱讀理解（根據本課內容回答問題）

1. 從哪些方面可以看出中國現在的消費市場發展得一天比一天繁榮？（簡單説明）

2. 從本課列出(listed)的蔬菜類中，寫出
    a. 你喜歡吃的蔬菜，

b.你不喜歡吃的蔬菜，

　　c.你認爲是營養價值比較低的蔬菜。

3.寫出兩種你比較喜歡吃的中國快餐。

4.你認爲中國的快餐和美國的有甚麼不同？

5.在你休閒的活動中最常作的是甚麼？

6.在本課的休閒活動中你不會去作的是甚麼？

7.簡單説明中國人對飲食的要求，過去和現在有甚麼不同？

8.你認爲，爲甚麼現在中國北方居民在吃蔬菜上不再受到季節的限制？

9.中國人以前沒有"快餐"的觀念，現在"快餐"却成爲一種平常的生活方式，這是爲甚麼？你認爲這是不是一種好的現象？

10.簡單説明現在的中國姑娘對服裝的看法：

　　a.甚麼是流行的服裝？

　　b.甚麼是得體的裝扮？

　　c.應該怎麼選擇自己的服裝？

11.甚麼是"雙修制"？是甚麼時候才實際開始實行的？

12."雙修制"對經濟發展有甚麼影響？對人民的生活有甚麼影響？

13.以前到中國各地去旅遊的差不多都是外國人，現在去旅遊的是中國人比外國人多。這是甚麼原因？

14.你認爲本課的目的是甚麼？

四、閱讀下面的短文：

"榮華雞" 大戰 "肯德基"

　　北京的快餐業近幾年來幾乎被 "洋快餐" 壟斷了。主要原因是 "洋快餐" 已形成了一套完整的製作服務體系，而且店裡裝潢漂亮，乾淨衛生，而傳統的中式快餐還停在路邊擺攤的水平。"洋快餐" 在中國的大發展，一方面對中國的飲食業衝擊很大，另一方面又爲他們提供了很好的經驗。這些情況，使具有中國特別風味的中式快餐雞——上海 "榮華雞"，1989 年底在上海出現了。

　　上海榮華雞快餐公司從成立那天起，就把 "肯德基" 作爲自己的競爭對手。他們既學習 "肯德基" 服務和管理上的長處，又利用比較便宜的價格和中國人喜歡的口味跟"肯德基"競爭市場，一場"榮華雞"和"肯德基"的大戰就從此開始了。這場"斗雞"首先是從上海的南京路上開始的。在南京路上有一家肯德基炸雞店。"榮華雞"也把快餐店開在那裡。兩種雞斗了起來。在短短的三年間，"榮華雞"就在上海開了九家連鎖店，跟"肯德基"斗了個旗鼓相當。"榮華雞"從那個時候起就開始有名起來了，上海人都把它叫做"上海第一炸雞"。

勇敢的"榮華雞"，不僅在上海跟"肯德基"斗，而且跑到北京去跟"肯德基"競爭市場。1992年10月8日上午，北京"上海榮華雞"快餐廳開業了。它的店就開在"肯德基"東四分店的對面。

北京"上海榮華雞"快餐廳是上海和北京兩家公司合作，投資150萬元蓋成的有100平方米營業面積的快餐廳。店裡裝潢漂亮，幾名穿着統一工作服的服務員在緊張地工作着。他們態度熱情，服務週到，所以每天顧客都很多，而且常常有幾十位顧客在大門口外等着。據統計，從1992年10月8日開業以來，日平均營業額為1.6萬元，最高時達2.1萬元。

在熱鬧的"榮華雞"對面，是"肯德基"東四分店。店裡的那位"老先生"，好像對競爭對手不太在乎。"肯德基"的經理說歡迎有競爭對手，店裡職工也認為顧客並沒有因為"榮華雞"而減少。

"榮華雞"和"肯德基"的大戰還在繼續。兩雞相斗，誰最後能牲還不知道。不過人們都很關心這場大戰。

在快節奏的現代生活中，人們希望有更多的快餐來競爭。

1.大戰	dàzhàn	to battle	
2.榮華雞	Rónghuájī	Ronghua Fried Chicken	
3.肯德基	Kěndéjī	Kentucky Fried Chicken	
4.壟斷	lǒngduàn	to monopolize	
5.一套完整的體系	yī tào wánzhěng de tǐxì	a complete system	
6.製作	zhìzuò	operating	
7.擺攤	bǎitān	to set up a stall	
8.衝擊	chōngjī	impact	
9.競爭	jìngzhēng	to compete	
10.競爭對手	jìngzhēng duìshǒu	competitor	

11. 長處	chángchù	strong points
12. 口味	kǒuwèi	a person's taste
13. 斗雞	dòujī	cockfighting
14. 炸雞	zhájī	fried chicken
15. 連鎖店	lián-suǒ-diàn	chain stores
16. 旗鼓相當	qí gǔ xiāngdāng	be well-matched
17. 東四分店	dōng sì fēndiàn	the Dōng-sì branch
18. 合作	hézuò	to work together
19. 服務週到	fúwù zhōudào	to provide good services
20. 不在乎	bù zàihū	not mind; to take no notice

A

挨饿	ái è	VO. suffer from hunger	5.0
爱情	àiqíng	N. love (between man and woman)	3.3
安宁	ānníng	N/SV. tranquillity; peaceful	3.3
安慰	ānwèi	V. comfort; console	4.2
案	àn	N. (law) case	5.2
按照	ànzhào	Prep. according to; on the basis of	5.2

B

白菜	báicài	N. Chinese cabbage	5.3
摆	bǎi	V. put; place; arrange	4.3
百货商店	bǎihuò shāngdiàn	N. department store	1.1
百万大军	bǎiwàn dàjūn	N. a veritable army of soldiers (a metaphor)	1.1
百万富翁	bǎiwàn fùwēng	N. millionaire	5.1
伴侣	bànlǚ	N. companion	3.1
办学	bànxué	VO. run a school	2.0
棒	bàng	SV. excellent	4.3
包子	bāozǐ	N. steamed stuffed bun	
宝贝	bǎobèi	N. darling; treasure	3.2
保护	bǎohù	V. protect; safeguard	5.2
保守	bǎoshǒu	SV. conservative	3.0
保重	bǎozhòng	V. take good care of yourself;	3.3
抱	bào	V. hug; hold...in the arms	4.3
报道	bàodào	N. (news) report	1.0
报名	bàomíng	VO. sign up; enter one's name	5.3
报名处	bàomíng chù	N. registration office	2.2
爆炸	bàozhà	N. explosion	1.0
倍增	bèizēng	VP. has doubled and redoubled	5.1
本	běn	Det. this	1.0
本科生	běnkēshēng	N. undergraduate (degree)	2.2
比例	bǐlì	N. proportion; scale	3.3
比如	bǐrú	VP. (take) for example	1.0
避免	bìmiǎn	V. avoid; refrain from	3.3
必须	bìxū	Adv. must; have to	2.2
变化	biànhuà	N/V. change	2.3

标准	biāozhǔn	N. standard; criterion	1.2
表态	biǎotài	VO. make known one's position	3.3
表演	biǎoyǎn	V. perform	3.2
表扬	biǎoyáng	V. praise	4.1
别扭	biéniǔ	SV. awkward; uncomfortable	3.2
宾馆	bīnguǎn	N. hotel	2.3
冰箱	bīngxiāng	N. refrigerator	2.3
博士	bóshì	N. Doctor (of Philosophy, etc.)	2.2
补	bǔ	V. compensate	4.2
不断地	búduàndě	Adv. uninterruptedly; continuously	1.0
不安	bù'ān	SV. uneasy; disturbed; restless	4.2
不管	bùguǎn	Con. no matter	3.0
不好过	bù hǎoguò	V. difficult to get through	3.2
不仅	bùjǐn	Con. not only	4.2
不禁	bújìn	Adv. can't help	3.2
不如	bùrú	VP. not as good as; not equal to	4.2
不自然	bú zìrán	SV. awkward	3.2
部分	bùfèn	N. section; part; some	3.3
部门	bùmén	N. department; branch (of an organization)	2.2

C

财产	cáichǎn	N. property	3.3
财会	cáikuài	N. finance and accounting	2.1
彩电	cǎidiàn	N. color television	2.3
餐桌	cānzhuō	N. dining table	5.3
仓库	cāngkù	N. warehouse	2.1
差	chà	SV. not up to standard; bad	2.0
产生	chǎnshēng	V. produce	1.0
产品	chǎnpǐn	N. product	5.2
产业	chǎnyè	N. estate; property	5.1
超过	chāoguò	V. exceed	1.0
吵	chǎo	V. disturb; quarrel	4.1
陈旧	chénjiù	SV. old-fashioned; outmoded; obsolete	1.3
趁	chèn	Prep. while	4.2
承担	chéngdān	V. bear; assume	3.3
成交额	chéngjiāo'é	N. volume of business; amount of deals struck	5.2
成立	chénglì	V. found; establish; set up	5.2

城镇	chéngzhèn	N. cities and towns	5.0
吃大锅饭	chī dàguōfàn	VO. eat from the big pot	5.2
崇拜	chóngbài	V. worship	5.0
重庆市	Chóngqìng shì	N. Chungking city	5.2
筹资	chóuzī	VO. raise money	5.1
出现	chūxiàn	V. appear; emerge; arise	2.2
初中	chūzhōng	N. junior high school	2.1
处理	chǔlǐ	V. handle	5.3
除非...要不然	chúfēi...yào bùrán	Con. unless...otherwise...	1.3
厨房	chúfáng	N. kitchen	3.1
传统	chuántǒng	SV. traditional	3.0
喘不过气来	chuǎn bú guò qì lái	VP. out of breath	2.1
喘气	chuǎnqì	VO. breathe heavily	4.3
春季	chūnjì	N. spring	1.1
辞职	cízhí	VO. resign	5.3
脆响	cuìxiǎng	Adv. crisply	4.3
存款	cúnkuǎn	V/N. deposit in the bank; savings in the bank	1.2
存在	cúnzài	V. exist	3.0
寸土如金	cùn tǔ rú jīn	Ph. land as dear as gold	5.1

D

搭	dā	V. build; put up	1.2
达	dá	V. reach	1.1
达到	dádào	V. reach; come up to	2.0
打扮	dǎbàn	V. to make up (said of a woman, an actor or actress); to dress up	5.3
打太极拳	dǎ tàijíquán	VO. do tàijí (shadow boxing)	4.1
大包	dàbāo	N. a big bag	4.3
大量	dàliáng	Attr. a large quantity	5.3
大批	dàpī	Attr. large numbers of	1.2
大型	dàxíng	Attr. large-scale	5.0
贷款	dàikuǎn	VO\N. to borrow money (from a bank); (bank) loan	5.2
待业	dàiyè	VO. await job assignment	2.1
待遇	dàiyù	N. pay and benefits	2.3
单调	dāndiào	SV. monotonous; dull	2.2
单位	dānwèi	N. unit; (In mainland China, it refers to an	2.2

249

		organization; institution, etc.)	
单元	dānyuán	N. unit (a single thing or person; one of the individuals or groups that together constitute a whole)	1.0
当前	dāngqián	TW. at present; current	1.0
倒	dǎo	V. fall; collapse	4.2
倒	dào	Adv. but actually; contrary to what you might think	4.2
得体	détǐ	SV. suitable; befitting	5.3
得意	déyì	SV· complacent	4.3
登记	dēngjì	V. register	3.2
等待	děngdài	V. wait	2.1
瞪大眼睛	dèng dà yǎnjīng	VP. open the eyes wide	4.2
的确	díquè	Adv. really; indeed	5.3
底价	dǐjià	N. minimum price; opening price	5.2
抵押品	dǐyāpǐn	N. collateral for a loan	5.2
地位	dìwèi	N. position; status	5.0
电报	diànbào	N. telegram; cable	3.1
电视大学	diànshì dàxué	N. television university	3.1
电视台	diànshìtái	N. television station	1.1
调查	diàochá	N. surveys; investigations	3.3
跌	diē	V. fall down	4.3
定做	dìngzuò	VP. have something made to order	5.3
东奔西跑	dōng-bēn-xī-pǎo	Idiom. run around here and there; rush about	4.2
栋	dòng	M. for building	2.3
动产	dòngchǎn	N. movables (personal property)	3.3
动物园	dòngwù yuán	N. zoo	4.3
动作	dòngzuò	N. movement; action	4.1
都怪你	dōu guài nǐ	VP. it's all your fault	3.2
逗	dòu	V. tease; play with	4.3
豆子	dòuzǐ	N. bean; legume	5.3
都市	dūshì	N. city; metropolis	5.3
独立	dúlì	V/N. independent; independence; on one's own	4.0
读书人	dúshūrén	N. literate person; educated person	5.0
度	dù	N. degree	1.1
度过	dùguò	V. spend	3.1
锻炼	duànliàn	V. train and form (character); forge	4.2

对象	duìxiàng	N. aim(of study); marriage prospect	3.0
多彩	duōcǎi	SV. varied; many-splendored; colorful	5.3

E.

而	ér	Con. connects two verb phrases or clauses	1.2
儿孙	érsūn	N. children and grandchildren	4.0
儿童	értóng	N. children	2.0
儿媳	érxí	N. daughter-in-law	3.2

F

发财	fācái	VO. get rich; make big money	5.1
发明	fāmíng	V. invent	4.1
发生	fāshēng	V. take place; occur	2.3
发现	fāxiàn	V/N. discover; discovery	1.1
发展	fāzhǎn	V/N. develop; grow; development; growth	1.2
法院	fǎyuàn	N. court (of law)	5.2
烦恼	fánnǎo	N/SV. trouble; vexation	2.1
繁荣	fánróng	SV. prosperity	5.1
反对	fǎnduì	V. oppose	3.0
反而·	fǎnér	Con. on the contrary	2.1
反映	fǎnyìng	V. reflect; mirror	2.0
反正	fǎnzhèng	Adv. anyway	4.3
饭票	fànpiào	N. food coupon; meal ticket	4.3
方便面	fāngbiànmiàn	N. instant noodles	5.3
方式	fāngshì	N. way; fashion	3.0
房东	fángdōng	N. the owner of the house or apartment	5.1
分配	fēnpèi	V. assign; allocate	1.2
风（气）	fēng(qì)	N. fad; common practice; general mood	2.2
丰富	fēngfù	SV. rich; abundant	2.2
封建	fēngjiàn	N. feudalism	3.0
否认	fǒurèn	V. deny	2.1
夫妇	fūfù	N. husband and wife	3.3
服从	fúcóng	V. submit (oneself) to	4.0
服装	fúzhuāng	N. dress; clothing	5.3
腐败	fǔbài	SV. corrupt	1.0
附近	fùjìn	N. in the vicinity of	3.2
副教授	fù-jiàoshòu	N. associate professor	2.3

富裕	fùyù	SV. rich	5.1
复杂	fùzá	SV. complicated; complex	3.3
负债率	fùzhàilǜ	NP. ratio of liabilities (to assets)	5.2

G

该	gāi	Det. the said; this; that; the above-mentioned	5.2
改行	gǎiháng	VO. change one's profession	4.1
改革	gǎigé	V/N. reform	1.2
改革开放	gǎigé kāifàng	Ph. the reform and opening door policy	1.2
改进	gǎijìn	V. improve	5.2
盖	gài	V. build	1.0
感到	gǎndào	V. felt	2.2
感情	gǎnqíng	N. feeling; emotion	3.0
感兴趣	gǎn xīngqù	VO. have interest in	3.1
干活	gànhuó	VO. work	3.2
高等学校	gāoděng xuéxiào	N. colleges and universities	2.1
高考	gāokǎo	N. college entrance examination	2.3
高粱	gāoliáng	N. Chinese red sorghum	5.3
高中生	gāozhōng shēng	N. senior high school student - In China as well as in Taiwan, the 6 years of high school education are regularly divided into 2 stages. The first 3 years are designated junior high high school (初中), the second 3 years senior high school (高中).	2.1
告别	gàobié	VO. to say farewell; to take leave; to announce one's departure	5.0
歌舞厅	gēwǔtīng	N. night club (lit., song and dance hall)	
隔周	gézhōu	VO. every other week (隔 V.separate; at an interval of; away from)	5.3
各	gè	Det. each; every; various; different	3.2
个体户	gètǐhù	N. a small private business; individual entrepreneur (a term used in China only)	2.1
个性	gèxìng	N. individuality	5.3
根本	gēnběn	SV/Adv. basic; fundamental; radically; thoroughly	1.2
工程师	gōngchéngshī	N. engineer	2.3
攻读	gōngdú	VP. work for (actively study)	2.2

公共关系	gōnggòng guānxì	N. public relations	3.1
工厂	gōngchǎng	N. factory; plant	4.2
公司	gōngsī	N. company; corporation	5.2
公证	gōngzhèng	N/V. notarization; notarize	3.3
工资	gōngzī	N. wages; pay	2.2
贡献	gòngxiàn	V/N. contribute; contribution	4.0
鼓掌	gǔzhǎng	VO. clap one's hands	4.1
固定	gùdìng	V. fixed; permanent	5.0
顾客	gùkè	N. customer	1.1
关键	guānjiàn	N. the key to the question; the crux of the matter; what counts is....	4.3
观念	guānniàn	N. sense; idea; concept	3.0
关系到	guānxì dào	VP. affects; related to	1.0
关于	guānyú	Prep. concerning; about; on; with regard to	5.2
管理	guǎnlǐ	VP. manage; run; administer; supervise	5.2
光荣	guāngróng	N. glory; honor	2.2
广场	guǎngcháng	N. public square	1.1
广大	guǎngdà	SV. vast	5.0
广东省	Guǎngdōng shěng	N. Kwangtung province	5.2
广州市	Guǎngzhōu shì	N. Canton city	5.2
广告	guǎnggào	N. advertisement	2.1
逛街	guàngjiē	VP. strolling; window-shopping	5.3
规定	guīdìng	V/N. stipulate; make it a rule that; regulation	2.1
柜台	guìtái	N. counter	5.1
国产	guóchǎn	N. domestic product	5.1
过程	guòchéng	N. process; course	5.2
国际	guójì	Attr. international	1.2
国有企业	guóyǒu qǐyè	NP. state-owned enterprise	5.2

H

害怕	hàipà	SV. feel afraid	4.2
汗气	hànqì	N. sweaty atmosphere	1.1
汗珠	hànzhū	N. beads of sweat	3.1
何不	hébù	QW. why not (do something)? (a rhetorical question)	5.1
合得来	hédélái	RVC. get along well; compatible	3.2
合法	héfǎ	SV. legal; lawful	5.2

253

盒饭	héfàn	N. box lunch	5.3
候车室	hòuchē shì	N. waiting room in a railway or bus station	1.1
花本钱	huā běnqián	VO. invest capital in.....(lit. spend money/ time/energy on...)	4.3
花草	huācǎo	N. flowers and plants	3.2
...化	...huà	Suffix. -ize; -ify	1.2
话题	huàtí	N. topic of the conversation	3.3
怀疑	huáiyí	V. suspect; doubt	3.3
还	huán	V. pay back	5.2
蝗虫	huángchóng	N. locust	1.1
皇帝	huángdì	N. emperor	4.0
黄瓜	huángguā	N. cucumber	5.3
黄昏	huánghūn	N. dusk	1.1
挥	huī	V. wave	4.1
婚事	hūnshì	N. marriage (matters); wedding	4.0
婚姻	hūnyīn	N. marriage	3.0
活动	huódòng	N. activity	2.1
活动量	huódòngliàng	N. physical endurance for exercise (to benefit one's health)	4.1

J

鸡蛋羹	jīdàngēng	N. egg custard (usually salty)	3.2
几乎	jīhū	Adv. almost; nearly	3.3
积极	jījí	Adv. work with all one's energy	3.2
及格	jígé	V. pass (a test)	2.1
急迫	jípò	SV. urgent; pressing; imperative	1.0
即使...也...	jíshǐ...yě...	Con. even if	2.1
几辈人	jībèi rén	N. several generations	4.0
季节	jìjié	N. season	5.3
既...又...	jì...yòu...	Con. both...and...	5.3
既然	jìrán	Con. such being the case	3.2
记者	jìzhě	N. reporter	1.1
家务	jiāwù	N. household duties	5.3
家长	jiāzhǎng	N. the head of a family	4.0
价格	jiàgé	N. price	1.2
坚持	jiānchí	Adv. insistently	4.2
兼职	jiānzhí	VO. hold two or more jobs concurrently	2.3

检查	jiǎnchá	V. check up on; inspect	2.1
检查仓库	jiǎnchá cāngkù	VO. check warehouse stocks	2.1
检票厅	jiǎnpiàotīng	N. a hall/room where tickets are checked	1.1
简直	jiǎnzhí	Adv. simply	2.1
建立	jiànlì	V. found; set up	4.0
健身中心	jiànshēn zhōngxīn	N. fitness center/health club	5.3
将	jiāng	Adv. will; Prep. same as 把	1.2; 5.1
奖品	jiǎngpǐn	N. award; prize	4.3
骄傲	jiāo'ào	SV. proud	2.3
交房租	jiāo fángzū	VO. pay rent	1.2
交学费	jiāo xuéfèi	VO. pay tuition	2.2
交通	jiāotōng	N. traffic	1.0
交易	jiāoyì	N. trade	1.1
教师	jiàoshī	N. teacher	2.0
教室	jiàoshì	N. classroom	2.2
教育	jiàoyù	N. education	2.0
结构	jiégòu	N. structure	4.0
结果	jiéguǒ	N. result	1.1
结合	jiéhé	V. combine; integrate	4.1
结束	jiéshù	V. end; conclude	5.2
结帐	jiézhàng	VO. to settle accounts	2.1
节奏	jiézòu	N. beat; (生活节奏 "the pace of life")	4.1
解放	jiěfàng	V/N. liberate; liberation	5.0
解决	jiějué	V. solve	1.0
借口	jièkǒu	VO. (use as an) excuse; pretext	3.3
借款	jièkuǎn	VO. borrow money	5.1
斤	jīn	M. Chinese unit of weight = 1/2 kilogram	4.1
尽管...也...	jǐnguǎn...yě...	Con. in spite of; despite	4.2
V尽	V+jìn	RVE. exhausted all the possible means	4.2
仅	jǐn	Adv. only; solely; merely	2.2
仅仅	jǐnjǐn	Adv. only; solely; merely	5.0
进行	jìnxíng	V. proceed with; go ahead with	3.3
进展	jìnzhǎn	N. progress	5.0
经常	jīngcháng	Adv. constantly	5.1
经费	jīngfèi	N. funds; outlay	2.0
惊呼	jīng hū	V. cry out in amazement	1.1
经济	jīngjì	N. economy	3.0

255

经济学	jīngjìxué	N. economics (as a study)	2.1
经纪商	jīngjìshāng	N. broker; agent	5.1
经理	jīnglǐ	N. manager	2.3
精疲力尽	jīngpí lìjìn	Ph. totally exhausted	4.3
经商	jīngshāng	VO. engage in trade	5.0
惊讶地	jīngyà dě	Adv. amazingly	5.1
经营	jīngyíng	V. manage; run	5.2
竟然	jìngrán	Adv. (it) actually (happened that); surprisingly	2.2
纠纷	jiūfēn	N. dispute; issue	3.3
救活无望	jiùhuó-wúwàng	VP. beyond hope of saving	5.2
就业	jiùyè	VO. obtain employment; take up an occupation	2.0
居民	jūmín	N. resident	1.0
居然	jūrán	Adv. unexpectedly; to one's surprise	2.2
举手	jǔshǒu	VO. put up one's hand or hands	3.2
据	jù	Prep. according to; on the grounds of	3.3
聚	jù	V. assemble; get together; gather	4.1
巨大	jùdà	SV. huge; big	4.3
具有	jùyǒu	V. have	3.1

K

咖啡馆	kāfēiguǎn	N. cafe	3.1
开眼界	kāi yǎnjiè	VO. widen one's view; broaden one's mind	4.3
看管	kānguǎn	V. look after; attend to	3.3
考虑	kǎolǜ	V. consider; weigh (problem in mind)	2.2
靠	kào	Prep/V. depend on; rely on	5.3
科研	kēyán	N. scientific research	2.2
可耻	kěchǐ	SV. shameful	5.0
可口	kěkǒu	SV. tasty	4.2
课程	kèchéng	N. course of study	2.1
肯	kěn	V. be willing to	3.2
枯燥	kūzào	SV. uninteresting	2.2
苦恼	kǔnǎo	SV. depressed	2.1
快餐	kuàicān	N. fast food	5.3
会计	kuàijì	N. accountant	2.1
快速	kuàisù	N. swiftness; rapidity	5.0
亏损	kuīsǔn	N/V. loss (in business); lose	

L

拉	lā	V. pull	3.2
老百姓	lǎobǎixìng	N. the common people	1.2
老伴	lǎobàn	N.(of an old married couple) husband and wife	4.1
老公	lǎogōng	N. husband (informal)	4.2
类	lèi	M. kind; type	2.0
楞	léng	V. be stupefied (caught by surprise)	3.2
离婚	líhūn	VO. divorce	3.0
礼物	lǐwù	N. present; gift	5.3
理想	lǐxiǎng	SV. ideal	2.2
理直气壮	lǐzhí-qìzhuàng	Ph. with perfect assurance; being bold and assured	4.3
厉害	lìhài	SV. devastating	1.1
立刻	lìkè	Adv. immediately	1.1
利润	lìrùn	N. profit	5.1
例外	lìwài	N. exception	5.3
利益	lìyì	N. interests; gain; benefits	3.3
恋	liàn	N. love	3.2
恋恋不舍	liànliànbùshě	VP. very unwilling to part with	4.2
临时	línshí	Attr. temporary	1.1
领工资	lǐng gōngzī	VO. get paid	4.3
领域	lǐngyù	N. domain; dimension	5.1
令	lìng	V. make; cause	5.0
令人	lìngrén	VO. it makes one	1.3
流量	liúliáng	N. rate of flow	1.1
流行	liúxíng	SV. fashionable; in vogue	5.3
留学	liúxué	VO. go study abroad	2.2
搂	lǒu	V. hug; embrace	3.2
论	lùn	N. theory	2.3
萝卜	luóbǒ	N. turnip	5.3
落后	luòhòu	SV. fall behind	2.0
旅游	lǚyóu	V. sightseeing	5.3

M

麻将牌	májiàngpái	N. mahjong	5.3
满意	mǎnyì	SV. be satisfied	4.3
冒险	màoxiǎn	V. take a risk	3.1

媒体	méitǐ	N. media	3.3
美差事	měi chāishì	N. a terrific job	2.1
美术	měishù	N. arts and crafts	2.1
猛然	měngrán	Adv. suddenly	3.2
猛增	měng zēng	V. increase drastically	1.3
迷上了	míshànglě	RVC. infatuated with (person); obsessed with (things)	4.1
密	mì	SV. dense; thick	1.1
秘书	mìshū	N. secretary	3.1
面积	miànjī	N. area	1.0
面面观	miànmiànguān	VP. view from various angles	1.1
谋生	móushēng	VO. make a living	5.0
某	mǒu	Det. such and such (N); a certain (N)	2.3

N

拿...来说	ná…láishuō	VP. take...for example	2.0
奶奶	nǎinǎi	N. grandmother	4.1
闹得翻天	nào děi fāntiān	VP. raise a rumpus	3.2
内容	nèiróng	N. contents	3.3
年代	niándài	N. a decade of a century	2.2
年轻人	niánqīngrén	N. young people	5.3
年薪	nián xīn	N. annual pay	3.1
扭	niǔ	V. (of body movement)sway from side to side	4.1
农村	nóngcūn	N. rural area; village	2.0

P

拍卖	pāimài	V/N auction	5.0
怕老婆	pàlǎopó	VO. henpecked	4.2
派	pài	N. group; faction	4.1
判决	pànjué	V. make (court's) decision	5.2
抛出	pāochū	RVC. sell off (a term used especially in the stock market)	5.1
跑遍	pǎobiàn	VP. searched over (an entire area)	4.3
跑一圈	pǎo yīquān	VP. run a lap	4.2
培养	péiyǎng	V. cultivate (the mind; manner, etc.)	2.3
屁股	pìgǔ	N. buttocks; bottom	4.1
篇	piān	M. for report; chapter	1.0

飘	piāo	V. flutter; wave	5.3
凭	píng	V. rely on; base on	5.1
平常	píngcháng	SV. ordinary; common	5.3
平方米	píngfāngmǐ	N. square meter	1.0
平方	píngfáng	N. single-story house	2.3
评价	píngjià	V. comment	1.1
平均	píngjūn	V. average	1.0
平平淡淡	píngpíngdàndàn	SV. insipid	3.1
破产	pòchǎn	V/N. bankrupt; bankruptcy	4.2
破裂	pòliè	V. break down; broken up	3.3
普遍	pǔbiàn	SV. widespread; universal	1.0
普通	pǔtōng	SV. general; common	2.1

Q

期间	qījiān	N. a period of time	1.1
七十年代末	qīshí niándài mò	TW. the end of the 70's	1.0
妻子	qīzǐ	N. wife	1.2
奇观	qíguān	N. a spectacular sight	1.1
其实	qíshí	Adv. in fact	3.1
启事	qǐshì	N. announcement	3.1
企业	qǐyè	N. enterprise	2.2
企业管理	qǐyè guǎnlǐ	N. business management	2.1
企业家	qǐyèjiā	N. entrepreneur	3.0
气温	qìwēn	N. (air) temperature	1.1
千家万户	qiānjiā wànhù	N. thousands and thousands of families	1.0
前所未有	qián-suǒ-wèi-yǒu	Ph. unprecedented; hitherto unknown	2.2
钱财	qiáncái	N. wealth; money	4.0
前途	qiántú	N. future; prospect	4.0
巧克力	qiǎokèlì	N. chocolate	4.1
亲	qīn	V. kiss	4.3
青菜	qīngcài	N. fresh vegetables in gen.; greens	5.3
轻浮	qīngfú	SV. frivolous	4.1
清苦	qīngkǔ	SV. penurious; in straitened circumstances	2.0
轻视	qīngshì	V. look down on	5.0
轻松	qīngsōng	SV. relaxed; light (work)	2.1
清算	qīngsuàn	V. clear; settle (accounts)	5.2
倾向	qīngxiàng	V. inclined to	5.0

情况	qíngkuàng	N. condition; circumstances	1.2
情绪	qíngxù	N. mood; state of mind	4.2
求职	qiúzhí	VO. seek employment; look for a job	2.2
取而代之	qǔ-ér-dài-zhī	VP. take its place	5.3
娶媳妇	qǔ xífù	VO. to take a wife	2.2
取消	qǔxiāo	V. cancel; nullify	2.1
权力	quánlì	N. power	1.2
权益	quányì	N. rights and interests	5.2
劝	quàn	V. urge; try to persuade	4.2
缺	quē	V. be short of	2.1
却	què	Adv. however; but (same as "可是"; which, however, may appear before a subject or a verb, while 却 can only be placed before a verb, never a subject)	1.2
裙子	qúnzi	N. skirt	5.3

R

让	ràng	V. give in and let	5.3
热浪	rèlàng	N. heat wave	1.1
热门	rèmén	SV. popular; in great demand	3.3
货	huò	N. goods; commodity	2.1
热气	rèqì	N. steam (lit., hot air); heat	1.1
热心	rèxīn	SV. enthusiastic; warm hearted	5.2
人才	réncái	N. a person of ability; a talented person	2.2
人口	rénkǒu	N. population	1.0
人数	rénshù	N. (total) number of people; figure (referring to people)	2.0
人员	rényuán	N. personnel	1.1
认为	rènwéi	V. consider	1.1
仍然	réngrán	Adv. still	1.1
日常	rìcháng	Attr. daily; day-to-day	5.3
如何	rúhé	QW. how (literary)	5.0
如今	rújīn	TW. now; nowadays	5.0
入学率	rùxué lǜ	N. the rate of (students) attending school	2.0

S

沙发	shāfā	N. sofa	4.2

赡养	shànyǎng	V. support; provide for	3.3
商品	shāngpǐn	N. merchandise	2.1
商品化	shāngpǐnhuà	V. to commercialize...	1.2
商人	shāngrén	N. merchant; businessman	4.0
伤心	shāngxīn	SV. sad; grieved	4.3
上升	shàngshēng	V. rise; go up	2.2
社会	shèhuì	N. society	1.2
社会地位	shèhuì dìwèi	N. social status	3.0
设计	shèjì	V/N. design	1.1
社交	shèjiāo	N. social intercourse	3.1
摄氏	shèshì	N. Celsius	1.1
申请	shēnqǐng	V/N. apply for; application	2.2
身子	shēnzi	N. body	4.1
神秘	shénmì	SV. mysterious	3.1
神圣	shénshèng	SV. sacred; holy	5.0
审理	shěnlǐ	V. try; hear (a case)	5.2
甚至	shènzhì	Con. even; so far as to	1.2
生活水平	shēnghuó shuǐpíng	N. standard of living	2.3
生产	shēngchǎn	N. production	1.0
省	shěng	N. province	5.1
省得	shěngdé	V. so as to avoid (doing something)	4.1
剩	shèng	V. be left (over)	4.3
失利	shīlì	VO. suffer a setback	2.3
失业	shīyè	VO/N. lose one's job; unemployment	1.0
实际	shíjì	SV. practical	2.1
实践	shíjiàn	V. carry out; practise	3.1
实行	shíxíng	V. put into effect; implement	2.0
使	shǐ	V. cause; enable; make	1.1
市场经济	shìcháng jīngjì	N. market economy	3.3
世纪	shìjì	N. century	3.0
事业	shìyè	N. career	3.1
收获	shōuhuò	N. gains; results	4.3
收入	shōurù	N. income	1.0
受不了	shòubùliǎo	RVC. cannot bear; be unable to endure	1.1
受到	shòudào	V. be subjected to	3.0
受理	shòulǐ	V. accept and hear (a case)	5.2
蔬菜	shūcài	N. vegetables	5.3

暑假	shǔjiǎ	N. summer vacation	2.1
数目	shùmù	N. number; amount	3.3
双方	shuāngfāng	N. both sides; the two parties	3.0
水平	shuǐpíng	N. level	1.0
说服	shuófú	V. convince; persuade	5.1
顺利	shùnlì	SV. smoothly; successfully; without a hitch	5.3
硕士	shuòshì	N. Master of Arts (M.A.)	2.2
私人	sīrén	Attr. personal (privately owned)	1.2
私人企业	sīrén qǐyè	N. private enterprise (distinct from 国有企业 "state-owned enterprise")	5.0
私下	sīxià	Adv. privately; secretly	1.2
私有财产	sīyǒu cáichǎn	N. private property	3.3
四川省	Sìchuān shěng	N. Szechwan province	5.2
速冻饺子	sùdòng jiǎozi	N. quick-frozen dumpling	5.3
随着	suízhě	V. along with	3.0
孙女	sūnnǚ	N. granddaughter	4.1
所	suǒ	M. for buildings	2.0

T

台胞	tái bāo	N. our compatriots in Taiwan	3.3
摊	tān	N. vendor's stand; stall	2.3
叹	tàn	V. sigh	4.3
探亲	tànqīn	VO. go back home to visit one's family	5.1
叹息	tànxī	V. sigh	3.2
掏	tāo	V. pull out; draw out	4.3
套	tào	M. a suite of rooms	1.0
提出	tíchū	RVC. put forward (a proposal); propose (a policy)	1.0
提高	tígāo	V. raise; increase	1.0
提供	tígōng	V. provide; furnish	5.0
体制	tǐzhì	N. system; system of organization	
甜	tián	SV. sweet	3.2
条件	tiáojiàn	N. condition (of an agreement, etc.)	2.0
跳舞	tiàowǔ	V. dance	4.1
铁饭碗	tiěfànwǎn	N. (lit., iron rice bowl) guaranteed livelihood	5.0
听话	tīnghuà	VO. heed what an elder says	3.2
挺	tǐng	Adv. very; rather	4.2

同龄	tónglíng	N. of the same age	2.1
同事	tóngshì	N. coworker	4.2
同意	tóngyì	N. agreement; approval; consent	3.2
统计	tǒngjì	V. count (up the number of people)	1.1
统一招生	tǒngyī-zhāoshēng	VP/NP. to announce/an announcement of the national unified entrance examination for college students	2.1
痛苦	tòngkǔ	N/SV. pain; suffering	3.3
痛快	tòngkuài	SV. straightforward	3.1
头脑	tóunǎo	N. (a person's) mind	5.0
投资	tóuzī	VO/N. to invest; investment	4.3
土豆	tǔdòu	N. potato (coll.)	5.3
团	tuán	N. regiment	3.2
推	tuī	V. push	3.2
推辞	tuīcí	V. decline (an appointment; invitation)	4.1
退学	tuìxué	VO. withdraw from school	2.0
拖欠	tuōqiàn	V. be behind in payment	5.2

W

外表	wàibiǎo	N. exterior appearance	5.3
顽固	wángù	SV. stubborn; bitterly opposed to change	4.1
完善	wánshàn	SV. perfect; excellent	5.2
玩具柜	wánjùguì	N. toy case	4.3
晚辈	wǎnbèi	N. the younger generation; one's juniors (by one generation)	4.0
晚年	wǎnnián	N. twilight years; one's later years	4.0
惋惜	wǎnxī	V. feel sorry for a person over something that should have happened but did not	2.1

万般皆下品 惟有读书高 wànbàn jiē xiàpǐn wéiyǒu dúshū gāo   5.0
(a Chinese saying) Learning is the noblest of human pursuits (lit., Everything else is inferior, only studying is high.)

王府井	Wángfǔjǐng	N. a commercial center in Beijing	5.3
危房	wēi fáng	N. decrepit house	2.0
为	wéi	V. is; was; are; were (literary)	1.0
维护	wéihù	V. defend; safeguard	4.0
维修	wéixiū	V. keep in good repair; maintain	5.1
未婚	wèihūn	VP. unmarried	3.1

卫生间	wèishēngjiān	N. bathroom	3.1
文化	wénhuà	N. culture	2.3
文盲	wénmáng	N. illiterate; illiteracy	2.0
稳定	wěndìng	SV. be calm; steady	4.2
五花八门	wǔ-huā-bā-mén	Ph. of rich variety; multifarious	5.0
无可奈何	wú-kě-nàihé	Ph. be utterly helpless; having no way out	4.3
物价	wùjià	N. prices of commodities	1.0

X

西红柿	xīhóngshì	tomato	5.3
牺牲	wīshēng	V. sacrifice; do sth. at the expense of ...	3.0
吸引	xīyǐn	V. attract	3.1
细	xì	SV. very fine	3.1
下班	xiàbān	VO. get off work	3.2
下降	xiàjiàng	V. fall; decline	2.0
鲜	xiān	SV. fresh	5.3
咸菜	xiáncài	N. pickles; salted vegetables	4.3
闲谈	xiántán	V. chat	5.1
现代化	xiàndàihuà	SV. modernized	2.3
羡慕	xiànmù	V. envy	5.0
献身	xiànshēn	V. give one's life for; dedicate oneself to	2.3
现象	xiànxiàng	N. phenomenon	1.2
现行	xiànxíng	VP. presently in effect (presently operative)	2.2
限制	xiànzhì	N. restriction	3.0
相当数目	xiāngdāng shùmù	NP. considerable number of	3.3
消费	xiāofèi	V. consume	5.3
小卖部	xiǎomàibù	N. a small shop (attached to a school or work place)	2.3
协议	xiéyì	V/N. agree on; agreement	3.0
辛苦	xīnkǔ	SV. harsh; hardship	2.3
心理状态	xīnlǐ zhuàngtài	N. state of mind; psychological state	3.3
心痛	xīntòng	SV. (makes one's) heart ache (to see such a...)	4.2
新鲜	xīnxiān	SV. new/fresh (experience)	2.1
心血	xīnxuè	N. painstaking care; painstaking labor	4.3
形成	xíngchéng	V. form; take place	3.3
形态	xíngtài	N. pattern	5.0
幸福	xìngfú	SV. happy	3.0

性格	xìnggé	N. temperament; character	5.3
幸运儿	xìngyùnér	N. a lucky person	2.1
兄弟	xiōngdì	N. brothers	2.3
休闲	xiūxián	N. time free from work	5.3
需要	xūyào	V. need; require	1.0
需求	xūqiú	N. demand; requirement	2.2
宣布	xuānbù	V. declare; proclaim	4.2
宣传	xuānchuán	N. publicity	3.3
选用	xuǎnyòng	V. select; make a choice of	3.3
选择	xuǎnzé	V. choose; select	4.0
学历	xuélì	N. record of schooling	2.2
学龄	xuélíng	N. school age	2.0
学位	xuéwèi	N. (academic) degree	2.2
学业	xuéyè	N. one's studies	2.2
迅速	xùnsù	Adv. rapid; speedy	2.0

Y

压	yā	V. press	2.1
压抑	yāyì	V. hold back (one's emotion); (feel) constrained	3.0
研究生	yánjiùshēng	N. graduate student	2.2
严重	yánzhòng	SV. serious	1.0
眼界	yǎnjiè	N. vision	5.1
洋务派	yángwùpài	N. a group that acts in an ostentatiously foreign style	4.1
要求	yàoqiú	V. request	2.2
爷爷	yéyě	N. grandfather	4.1
夜班	yèbān	N. night shift	4.2
夜大学	yèdàxué	N. evening university	3.1
业余	yèyú	Attr. after work	5.1
业余大学	yèyú dàxué	N. college for people who attend after work	2.0
一分为二	yī fēn wéi èr	Ph. one divided into two	3.2
一举两得	yījǔ liǎngdé	Idiom. kill two birds with one stone	2.1
一穷二白	yīqióng èrbái	Idiom. completely without money	3.3
衣食住行	yī-shí-zhù-xíng	Idiom. daily necessities (lit., food, clothing, shelter and transportation)	5.1
一塌糊涂	yītā hútǔ	Idiom. in a complete mess	4.2
一向	yíxiàng	Adv. all along; consistently	5.2

遗憾	yíhàn	SV. regrettable (that something happened or did not happen)	2.1
亿	yì	Nu. a hundred million	1.0
意见	yìjiàn	N. opinion	3.2
意图	yìtú	N. intention	3.3
意味	yìwèi	V imply	5.0
义务	yìwù	N. duty; obligation	3.3
义务教育	yìwù-jiàoyù	N. compulsory education	2.0
因此	yīncǐ	Con. because of this..... (implied: therefore....)	1.2
音乐	yīnyuè	N. music	4.1
盈利	yínglì	V/N. net a profit; profit; gains	5.1
营养	yíngyǎng	N. nutrition; nourishment	4.3
营业	yíngyè	V. do business	3.3
营业员	yíngyèyuán	N. salesperson; clerk	4.3
应征者	yìngzhēngzhě	N. respondents	3.1
勇敢	yǒnggǎn	SV. brave	3.0
拥有	yōngyǒu	V. possess; have; own	3.3
优越	yōuyuè	SV. superior; excellent	3.1
由	yóu	Prep. by (see 1.2 grammar)	1.2
游览参观	yóulǎn cānguān	Ph. sightseeing; touring famous places	5.3
由于	yóuyú	Prep. due to; owing to	1.2
有出息	yǒu chūxī	SV. promising; high-minded	4.3
有趣	yǒuqù	SV. interesting	5.3
有所作为	yǒu-suǒ-zuò-wéi	Ph. accomplished	3.1
幼儿园	yòu'éryuán	N. nursery school	3.2
余	yú	Suffix. more than.....	3.2
于	yú	V Suffix. in; on; at; to; from; than; by	5.2
于是	yúshì	Con. thereupon; from this; and then; and so	3.3
与	yǔ	Con. and	3.1
与...见面	yǔ...jiànmiàn	Prep Ph. meet with	3.1
遇到	yùdào	V. met	3.2
玉米	yùmǐ	N. corn; maize	5.3
原来	yuánlái	Con. it turns out that	3.2
原理	yuánlǐ	N. principle (basic truth); tenet; general law shown in the working of a machine	2.1
原因	yuányīn	N. cause; reason	1.2
原则	yuánzé	N. principle (guiding rule for behavior)	5.2

约好	yuēhǎo	RVC. agreed to	3.2
允许	yǔnxǔ	V. permit; allow	1.2

Z

在...心目中	zài...xīnmù zhōng	Prep.Ph. in people's view; to sb. mind	5.0
赞成	zànchéng	V. endorse; approve of; favour	3.2
赞同	zàntóng	V. agree with	4.3
脏	zāng	SV. dirty; filthy	5.3
造成	zàochéng	VP. create; bring about	3.3
则	zé	M. for notice; advertisement	3.1
则	zé	Adv. however; then	4.1
责任	zérèn	N. duty; responsibility	4.0
增加	zēngjiā	V. increase; add	2.2
增长	zēngzhǎng	V. increase; rise	1.0
扎根在	zhāgēn zài	VP. take root in	5.0
债权	zhàiquán	N. creditor's rights	5.2
债务	zhàiwù	N. debt; liabilities	2.3
沾满	zhānmǎn	RVC. completely covered with	4.1
占	zhàn	V. makes up (such and such percent)	2.0
长辈	zhǎngbèi	N. senior; elder member of a family	4.0
掌握	zhǎngwò	V. master; have...well in hand; control	4.0
障碍	zhàng'ài	N. obstacle	2.2
招收工人	zhāoshōu gōngrén	VO. recruit workers	5.0
者	zhě	Suffix. those who; he who	3.3
这辈子	zhè bèizi	N. this generation; this lifetime	4.3
这倒是	zhè dǎoshì	Ph. (you are) right, this is actually the case	4.3
真舍得	zhēnshědé	VP. generous; truly not grudging	4.3
	(in this lesson:你真舍得! "You really don't care about money!"		
针织厂	zhēnzhī chǎng	N. knitting mill	5.2
征婚	zhēnghūn	VO. to advertise for a (marriage) partner	3.1
争论	zhēnglùn	V/N. debate; dispute; argue	4.1
整理	zhěnglǐ	V. put in order; straighten out	5.2
政策	zhèngcè	N. policy	1.0
政府	zhèngfǔ	N. government	1.2
证明	zhèngmíng	V. prove; testify	3.3
挣钱	zhèngqián	VO. earn money	2.0
知识	zhīshi	N. knowledge	4.3

知识分子	zhīshifènzǐ	N. intellectual; the intelligentsia	2.0
值得	zhídě	V. be worth; deserve	3.3
职工	zhígōng	N. staff and workers	5.2
值钱	zhíqián	SV. valuable; costly	2.3
直线上升	zhíxiàn shàngshēng	Ph. sharp rise (lit., shoot up in a straight line)	5.1
职业	zhíyè	N. profession; professional	2.1
职业中学	zhíyèzhōngxué	N. vocational high school	2.0
指出	zhǐchū	V. point out	1.2
指挥	zhǐhuī	V. command; direct	3.2
制度	zhìdù	N. system	1.2
智力	zhìlì	N. intelligence	4.3
中断	zhōngduàn	V. discontinue; interrupt	2.2
中华人民共和国	Zhōnghuá rénmín gònghé guó	N. the People's Republic of China	5.0
中期	zhōngqī	N. mid- period	3.0
终身	zhōngshēn	N. all one's life	5.0
中外合资	zhōngwài hézī	NP. Chinese-foreign joint venture	2.2
终于	zhōngyú	Adv. at long last; finally	4.2
肿	zhǒng	SV. swollen; swelling	4.2
重点大学	zhòngdiǎn dàxué	N. top-ranked university	2.2
重视	zhòngshì	V. lay emphasis; emphasize	2.0
周围	zhōuwéi	N. around; surroundings	3.0
皱眉头	zhòuméitóu	VO. knit one's brows; frown	4.3
逐步	zhúbù	Adv. step by step; progressively	5.2
逐渐	zhújiàn	Adv. gradually	3.3
主动	zhǔdòng	V/N. take the initiative; initiative	4.2
主科	zhǔkē	N. required courses in the major subject	2.1
主张	zhǔzhāng	V. advocate; maintain	3.3
住房	zhùfáng	N. housing; lodgings	1.0
助手	zhùshǒu	N. assistant	2.3
住宅	zhùzhái	N. residence; dwelling	1.2
著作	zhùzuò	N. publications	2.3
抓	zhuā	V. grab; clutch	4.3
抓住时间	zhuāzhù shíjiān	VO. make the best use of one's time	4.2
赚钱	zhuànqián	VO. make money	2.3
装扮	zhuāngbàn	N. attire; costume	5.3
装潢	zhuānghuáng	V. decorate	5.1

状态	zhuàngtài	N. condition; state	5.2
追求	zhuīqiú	V. seek	3.0
资产	zīchǎn	N. assets (in accounting)	5.2
资格	zīgé	N. qualification; seniority of a person	2.1
资料	zīliào	N. data; reference material	3.3
咨询	zīxún	V. consult; inquire; seek advice from	3.3
紫茄子	zǐqiézi	N. (purple) eggplant	5.3
自动	zìdòng	SV. of one's own accord	2.2
自费	zìfèi	V. pay at one's own expense	2.2
自豪	zìháo	V. pride oneself on	4.0
自然	zìrán	Adv. naturally	3.3
自由恋爱	zìyóuliàn'ài	VP. to love based on one's own feelings (without parents' constraint)	3.0
总额	zǒng'é	N. total (amount)	5.2
走亲访友	zǒu-qīn-fǎng-yǒu	Ph. calling on friends and relatives	5.3
组成	zǔchéng	V. make up; compose; form	5.2